James Russell Lowell

Political Essays

James Russell Lowell

Political Essays

ISBN/EAN: 9783337068660

Printed in Europe, USA, Canada, Australia, Japan

Cover: Foto ©Suzi / pixelio.de

More available books at **www.hansebooks.com**

Riverside Edition

THE WRITINGS

OF

JAMES RUSSELL LOWELL

IN TEN VOLUMES

VOLUME V.

POLITICAL ESSAYS

BY

JAMES RUSSELL LOWELL

LONDON
MACMILLAN AND CO
1890

The Riverside Press, Cambridge, Mass., U. S. A.
Printed by H. O. Houghton & Company.

CONTENTS

POLITICAL ESSAYS

THE AMERICAN TRACT SOCIETY

1858

THERE was no apologue more popular in the Middle Ages than that of the hermit, who, musing on the wickedness and tyranny of those whom the inscrutable wisdom of Providence had intrusted with the government of the world, fell asleep, and awoke to find himself the very monarch whose abject life and capricious violence had furnished the subject of his moralizing. Endowed with irresponsible power, tempted by passions whose existence in himself he had never suspected, and betrayed by the political necessities of his position, he became gradually guilty of all the crimes and the luxury which had seemed so hideous to him in his hermitage over a dish of water-cresses.

The American Tract Society from small beginnings has risen to be the dispenser of a yearly revenue of nearly half a million. It has become a great establishment, with a traditional policy, with the distrust of change and the dislike of disturbing questions (especially of such as would lessen its revenues) natural to great establishments.

It had been poor and weak; it has become rich and powerful.   The hermit has become king.

If the pious men who founded the American Tract Society had been told that within forty years they would be watchful of their publications, lest, by inadvertence, anything disrespectful might be spoken of the African Slave-trade, — that they would consider it an ample equivalent for compulsory dumbness on the vices of Slavery, that their colporteurs could awaken the minds of Southern brethren to the horrors of St. Bartholomew, — that they would hold their peace about the body of Cuffee dancing to the music of the cart-whip, provided only they could save the soul of Sambo alive by presenting him a pamphlet, which he could not read, on the depravity of the double shuffle, — that they would consent to be fellow members in the Tract Society with him who sold their fellow members in Christ on the auction block, if he agreed with them in condemning Transubstantiation (and it would not be difficult for a gentleman who ignored the real presence of God in his brother man to deny it in the sacramental wafer), — if those excellent men had been told this, they would have shrunk in horror, and exclaimed, " Are thy servants dogs, that they should do these things ? "

Yet this is precisely the present position of the Society.

There are two ways of evading the responsibility of such inconsistency.   The first is by an appeal to the Society's Constitution, and by claiming to interpret it strictly in accordance with the rules of law as applied to contracts, whether between individuals or States. The second is by denying that Slavery is opposed to the genius of Christianity, and that any moral wrongs are the necessary results of it. We will not be so unjust to the Society as to suppose that any of its members would rely on this latter plea, and shall therefore confine ourselves to a brief consideration of the other.

In order that the same rules of interpretation should be considered applicable to the Constitution of the Society and to that of the United States, we must attribute to the former a solemnity and importance which involve a palpable absurdity. To claim for it the verbal accuracy and the legal wariness of a mere contract is equally at war with common sense and the facts of the case ; and even were it not so, the party to a bond who should attempt to escape its ethical obligation by a legal quibble of construction would be put in coventry by all honest men. In point of fact, the Constitution was simply the minutes of an agreement among certain gentlemen, to define the limits within which they would accept trust funds, and the objects for which they should expend them.

But if we accept the alternative offered by the advocates of strict construction, we shall not find that their case is strengthened. Claiming that where the meaning of an instrument is doubtful, it should be interpreted according to the contemporary understanding of its framers, they argue that it would be absurd to suppose that gentlemen from the Southern States would have united to form a society that included in its objects any discussion of the moral duties arising from the institution of Slavery. Admitting the first part of their proposition, we deny the conclusion they seek to draw from it. They are guilty of a glaring anachronism in assuming the same opinions and prejudices to have existed in 1825 which are undoubtedly influential in 1858. The Anti-slavery agitation did not begin until 1831, and the debates in the Virginia Convention prove conclusively that six years after the foundation of the Tract Society, the leading men in that State, men whose minds had been trained and whose characters had been tempered in that school of action and experience which was open to all during the heroic period of our history, had not yet suffered such distortion of the intellect through passion and such deadening of the conscience through interest, as would have prevented their discussing either the moral or the political aspects of Slavery, and precluded them from uniting in any effort to make the relation between master and slave less demoralizing to the one and less imbruting to the other.

Again, it is claimed that the words of the Constitution are conclusive, and that the declaration that the publications of the Society shall be such as are "satisfactory to all Evangelical Christians" forbids by implication the issuing of any tract which could possibly offend the brethren in Slave States. The Society, it is argued, can publish only on topics about which all Evangelical Christians are agreed, and must, therefore, avoid everything in which the question of politics is involved. But what are the facts about matters other than Slavery? Tracts have been issued and circulated in which Dancing is condemned as sinful; are all Evangelical Christians agreed about this? On the Temperance question, against Catholicism, — have these topics never entered into our politics? The simple truth is that Slavery is the only subject about which the Publishing Committee have felt Constitutional scruples. Till this question arose, they were like men in perfect health, never suspecting that they had any constitution at all; but now, like hypochondriacs, they feel it in every pore, at the least breath from the eastward.

If a strict construction of the words "all Evangelical Christians" be insisted on, we are at a loss to see where the committee could draw the dividing line between what might be offensive and what allowable. The Society publish tracts in which the study of the Scriptures is enforced and their denial to the laity by Romanists assailed. But throughout the South it is criminal to teach a slave to read; throughout the South no book could be distributed among the servile population more incendiary than the Bible, if they could only read it. Will not our Southern brethren take alarm? The Society is reduced to the dilemma of either denying that the African has a soul to be saved, or of consenting to the terrible mockery of assuring him that the way of life is to be found only by searching a book which he is forbidden to open.

If we carry out this doctrine of strict construction to its legitimate results, we shall find that it involves a logical absurdity. What is the number of men whose outraged sensibilities may claim the suppression of a tract? Is the *taboo* of a thousand valid? Of a hundred? Of ten? Or are tracts to be distributed only to those who will find their doctrine agreeable, and are the Society's colporteurs to be instructed that a Temperance essay is the proper thing for a total-abstinent infidel, and a sermon on the Atonement for a distilling deacon? If the aim of the Society be only to convert men from sins they have no mind to, and to convince them of errors to which they have no temptation, they might as well be spending their money to persuade schoolmasters that two and two make four, or geometricians that there cannot be two obtuse angles in a triangle. If this be their notion of the way in which the gospel is to be preached, we do not wonder that they have found it necessary to print a tract upon the impropriety of sleeping in church.

But the Society are concluded by their own action; for in 1857 they unanimously adopted the following resolution: "That those moral duties which grow out of the existence of Slavery, as well as those moral evils and vices which it is known to promote and which are condemned in Scripture, and so much deplored by Evangelical Christians, undoubtedly do fall within the province of this Society, and can and ought to be discussed in a fraternal and Christian spirit." The Society saw clearly that it was impossible to draw a Mason and Dixon's line in the world of ethics, to divide Duty by a parallel of latitude. The only line which Christ drew is that which parts the sheep from the goats, that great horizon-line of the moral nature of man, which is the boundary between light and darkness. The Society, by yielding (as they have done in 1858) to what are pleasantly called the "objections" of the South (objections of so forcible a nature that we are told the colporteurs were "forced to flee") virtually exclude the black man, if born to the southward of a certain arbitrary line, from the operation of God's providence, and thereby do as great a wrong to the Creator as the Episcopal Church did to the artist when without public protest they allowed Ary Scheffer's *Christus Consolator*, with the figure of the slave left out, to be published in a Prayer-Book.

The Society is not asked to disseminate Anti-slavery doctrines, but simply to be even-handed between master and slave, and, since they have recommended Sambo and Toney to be obedient to Mr. Legree, to remind him in turn that he also has duties toward the bodies and souls of his bondmen. But we are told that the time has not yet arrived, that at present the ears of our Southern brethren are closed against all appeals, that God in his good time will turn their hearts, and that then, and not till then, will be the fitting occasion to do something in the premises. But if the Society is to await this golden opportunity with such exemplary patience in one case, why not in all? If it is to decline any attempt at converting the sinner till after God has converted him, will there be any special necessity for a tract society at all? Will it not be a little presumptuous, as well as superfluous, to undertake the doing over again of what He has already done? We fear that the studies of Blackstone, upon which the gentlemen who argue thus have entered in order to fit themselves for the legal and constitutional argument of the question, have confused their minds, and that they are misled by some fancied analogy between a tract and an action of trover, and conceive that the one, like the other, cannot be employed till after an actual conversion has taken place.

The resolutions reported by the Special Committee at the annual meeting of 1857, drawn up with great caution and with a sincere desire to make whole the breach in the Society, have had the usual fate of all attempts to reconcile incompatibilities by compromise. They express confidence in the Publishing Committee, and at the same time impliedly condemn them by recommending them to do precisely what they had all along scrupulously avoided doing. The result was just what might have been expected. Both parties among the Northern members of the Society, those who approved the former action of the Publishing Committee and those who approved the new policy recommended in the resolutions, those who favored silence and those who favored speech on the subject of Slavery, claimed the victory, while the Southern brethren, as usual, refused to be satisfied with anything short of unconditional submission. The word Compromise, as far as Slavery is concerned, has always been of fatal augury. The concessions of the South have been like the " With all my worldly goods I thee endow" of a bankrupt bridegroom, who thereby generously bestows all his debts upon his wife, and as a small return for his magnanimity consents to accept all her personal and a life estate in all her real property. The South is willing that the Tract Society should expend its money to convince the slave that he has a soul to be saved so far as he is obedient to his master, but not to persuade the master that he has a soul to undergo a very different process so far as he is unmerciful to his slave.

We Americans are very fond of this glue of compromise. Like so many quack cements, it is advertised to make the mended parts of the vessel stronger than those which have never been broken, but, like them, it will not stand hot water, — and as the question of slavery is sure to plunge all who approach it, even with the best intentions, into that fatal element, the patched-up brotherhood, which but yesterday was warranted to be better than new, falls once more into a heap of incoherent fragments. The last trial of the virtues of the Patent Redintegrator by the Special Committee of the Tract Society has ended like all the rest, and as all attempts to buy peace at too dear a rate must end. Peace is an excellent thing, but principle and pluck are better; and the man who sacrifices them to gain it finds at last that he has crouched under the Caudine yoke to purchase only a contemptuous toleration, that leaves him at war with his own self-respect and the invincible forces of his higher nature.

But the peace which Christ promised to his followers was not of this world; the good gift he brought them was not peace, but a sword. It was no sword of territorial conquest, but that flaming blade of conscience and self-conviction which lightened between our first parents and their lost Eden, — that sword of the Spirit that searcheth all things, — which severs one by one the ties of passion, of interest, of self-pride, that bind the soul to earth, — whose implacable edge may divide a man from family, from friends, from whatever is nearest and dearest, — and which hovers before him like the air-drawn dagger of Macbeth, beckoning him, not to crime, but to the legitimate royalties of self-denial and self-sacrifice, to the freedom which is won only by surrender of the will. Christianity has never been concession, never peace; it is continual aggression; one province of wrong conquered, its pioneers are already in the heart of another. The mile-stones of its onward march down the ages have not been monuments of material power, but the blackened stakes of martyrs, trophies of individual fidelity to conviction. For it is the only religion which is superior to all endowment, to all authority, — which has a bishopric and a cathedral wherever a single human soul has surrendered itself to God. That very spirit of doubt, inquiry, and fanaticism for private judgment, with which Romanists reproach Protestantism, is its stamp and token of authenticity, — the seal of Christ, and not of the Fisherman.

We do not wonder at the division which has

taken place in the Tract Society, nor do we regret it. The ideal life of a Christian is possible to very few, but we naturally look for a nearer approach to it in those who associate together to disseminate the doctrines which they believe to be its formative essentials, and there is nothing which the enemies of religion seize on so gladly as any inconsistency between the conduct and the professions of such persons. Though utterly indifferent to the wrongs of the slave, the scoffer would not fail to remark upon the hollowness of a Christianity which was horror-stricken at a dance or a Sunday drive, while it was blandly silent about the separation of families, the putting asunder whom God had joined, the selling Christian girls for Christian harems, and the thousand horrors of a system which can lessen the agonies it inflicts only by debasing the minds and souls of the race on which it inflicts them. Is your Christianity, then, he would say, a respecter of persons, and does it condone the sin because the sinner can contribute to your coffers? Was there ever a simony like this, — that does not sell, but withholds, the gift of God for a price?

The world naturally holds the Society to a stricter accountability than it would insist upon in ordinary cases. Were they only a club of gentlemen associated for their own amusement, it would be very natural and proper that they should exclude all questions which would introduce controversy, and that, however individually interested in certain reforms, they should not force them upon others who would consider them a bore. But a society of

professing Christians, united for the express purpose of carrying both the theory and the practice
of the New Testament into every household in the
land, has voluntarily subjected itself to a graver
responsibility, and renounced all title to fall back
upon any reserved right of personal comfort or
convenience.

We say, then, that we are glad to see this division in the Tract Society; not glad because of the
division, but because it has sprung from an earnest
effort to relieve the Society of a reproach which
was not only impairing its usefulness, but doing
an injury to the cause of truth and sincerity everywhere. We have no desire to impugn the motives
of those who consider themselves conservative
members of the Society; we believe them to be
honest in their convictions, or their want of them;
but we think they have mistaken notions as to what
conservatism is, and that they are wrong in supposing it to consist in refusing to wipe away the
film on their spectacle-glasses which prevents their
seeing the handwriting on the wall, or in conserving reverently the barnacles on their ship's bottom
and the dry-rot in its knees. We yield to none of
them in reverence for the Past; it is there only
that the imagination can find repose and seclu-
sion; there dwells that silent majority whose experience guides our action and whose wisdom shapes
our thought in spite of ourselves;— but it is not
length of days that can make evil reverend, nor
persistence in inconsistency that can give it the
power or the claim of orderly precedent. Wrong,

though its title-deeds go back to the days of Sodom,
is by nature a thing of yesterday, — while the
right, of which we became conscious but an hour
ago, is more ancient than the stars, and of the
essence of Heaven. If it were proposed to establish Slavery to-morrow, should we have more
patience with its patriarchal argument than with
the parallel claim of Mormonism? That Slavery
is old is but its greater condemnation ; that we
have tolerated it so long, the strongest plea for our
doing so no longer. There is one institution to
which we owe our first allegiance, one that is more
sacred and venerable than any other, — the soul
and conscience of Man.

What claim has Slavery to immunity from discussion? We are told that discussion is dangerous. Dangerous to what? Truth invites it, courts
the point of the Ithuriel-spear, whose touch can
but reveal more clearly the grace and grandeur
of her angelic proportions. The advocates of
Slavery have taken refuge in the last covert of
desperate sophism, and affirm that their institution
is of Divine ordination, that its bases are laid in
the nature of man. Is anything, then, of God's
contriving endangered by inquiry? Was it the
system of the universe, or the monks, that trembled
at the telescope of Galileo? Did the circulation
of the firmament stop in terror because Newton
laid his daring finger on its pulse? But it is idle
to discuss a proposition so monstrous. There is
no right of sanctuary for a crime against humanity,
and they who drag an unclean thing to the horns

of the altar bring it to vengeance, and not to safety.

Even granting that Slavery were all that its apologists assume it to be, and that the relation of master and slave were of God's appointing, would not its abuses be just the thing which it was the duty of Christian men to protest against, and, as far as might be, to root out? Would our courts feel themselves debarred from interfering to rescue a daughter from a parent who wished to make merchandise of her purity, or a wife from a husband who was brutal to her, by the plea that parental authority and marriage were of Divine ordinance? Would a police-justice discharge a drunkard who pleaded the patriarchal precedent of Noah? or would he not rather give him another month in the House of Correction for his impudence?

The Anti-slavery question is not one which the Tract Society can exclude by triumphant majorities, nor put to shame by a comparison of respectabilities. Mixed though it has been with politics, it is in no sense political, and springing naturally from the principles of that religion which traces its human pedigree to a manger, and whose first apostles were twelve poor men against the whole world, it can dispense with numbers and earthly respect. The clergyman may ignore it in the pulpit, but it confronts him in his study; the church-member, who has suppressed it in parish-meeting, opens it with the pages of his Testament; the merchant, who has shut it out of his house and his heart, finds it lying in wait for him, a gaunt fugitive, in the hold of his ship; the lawyer, who has declared that it is no concern of his, finds it thrust upon him in the brief of the slave-hunter; the historian, who had cautiously evaded it, stumbles over it at Bunker Hill. And why? Because it is not political, but moral, — because it is not local, but national, — because it is not a test of party, but of individual honesty and honor. The wrong which we allow our nation to perpetrate we cannot localize, if we would; we cannot hem it within the limits of Washington or Kansas; sooner or later, it will force itself into the conscience and sit by the hearthstone of every citizen.

It is not partisanship, it is not fanaticism, that has forced this matter of Anti-slavery upon the American people; it is the spirit of Christianity, which appeals from prejudices and predilections to the moral consciousness of the individual man; that spirit elastic as air, penetrative as heat, invulnerable as sunshine, against which creed after creed and institution after institution have measured their strength and been confounded; that restless spirit which refuses to crystallize in any sect or form, but persists, a Divinely commissioned radical and reconstructor, in trying every generation with a new dilemma between ease and interest on the one hand, and duty on the other. Shall it be said that its kingdom is not of this world? In one sense, and that the highest, it certainly is not; but just as certainly Christ never intended those words to be used as a subterfuge by which to escape our responsibilities in the life of business and politics.

Let the cross, the sword, and the arena answer, whether the world, that then was, so understood its first preachers and apostles. Cæsar and Flamen both instinctively dreaded it, not because it aimed at riches or power, but because it strove to conquer that other world in the moral nature of mankind, where it could establish a throne against which wealth and force would be weak and contemptible. No human device has ever prevailed against it, no array of majorities or respectabilities; but neither Cæsar nor Flamen ever conceived a scheme so cunningly adapted to neutralize its power as that graceful compromise which accepts it with the lip and denies it in the life, which marries it at the altar and divorces it at the church-door.

THE ELECTION IN NOVEMBER

1860

WHILE all of us have been watching, with that admiring sympathy which never fails to wait on courage and magnanimity, the career of the new Timoleon in Sicily ; while we have been reckoning, with an interest scarcely less than in some affair of personal concern, the chances and changes that bear with furtherance or hindrance upon the fortune of united Italy, we are approaching, with a quietness and composure which more than anything else mark the essential difference between our own form of democracy and any other yet known in history, a crisis in our domestic policy more momentous than any that has arisen since we became a nation. Indeed, considering the vital consequences for good or evil that will follow from the popular decision in November, we might be tempted to regard the remarkable moderation which has thus far characterized the Presidential canvass as a guilty indifference to the duty implied in the privilege of suffrage, or a stolid unconsciousness of the result which may depend upon its exercise in this particular election, did we not believe that it arose chiefly from the · general persuasion that the success of the Republican party was a foregone conclusion.

In a society like ours, where every man may transmute his private thought into history and destiny by dropping it into the ballot-box, a peculiar responsibility rests upon the individual. Nothing can absolve us from doing our best to look at all public questions as citizens, and therefore in some sort as administrators and rulers. For though during its term of office the government be practically as independent of the popular will as that of Russia, yet every fourth year the people are called upon to pronounce upon the conduct of their affairs. Theoretically, at least, to give democracy any standing-ground for an argument with despotism or oligarchy, a majority of the men composing it should be statesmen and thinkers. It is a proverb, that to turn a radical into a conservative there needs only to put him into office, because then the license of speculation or sentiment is limited by a sense of responsibility; then for the first time he becomes capable of that comparative view which sees principles and measures, not in the narrow abstract, but in the full breadth of their relations to each other and to political consequences. The theory of democracy presupposes something of these results of official position in the individual voter, since iu exercising his right he becomes for the moment an integral part of the governing power.

How very far practice is from any likeness to theory, a week's experience of our politics suffices to convince us. The very government itself seems an organized scramble, and Congress a boy's debating-club, with the disadvantage of being reported. As our party-creeds are commonly represented less by ideas than by persons (who are assumed, without too close a scrutiny, to be the exponents of certain ideas) our politics become personal and narrow to a degree never paralleled, unless in ancient Athens or mediæval Florence. Our Congress debates and our newspapers discuss, sometimes for day after day, not questions of national interest, not what is wise and right, but what the Honorable Lafayette Skreemer said on the stump, or bad whiskey said for him, half a dozen years ago. If that personage, outraged in all the finer sensibilities of our common nature, by failing to get the contract for supplying the District Court-House at Skreemeropolisville City with revolvers, was led to disparage the union of these States, it is seized on as proof conclusive that the party to which he belongs are so many Catalines, — for Congress is unanimous only in misspelling the name of that oft-invoked conspirator. The next Presidential Election looms always in advance, so that we seem never to have an actual Chief Magistrate, but a prospective one, looking to the chances of re-election, and mingling in all the dirty intrigues of provincial politics with an unhappy talent for making them dirtier. The cheating mirage of the White House lures our public men away from present duties and obligations; and if matters go on as they have gone, we shall need a Committee of Congress to count the spoons in the public plate-closet, whenever a President goes out of office, — with a policeman to watch every member of the Committee. We are kept normally in that most unprofitable of predicaments, a state of transition, and politicians measure their words and deeds by a standard of immediate and temporary expediency, — an expediency not as concerning the nation, but which, if more than merely personal, is no wider than the interests of party.

Is all this a result of the failure of democratic institutions? Rather of the fact that those institutions have never yet had a fair trial, and that for the last thirty years an abnormal element has been acting adversely with continually increasing strength. Whatever be the effect of slavery upon the States where it exists, there can be no doubt that its moral influence upon the North has been most disastrous. It has compelled our politicians into that first fatal compromise with their moral instincts and hereditary principles which makes all consequent ones easy; it has accustomed us to makeshifts instead of statesmanship, to subterfuge instead of policy, to party-platforms for opinions, and to a defiance of the public sentiment of the civilized world for patriotism. We have been asked to admit, first, that it was a necessary evil; then that it was a good both to master and slave; then that it was the corner-stone of free institutions; then that it was a system divinely instituted under the Old Law and sanctioned under the New. With a representation, three fifths of it based on the assumption that negroes are men, the South turns upon us and insists on our acknowledging that they are things. After compelling her Northern allies to pronounce the " free and equal " clause of the preamble to the Declaration of Independence (because it stood in the way of enslaving men) a manifest absurdity, she has declared, through the Supreme Court of the United States, that negroes are not men in the ordinary meaning of the word. To eat dirt is bad enough, but to find that we have eaten more than was necessary may chance to give us an indigestion. The slaveholding interest has gone on step by step, forcing concession after concession, till it needs but little to secure it forever in the political supremacy of the country. Yield to its latest demand, — let it mould the evil destiny of the Territories, — and the thing is done past recall. The next Presidential Election is to say *Yes* or *No*.

But we should not regard the mere question of political preponderancy as of vital consequence, did it not involve a continually increasing moral degradation on the part of the Non-slaveholding States, — for Free States they could not be called much longer. Sordid and materialistic views of the true value and objects of society and government are professed more and more openly by the leaders of popular outcry, — for it cannot be called public opinion. That side of human nature which it has been the object of all lawgivers and moralists to repress and subjugate is flattered and caressed; whatever is profitable is right; and already the slave-trade, as yielding a greater return on the capital invested than any other traffic, is lauded as the highest achievement of human reason and justice. Mr. Hammond has proclaimed the accession of King Cotton, but he seems to have forgotten that history is not without examples of kings who have lost their crowns through the folly and false security of their ministers. It is quite true that there is a large class of reasoners who would weigh all questions of right and wrong in the balance of trade ; but we cannot bring ourselves to believe that it is a wise political economy which makes cotton by unmaking men, or a far-seeing statesmanship which looks on an immediate money-profit as a safe equivalent for a beggared public sentiment. We think Mr. Hammond even a little premature in proclaiming the new Pretender. The election of November may prove a Culloden. Whatever its result, it is to settle, for many years to come, the question whether the American idea is to govern this continent, whether the Occidental or the Oriental theory of society is to mould our future, whether we are to recede from principles which eighteen Christian centuries have been slowly establishing at the cost of so many saintly lives at the stake and so many heroic ones on the scaffold and the battle-field, in favor of some fancied assimilation to the household arrangements of Abraham, of which all that can be said with certainty is that they did not add to his domestic happiness.

We believe that this election is a turning-point

in our history; for, although there are four candidates, there are really, as everybody knows, but
two parties, and a single question that divides
them. The supporters of Messrs. Bell and Everett have adopted as their platform the Constitution, the Union, and the enforcement of the Laws.
This may be very convenient, but it is surely not
very explicit. The cardinal question on which the
whole policy of the country is to turn — a question, too, which this very election must decide in
one way or the other — is the interpretation to
be put upon certain clauses of the Constitution.
All the other parties equally assert their loyalty
to that instrument. Indeed, it is quite the fashion.
The removers of all the ancient landmarks of our
policy, the violators of thrice-pledged faith, the
planners of new treachery to established compromise, all take refuge in the Constitution, —

> "Like thieves that in a hemp-plot lie,
> Secure against the hue and cry."

In the same way the first Bonaparte renewed his
profession of faith in the Revolution at every convenient opportunity; and the second follows the
precedent of his uncle, though the uninitiated
fail to see any logical sequence from 1789 to 1815
or 1860. If Mr. Bell loves the Constitution, Mr.
Breckinridge is equally fond; that Egeria of our
statesmen could be "happy with either, were
t' other dear charmer away." Mr. Douglas con-
fides the secret of his passion to the unloqua-
cious clams of Rhode Island, and the chief com-
plaint made against Mr. Lincoln by his opponents
is that he is *too* Constitutional.

Meanwhile, the only point in which voters are interested is, What do they mean by the Constitution? Mr. Breckinridge means the superiority of a certain exceptional species of property over all others; nay, over man himself. Mr. Douglas, with a different formula for expressing it, means practically the same thing. Both of them mean that Labor has no rights which Capital is bound to respect, — that there is no higher law than human interest and cupidity. Both of them represent not merely the narrow principles of a section, but the still narrower and more selfish ones of a caste. Both of them, to be sure, have convenient phrases to be juggled with before election, and which mean one thing or another, or neither one thing nor another, as a particular exigency may seem to require; but since both claim the regular Democratic nomination, we have little difficulty in divining what their course would be after the fourth of March, if they should chance to be elected. We know too well what regular Democracy is, to like either of the two faces which each shows by turns under the same hood. Everybody remembers Baron Grimm's story of the Parisian showman, who in 1789 exhibited the *royal* Bengal tiger under the new character of *national*, as more in harmony with the changed order of things. Could the animal have lived till 1848, he would probably have found himself offered to the discriminating public as the *democratic* and *social* ornament of the jungle. The Pro-slavery party of this country seeks the popular favor under even more frequent and incongruous *aliases :* it is now *national,* now *conservative,* now *constitutional ;* here it represents Squatter-Sovereignty, and there the power of Congress over the Territories; but, under whatever name, its nature remains unchanged, and its instincts are none the less predatory and destructive.

Mr. Lincoln's position is set forth with sufficient precision in the platform adopted by the Chicago Convention; but what are we to make of Messrs. Bell and Everett? Heirs of the stock in trade of two defunct parties, the Whig and Know-Nothing, do they hope to resuscitate them? or are they only like the inconsolable widows of Père la Chaise, who, with an eye to former customers, make use of the late Andsoforth's gravestone to advertise that they still carry on business at the old stand? Mr. Everett, in his letter accepting the nomination, gave us only a string of reasons why he should not have accepted it at all; and Mr. Bell preserves a silence singularly at variance with his patronymic. The only public demonstration of principle that we have seen is an emblematic bell drawn upon a wagon by a single horse, with a man to lead him, and a boy to make a nuisance of the tinkling symbol as it moves along. Are all the figures in this melancholy procession equally emblematic? If so, which of the two candidates is typified in the unfortunate who leads the horse?— for we believe the only hope of the party is to get one of them elected by some hocus-pocus in the House of Representatives. The little boy, we suppose, is intended to represent the party, which promises to be so conveniently small that there will be an office for every member of it, if its candidate should win. Did not the bell convey a plain allusion to the leading name on the ticket, we should conceive it an excellent type of the hollowness of those fears for the safety of the Union, in case of Mr. Lincoln's election, whose changes are so loudly rung, — its noise having once or twice given rise to false alarms of fire, till people found out what it really was. Whatever profound moral it be intended to convey, we find in it a similitude that is not without significance as regards the professed creed of the party. The industrious youth who operates upon it has evidently some notion of the measured and regular motion that befits the tongues of well-disciplined and conservative bells. He does his best to make theory and practice coincide; but with every jolt on the road an involuntary variation is produced, and the sonorous pulsation becomes rapid or slow accordingly. We have observed that the Constitution was liable to similar derangements, and we very much doubt whether Mr. Bell himself (since, after all, the Constitution would practically be nothing else than his interpretation of it) would keep the same measured tones that are so easy on the smooth path of candidacy, when it came to conducting the car of State over some of the rough places in the highway of Manifest Destiny, and some of those passages in our politics which, after the fashion of new countries, are rather *corduroy* in character.

But, fortunately, we are not left wholly in the

dark as to the aims of the self-styled Constitutional party. One of its most distinguished members, Governor Hunt of New York, has given us to understand that its prime object is the defeat at all hazards of the Republican candidate. To achieve so desirable an end, its leaders are ready to coalesce, here with the Douglas, and there with the Breckinridge faction of that very Democratic party of whose violations of the Constitution, corruption, and dangerous limberness of principle they have been the lifelong denouncers. In point of fact, then, it is perfectly plain that we have only two parties in the field : those who favor the extension of slavery, and those who oppose it, — in other words, a Destructive and a Conservative party.

We know very well that the partisans of Mr. Bell, Mr. Douglas, and Mr. Breckinridge all equally claim the title of conservative : and the fact is a very curious one, well worthy the consideration of those foreign critics who argue that the inevitable tendency of democracy is to compel larger and larger concessions to a certain assumed communistic propensity and hostility to the rights of property on the part of the working classes. But the truth is, that revolutionary ideas are promoted, not by any unthinking hostility to the *rights* of property, but by a well-founded jealousy of its usurpations ; and it is Privilege, and not Property, that is perplexed with fear of change. The conservative effect of ownership operates with as much force on the man with a hundred dollars in an old stocking as on his neighbor with a million in the funds.

During the Roman Revolution of '48, the beggars who had funded their gains were among the stanchest reactionaries, and left Rome with the nobility. No question of the abstract right of property has ever entered directly into our politics, or ever will, — the point at issue being, whether a certain exceptional kind of property, already privileged beyond all others, shall be entitled to still further privileges at the expense of every other kind. The extension of slavery over new territory means just this, — that this one kind of property, not recognized as such by the Constitution, or it would never have been allowed to enter into the basis of representation, shall control the foreign and domestic policy of the Republic.

A great deal is said, to be sure, about the rights of the South; but has any such right been infringed? When a man invests money in any species of property, he assumes the risks to which it is liable. If he buy a house, it may be burned; if a ship, it may be wrecked; if a horse or an ox, it may die. Now the disadvantage of the Southern kind of property is — how shall we say it so as not to violate our Constitutional obligations? — that it is exceptional. When it leaves Virginia, it is a thing; when it arrives in Boston, it becomes a man, speaks human language, appeals to the justice of the same God whom we all acknowledge, weeps at the memory of wife and children left behind, — in short, hath the same organs and dimensions that a Christian hath, and is not distinguishable from ordinary Christians, except, perhaps, by a simpler

and more earnest faith. There are people at the
North who believe that, beside *meum* and *tuum*,
there is also such a thing as *suum*, — who are old-
fashioned enough, or weak enough, to have their
feelings touched by these things, to think that human nature is older and more sacred than any claim
of property whatever, and that it has rights at least
as much to be respected as any hypothetical one of
our Southern brethren. This, no doubt, makes it
harder to recover a fugitive chattel ; but the existence of human nature in a man here and there is
surely one of those accidents to be counted on at
least as often as fire, shipwreck, or the cattle-dis-
ease ; and the man who chooses to put his money
into these images of his Maker cut in ebony should
be content to take the incident risks along with the
advantages. We should be very sorry to deem this
risk capable of diminution ; for we think that the
claims of a common manhood upon us should be at
least as strong as those of Freemasonry, and that
those whom the law of man turns away should find
in the larger charity of the law of God and Nature
a readier welcome and surer sanctuary. We shall
continue to think the negro a man, and on Southern evidence, too, so long as he is counted in the
population represented on the floor of Congress, —
for three fifths of perfect manhood would be a high
average even among white men ; so long as he is
hanged or worse, as an example and terror to
others, — for we do not punish one animal for the
moral improvement of the rest ; so long as he is
considered capable of religious instruction, — for

we fancy the gorillas would make short work with a missionary; so long as there are fears of insurrection, — for we never heard of a combined effort at revolt in a menagerie. Accordingly, we do not see how the particular right of whose infringement we hear so much is to be made safer by the election of Mr. Bell, Mr. Breckinridge, or Mr. Douglas, — there being quite as little chance that any of them would abolish human nature as that Mr. Lincoln would abolish slavery. The same generous instinct that leads some among us to sympathize with the sorrows of the bereaved master will always, we fear, influence others to take part with the rescued man.

But if our Constitutional Obligations, as we like to call our constitutional timidity or indifference, teach us that a particular divinity hedges the Domestic Institution, they do not require us to forget that we have institutions of our own, worth maintaining and extending, and not without a certain sacredness, whether we regard the traditions of the fathers or the faith of the children. It is high time that we should hear something of the rights of the Free States, and of the duties consequent upon them. We also have our prejudices to be respected, our theory of civilization, of what constitutes the safety of a state and insures its prosperity, to be applied wherever there is soil enough for a human being to stand on and thank God for making him a man. Is conservatism applicable only to property, and not to justice, freedom, and public honor? Does it mean merely drifting with the current of evil times and pernicious counsels, and carefully nursing the ills we have, that they may, as their nature it is, grow worse ?

To be told that we ought not to agitate the question of Slavery, when it is that which is forever agitating us, is like telling a man with the fever and ague on him to stop shaking, and he will be cured. The discussion of Slavery is said to be dangerous, but dangerous to what? The manufacturers of the Free States constitute a more numerous class than the slaveholders of the South : suppose they should claim an equal sanctity for the Protective System. Discussion is the very life of free institutions, the fruitful mother of all political and moral enlightenment, and yet the question of all questions must be tabooed. The Swiss guide enjoins silence in the region of avalanches, lest the mere vibration of the voice should dislodge the ruin clinging by frail roots of snow. But where is our avalanche to fall? It is to overwhelm the Union, we are told. The real danger to the Union will come when the encroachments of the Slave-Power and the concessions of the Trade-Power shall have made it a burden instead of a blessing. The real avalanche to be dreaded, — are we to expect it from the ever-gathering mass of ignorant brute force, with the irresponsibility of animals and the passions of men, which is one of the fatal necessities of slavery, or from the gradually increasing consciousness of the non-slaveholding population of the Slave States of the true cause

of their material impoverishment and political inferiority? From one or the other source its ruinous forces will be fed, but in either event it is not
the Union that will be imperilled, but the privileged Order who on every occasion of a thwarted
whim have menaced its disruption, and who will
then find in it their only safety.

We believe that the "irrepressible conflict"—
for we accept Mr. Seward's much-denounced phrase
in all the breadth of meaning he ever meant to
give it — is to take place in the South itself; because the Slave System is one of those fearful
blunders in political economy which are sure,
sooner or later, to work their own retribution.
The inevitable tendency of slavery is to concen-
trate in a few hands the soil, the capital, and
the power of the countries where it exists, to reduce the non-slaveholding class to a continually
lower and lower level of property, intelligence,
and enterprise, — their increase in numbers adding much to the economical hardship of their
position and nothing to their political weight in
the community. There is no home-encourage-
ment of varied agriculture, — for the wants of a
slave population are few in number and limited
in kind; none of inland trade, for that is devel-
oped only by communities where education in-
duces refinement, where facility of communication stimulates invention and variety of enterprise,
where newspapers make every man's improvement
in tools, machinery, or culture of the soil an in-
citement to all, and bring all the thinkers of the

world to teach in the cheap university of the
people. We do not, of course, mean to say that
slaveholding States may not and do not produce
fine men; but they fail, by the inherent vice of
their constitution and its attendant consequences,
to create enlightened, powerful, and advancing
communities of men, which is the true object of
all political organizations, and is essential to the
prolonged existence of all those whose life and
spirit are derived directly from the people. Every
man who has dispassionately endeavored to enlighten himself in the matter cannot but see,
that, for the many, the course of things in slaveholding States is substantially what we have
described, a downward one, more or less rapid,
in civilization and in all those results of material prosperity which in a free country show
themselves in the general advancement for the
good of all, and give a real meaning to the word
Commonwealth. No matter how enormous the
wealth centred in the hands of a few, it has no
longer the conservative force or the beneficent influence which it exerts when equably distributed,
— even loses more of both where a system of
absenteeism prevails so largely as in the South.
In such communities the seeds of an "irrepressible conflict" are surely if slowly ripening, and
signs are daily multiplying that the true peril to
their social organization is looked for, less in a
revolt of the owned labor than in an insurrection of intelligence in the labor that owns itself
and finds itself none the richer for it. To multiply such communities is to multiply weakness.

The election in November turns on the single and simple question, Whether we shall consent to the indefinite multiplication of them; and the only party which stands plainly and unequivocally pledged against such a policy, nay, which is not either openly or impliedly in favor of it, — is the Republican party. We are of those who at first regretted that another candidate was not nominated at Chicago; but we confess that we have ceased to regret it, for the magnanimity of Mr. Seward since the result of the Convention was known has been a greater ornament to him and a greater honor to his party than his election to the Presidency would have been. We should have been pleased with Mr. Seward's nomination, for the very reason we have seen assigned for passing him by, — that he represented the most advanced doctrines of his party. He, more than any other man, combined in himself the moralist's oppugnancy to Slavery as a fact, the thinker's resentment of it as a theory, and the statist's distrust of it as a policy, — thus summing up the three efficient causes that have chiefly aroused and concentrated the antagonism of the Free States. Not a brilliant man, he has that best gift of Nature, which brilliant men commonly lack, of being always able to do his best; and the very misrepresentation of his opinions which was resorted to in order to neutralize the effect of his speeches in the Senate and elsewhere was the best testimony to their power. Safe from the prevailing epidemic of Congressional eloquence as if he had been inoculated for it early in his career, he addresses himself to the reason, and what he says sticks. It was assumed that his nomination would have embittered the contest and tainted the Republican creed with radicalism; but we doubt it. We cannot think that a party gains by not hitting its hardest, or by sugaring its opinions. Republicanism is not a conspiracy to obtain office under false pretences. It has a definite aim, an earnest purpose, and the unflinching tenacity of profound conviction. It was not called into being by a desire to reform the pecuniary corruptions of the party now in power. Mr. Bell or Mr. Breckinridge would do that, for no one doubts their honor or their honesty. It is not unanimous about the Tariff, about State-Rights, about many other questions of policy. What unites the Republicans is a common faith in the early principles and practice of the Republic, a common persuasion that slavery, as it cannot but be the natural foe of the one, has been the chief debaser of the other, and a common resolve to resist its encroachments everywhen and everywhere. They see no reason to fear that the Constitution, which has shown such pliant tenacity under the warps and twistings of a forty-years' pro-slavery pressure, should be in danger of breaking, if bent backward again gently to its original rectitude of fibre. " All forms of human government," says Machiavelli, " have, like men, their natural term, and those only are long-lived which possess in themselves the power of returning to

the principles on which they were originally
founded."

It is in a moral aversion to slavery as a great
wrong that the chief strength of the Republican
party lies. They believe as everybody believed
sixty years ago; and we are sorry to see what appears to be an inclination in some quarters to blink
this aspect of the case, lest the party be charged
with want of conservatism, or, what is worse, with
abolitionism. It is and will be charged with all
kinds of dreadful things, whatever it does, and it
has nothing to fear from an upright and downright
declaration of its faith. One part of the grateful
work it has to do is to deliver us from the curse of
perpetual concession for the sake of a peace that
never comes, and which, if it came, would not be
peace, but submission, — from that torpor and imbecility of faith in God and man which have stolen
the respectable name of Conservatism. A question
which cuts so deep as that which now divides the
country cannot be debated, much less settled, without excitement. Such excitement is healthy, and
is a sign that the ill humors of the body politic are
coming to the surface, where they are comparatively harmless. It is the tendency of all creeds,
opinions, and political dogmas that have once defined themselves in institutions to become inoperative. The vital and formative principle, which
was active during the process of crystallization into
sects, or schools of thought, or governments, ceases
to act; and what was once a living emanation of
the Eternal Mind, organically operative in history,

becomes the dead formula on men's lips and the
dry topic of the annalist. It has been our good
fortune that a question has been thrust upon us
which has forced us to reconsider the primal principles of government, which has appealed to conscience as well as reason, and, by bringing the theories of the Declaration of Independence to the
test of experience in our thought and life and action, has realized a tradition of the memory into a
conviction of the understanding and the soul. It
will not do for the Republicans to confine themselves to the mere political argument, for the matter then becomes one of expediency, with two
defensible sides to it; they must go deeper, to
the radical question of right and wrong, or they
surrender the chief advantage of their position.
What Spinoza says of laws is equally true of party
platforms, — that those are strong which appeal
to reason, but those are impregnable which compel
the assent both of reason and the common affec-
tions of mankind.

No man pretends that under the Constitution
there is any possibility of interference with the domestic relations of the individual States ; no party
has ever remotely hinted at any such interference ;
but what the Republicans affirm is, that in every
contingency where the Constitution can be construed in favor of freedom, it ought to be and shall
be so construed. It is idle to talk of sectionalism,
abolitionism, and hostility to the laws. The principles of liberty and humanity cannot, by virtue of
their very nature, be sectional, any more than light

and heat. Prevention is not abolition, and unjust laws are the only serious enemies that Law ever had. With history before us, it is no treason to question the infallibility of a court ; for courts are never wiser or more venerable than the men composing them, and a decision that reverses precedent cannot arrogate to itself any immunity from reversal. Truth is the only unrepealable thing.

We are gravely requested to have no opinion, or, having one, to suppress it, on the one topic that has occupied caucuses, newspapers, Presidents' messages, and Congress for the last dozen years, lest we endanger the safety of the Union. The true danger to popular forms of government begins when public opinion ceases because the people are incompetent or unwilling to think. In a democracy it is the duty of every citizen to think ; but unless the thinking result in a definite opinion, and the opinion lead to considerate action, they are nothing. If the people are assumed to be incapable of forming a judgment for themselves, the men whose position enables them to guide the public mind ought certainly to make good their want of intelligence. But on this great question, the wise solution of which, we are every day assured, is essential to the permanence of the Union, Mr. Bell has no opinion at all, Mr. Douglas says it is of no consequence which opinion prevails, and Mr. Breckinridge tells us vaguely that " all sections have an equal right in the common Territories." The parties which support these candidates, however, all agree in affirming that the election of its

special favorite is the one thing that can give back
peace to the distracted country. The distracted
country will continue to take care of itself, as it
has done hitherto, and the only question that needs
an answer is, What policy will secure the most
prosperous future to the helpless Territories, which
our decision is to make or mar for all coming
time ? What will save the country from a Senate
and Supreme Court where freedom shall be forever
at a disadvantage ?

There is always a fallacy in the argument of the
opponents of the Republican party. They affirm
that all the States and all the citizens of the States
ought to have equal rights in the Territories. Undoubtedly. But the difficulty is that they cannot.
The slaveholder moves into a new Territory with
his *institution*, and from that moment the free
white settler is virtually excluded. *His* institutions he cannot take with him ; they refuse to root
themselves in soil that is cultivated by slave-labor.
Speech is no longer free; the post-office is Aus-
trianized ; the mere fact of Northern birth may be
enough to hang him. Even now in Texas, settlers
from the Free States are being driven out and mur-
dered for pretended complicity in a plot the evidence for the existence of which has been obtained
by means without a parallel since the trial of the
Salem witches, and the stories about which are
as absurd and contradictory as the confessions of
Goodwife Corey. Kansas was saved, it is true ;
but it was the experience of Kansas that disgusted
the South with Mr. Douglas's panacea of " Squat-
ter Sovereignty."

The claim of *equal* rights in the Territories is a specious fallacy. Concede the demand of the slavery-extensionists, and you give up every inch of territory to slavery, to the absolute exclusion of freedom. For what they ask (however they may disguise it) is simply this,—that their *local law* be made the law of the land, and coextensive with the limits of the General Government. The Constitution acknowledges no unqualified or interminable right of property in the labor of another; and the plausible assertion, that "that is property which the law makes property " (confounding *a* law existing anywhere with *the* law which is binding everywhere), can deceive only those who have either never read the Constitution, or are ignorant of the opinions and intentions of those who framed it. It is true only of the States where slavery already exists; and it is because the propagandists of slavery are well aware of this, that they are so anxious to establish by positive enactment the seemingly moderate title to a right of existence for their institution in the Territories,—a title which they do not possess, and the possession of which would give them the oyster and the Free States the shells. Laws accordingly are asked for to protect Southern property in the Territories,—that is, to protect the inhabitants from deciding for themselves what their frame of government shall be. Such laws will be passed, and the fairest portion of our national domain irrevocably closed to free labor, if the Non-slaveholding States fail to do their duty in the present crisis.

But will the election of Mr. Lincoln endanger the Union? It is not a little remarkable that, as the prospect of his success increases, the menaces of secession grow fainter and less frequent. Mr. W. L. Yancey, to be sure, threatens to secede; but the country can get along without him, and we wish him a prosperous career in foreign parts. But Governor Wise no longer proposes to seize the Treasury at Washington,— perhaps because Mr. Buchanan has left so little in it. The old Mumbo-Jumbo is occasionally paraded at the North, but, however many old women may be frightened, the pulse of the stock-market remains provokingly calm. General Cushing, infringing the patent-right of the late Mr. James, the novelist, has seen a solitary horseman on the edge of the horizon. The exegesis of the vision has been various, some thinking that it means a Military Despot, — though in that case the force of cavalry would seem to be inadequate, — and others the Pony Express. If it had been one rider on two horses, the application would have been more general and less obscure. In fact, the old cry of Disunion has lost its terrors, if it ever had any, at the North. The South itself seems to have become alarmed at its own scarecrow, and speakers there are beginning to assure their hearers that the election of Mr. Lincoln will do them no harm. We entirely agree with them, for it will save them from themselves.

To believe any organized attempt by the Republican party to disturb the existing internal policy of the Southern States possible presupposes a manifest absurdity. Before anything of the kind could take place, the country must be in a state of forcible revolution. But there is no premonitory symptom of any such convulsion, unless we except Mr. Yancey, and that gentleman's throwing a solitary somerset will hardly turn the continent head over heels. The administration of Mr. Lincoln will be conservative, because no government is ever intentionally otherwise, and because power never knowingly undermines the foundation on which it rests. All that the Free States demand is that influence in the councils of the nation to which they are justly entitled by their population, wealth, and intelligence. That these elements of prosperity have increased more rapidly among them than in communities otherwise organized, with greater advantages of soil, climate, and mineral productions, is certainly no argument that they are incapable of the duties of efficient and prudent administration, however strong a one it may be for their endeavoring to secure for the Territories the single superiority that has made themselves what they are. The object of the Republican party is not the abolition of African slavery, but the utter extirpation of dogmas which are the logical sequence of attempts to establish its righteousness and wisdom, and which would serve equally well to justify the enslavement of every white man unable to protect himself. They believe that slavery is a wrong morally, a mistake politically, and a misfortune practically, wherever it exists; that it has nullified our influence abroad and forced us to compromise with our better in-

stincts at home; that it has perverted our government from its legitimate objects, weakened the
respect for the laws by making them the tools of its
purposes, and sapped the faith of men in any
higher political morality than interest or any better
statesmanship than chicane. They mean in every
lawful way to hem it within its present limits.

We are persuaded that the election of Mr. Lincoln will do more than anything else to appease the
excitement of the country. He has proved both
his ability and his integrity; he has had experience
enough in public affairs to make him a statesman,
and not enough to make him a politician. That he
has not had more will be no objection to him in the
eyes of those who have seen the administration of
the experienced public functionary whose term of
office is just drawing to a close. He represents a
party who know that true policy is gradual in its
advances, that it is conditional and not absolute,
that it must deal with facts and not with sentiments,
but who know also that it is wiser to stamp out evil
in the spark than to wait till there is no help but in
fighting fire with fire. They are the only conservative party, because they are the only one based on
an enduring principle, the only one that is not willing to pawn to-morrow for the means to gamble with
to-day. They have no hostility to the South, but a
determined one to doctrines of whose ruinous tendency every day more and more convinces them.

The encroachments of Slavery upon our national
policy have been like those of a glacier in a Swiss
valley. Inch by inch, the huge dragon with its

glittering scales and crests of ice coils itself onward, an anachronism of summer, the relic of a by-gone world where such monsters swarmed.   But it has its limit, the kindlier forces of Nature work against it, and the silent arrows of the sun are still, as of old, fatal to the frosty Python.   Geology tells us that such enormous devastators once covered the face of the earth, but the benignant sunlight of heaven touched them, and they faded silently, leaving no trace, but here and there the scratches of their talons, and the gnawed boulders scattered where they made their lair.   We have entire faith in the benignant influence of Truth, the sunlight of the moral world, and believe that slavery, like other worn-out systems, will melt gradually before it. "All the earth cries out upon Truth, and the heaven blesseth it; ill works shake and tremble at it, and with it is no unrighteous thing."

E PLURIBUS UNUM

1861

WE do not believe that any government — no, not the Rump Parliament on its last legs — ever showed such pitiful inadequacy as our own during the past two months. Helpless beyond measure in all the duties of practical statesmanship, its members or their dependants have given proof of remarkable energy in the single department of peculation; and there, not content with the slow methods of the old-fashioned defaulter, who helped himself only to what there was, they have contrived to steal what there was going to be, and have peculated in advance by a kind of official post-obit. So thoroughly has the credit of the most solvent nation in the world been shaken, that an administration which still talks of paying a hundred millions for Cuba is unable to raise a loan of five millions for the current expenses of government. Nor is this the worst: the moral bankruptcy at Washington is more complete and disastrous than the financial, and for the first time in our history the Executive is suspected of complicity in a treasonable plot against the very life of the nation.

Our material prosperity for nearly half a century has been so unparalleled that the minds of men have

become gradually more and more absorbed in
matters of personal concern ; and our institutions
have practically worked so well and so easily that
we have learned to trust in our luck, and to take
the permanence of our government for granted.
The country has been divided on questions of temporary policy, and the people have been drilled to
a wonderful discipline in the manœuvres of party
tactics ; but no crisis has arisen to force upon them
a consideration of the fundamental principles of
our system, or to arouse in them a sense of national
unity, and make them feel that patriotism was anything more than a pleasant sentiment,— half Fourth
of July and half Eighth of January, — a feeble
reminiscence, rather than a living fact with a direct
bearing on the national well-being. We have had
long experience of that unmemorable felicity which
consists in having no history, so far as history is
made up of battles, revolutions, and changes of
dynasty ; but the present generation has never
been called upon to learn that deepest lesson of
politics which is taught by a common danger,
throwing the people back on their national instincts,
and superseding party-leaders, the peddlers of
chicane, with men adequate to great occasions and
dealers in destiny. Such a crisis is now upon us ;
and if the virtue of the people make up for the
imbecility of the Executive, as we have little doubt
that it will, if the public spirit of the whole country be awakened in time by the common peril, the
present trial will leave the nation stronger than
ever, and more alive to its privileges and the duties

they imply. We shall have learned what is meant
by a government of laws, and that allegiance to the
sober will of the majority, concentrated in established forms and distributed by legitimate channels,
is all that renders democracy possible, is its only
conservative principle, the only thing that has
made and can keep us a powerful nation instead of
a brawling mob.

The theory that the best government is that
which governs least seems to have been accepted
literally by Mr. Buchanan, without considering the
qualifications to which all general propositions are
subject. His course of conduct has shown up its
absurdity, in cases where prompt action is required,
as effectually as Buckingham turned into ridicule
the famous verse, —

"My wound is great, because it is so small,"

by instantly adding, —

"Then it were greater, were it none at all."

Mr. Buchanan seems to have thought, that, if to
govern little was to govern well, then to do nothing
was the perfection of policy. But there is a vast
difference between letting well alone and allowing
bad to become worse by a want of firmness at the
outset. If Mr. Buchanan, instead of admitting
the right of secession, had declared it to be, as it
plainly is, rebellion, he would not only have received the unanimous support of the Free States,
but would have given confidence to the loyal, re-
claimed the wavering, and disconcerted the plotters
of treason in the South.

Either we have no government at all, or else the very word implies the right, and therefore the duty, in the governing power, of protecting itself from destruction and its property from pillage. But for Mr. Buchanan's acquiescence, the doctrine of the right of secession would never for a moment have bewildered the popular mind. It is simply mob-law under a plausible name. Such a claim might have been fairly enough urged under the old Confederation; though even then it would have been summarily dealt with, in the case of a Tory colony, if the necessity had arisen. But the very fact that we have a National Constitution, and legal methods for testing, preventing, or punishing any infringement of its provisions, demonstrates the absurdity of any such assumption of right now. When the States surrendered their power to make war, did they make the single exception of the United States, and reserve the privilege of declaring war against them at any moment? If we are a congeries of mediæval Italian republics, why should the General Government have expended immense sums in fortifying points whose strategic position is of continental rather than local consequence? Florida, after having cost us nobody knows how many millions of dollars and thousands of lives to render the holding of slaves possible to her, coolly proposes to withdraw herself from the Union and take with her one of the keys of the Mexican Gulf, on the plea that her slave-property is rendered insecure by the Union. Louisiana, which we bought and paid for to secure the mouth of the Mississippi, claims the right to make her soil French or Spanish, and to cork up the river again, whenever the whim may take her. The United States are not a German Confederation, but a unitary and indivisible nation, with a national life to protect, a national power to maintain, and national rights to defend against any and every assailant, at all hazards. Our national existence is all that gives value to American citizenship. Without the respect which nothing but our consolidated character could inspire, we might as well be citizens of the toy-republic of San Marino, for all the protection it would afford us. If our claim to a national existence was worth a seven years' war to establish, it is worth maintaining at any cost; and it is daily becoming more apparent that the people, so soon as they find that secession means anything serious, will not allow themselves to be juggled out of their rights, as members of one of the great powers of the earth, by a mere quibble of Constitutional interpretation.

We have been so much accustomed to the Buncombe style of oratory, to hearing men offer the pledge of their lives, fortunes, and sacred honor on the most trivial occasions, that we are apt to allow a great latitude in such matters, and only smile to think how small an advance any intelligent pawnbroker would be likely to make on securities of this description. The sporadic eloquence that breaks out over the country on the eve of election, and becomes a chronic disease in the two houses of Congress, has so accustomed us to dissociate words

and things, and to look upon strong language as
an evidence of weak purpose, that we attach no
meaning whatever to declamation. Our Southern
brethren have been especially given to these orgies
of loquacity, and have so often solemnly assured us
of their own courage, and of the warlike propen-
sities, power, wealth, and general superiority of
that part of the universe which is so happy as to
be represented by them, that, whatever other useful
impression they have made, they insure our never
forgetting the proverb about the woman who talks
of her virtue. South Carolina, in particular, if she
has hitherto failed in the application of her enterprise to manufacturing purposes of a more practical
kind, has always been able to match every yard
of printed cotton from the North with a yard of
printed fustian, the product of her own domestic
industry. We have thought no harm of this, so
long as no Act of Congress required the reading of
the "Congressional Globe." We submitted to the
general dispensation of long-windedness and short-
meaningness as to any other providental visitation,
endeavoring only to hold fast our faith in the divine
government of the world in the midst of so much
that was past understanding. But we lost sight of
the metaphysical truth, that, though men may fail
to convince others by a never so incessant repetition
of sonorous nonsense, they nevertheless gradually
persuade themselves, and impregnate their own
minds and characters with a belief in fallacies that
have been uncontradicted only because not worth
contradiction. Thus our Southern politicians, by

dint of continued reiteration, have persuaded themselves to accept their own flimsy assumptions for valid statistics, and at last actually believe themselves to be the enlightened gentlemen, and the people of the Free States the peddlers and sneaks they have so long been in the habit of fancying. They have argued themselves into a kind of vague faith that the wealth and power of the Republic are south of Mason and Dixon's line; and the Northern people have been slow in arriving at the conclusion that treasonable talk would lead to treasonable action, because they could not conceive that anybody should be so foolish as to think of rearing an independent frame of government on so visionary a basis. Moreover, the so often recurring necessity, incident to our system, of obtaining a favorable verdict from the people has fostered in our public men the talents and habits of jury-lawyers at the expense of statesmanlike qualities; and the people have been so long wonted to look upon the utterances of popular leaders as intended for immediate effect and having no reference to principles, that there is scarcely a prominent man in the country so independent in position and so clear of any suspicion of personal or party motives that they can put entire faith in what he says, and accept him either as the leader or the exponent of their thoughts and wishes. They have hardly been able to judge with certainty from the debates in Congress whether secession were a real danger, or only one of those political feints of which they have had such frequent experience.

Events have been gradually convincing them that the peril was actual and near. They begin to see how unwise, if nothing worse, has been the weak policy of the Executive in allowing men to play at Revolution till they learn to think the coarse reality as easy and pretty as the vaudeville they have been acting. They are fast coming to the conclusion that the list of grievances put forward by the secessionists is a sham and a pretence, the veil of a long-matured plot against republican institutions. And it is time the traitors of the South should know that the Free States are becoming every day more united in sentiment and more earnest in resolve, and that, so soon as they are thoroughly satisfied that secession is something more than empty bluster, a public spirit will be aroused that will be content with no half-measures, and which no Executive, however unwilling, can resist.

The country is weary of being cheated with plays upon words. The United States are a nation, and not a mass-meeting; theirs is a government, and not a caucus, — a government that was meant to be capable, and is capable, of something more than the helpless *please don't* of a village constable; they have executive and administrative officers that are not mere puppet-figures to go through the motions of an objectless activity, but arms and hands that become supple to do the will of the people so soon as that will becomes conscious and defines its purpose. It is time that we turned up our definitions in some more trustworthy dictionary than that of avowed disunionists and their more dangerous because more timid and cunning accomplices. Rebellion smells no sweeter because it is called Secession, nor does Order lose its divine precedence in human affairs because a knave may nickname it Coercion. Secession means chaos, and Coercion the exercise of legitimate authority. You cannot dignify the one nor degrade the other by any verbal charlatanism. The best testimony to the virtue of coercion is the fact that no wrongdoer ever thought well of it. The thief in jail, the mob-leader in the hands of the police, and the murderer on the drop will be unanimous in favor of this new heresy of the unconstitutionality of constitutions, with its Newgate Calendar of confessors, martyrs, and saints. Falstaff's famous regiment would have volunteered to a man for its propagation or its defence. Henceforth let every unsuccessful litigant have the right to pronounce the verdict of a jury sectional, and to quash all proceedings and retain the property in controversy by seceding from the court-room. Let the planting of hemp be made penal, because it squints toward coercion. Why, the first great secessionist would doubtless have preferred to divide heaven peaceably, would have been willing to send commissioners, must have thought Michael's proceedings injudicious, and could probably even now demonstrate the illegality of hell-fire to any five-year-old imp of average education and intelligence. What a fine world we should have, if we could only come quietly together in convention, and declare by unanimous resolution, or even by a two-thirds vote, that edge-tools should hereafter cut everybody's fingers but his that played with them; that, when two men ride on one horse, the hindmost shall always sit in front; and that, when a man tries to thrust his partner out of bed and gets kicked out himself, he shall be deemed to have established his title to an equitable division, and the bed shall be thenceforth his as of right, without detriment to the other's privilege in the floor!

If secession be a right, then the moment of its exercise is wholly optional with those possessing it. Suppose, on the eve of a war with England, Michigan should vote herself out of the Union and declare herself annexed to Canada, what kind of a reception would her commissioners be likely to meet in Washington, and what scruples should we feel about coercion? Or, to take a case precisely parallel to that of South Carolina, suppose that Utah, after getting herself admitted to the Union, should resume her sovereignty, as it is pleasantly called, and block our path to the Pacific, under the pretence that she did not consider her institutions safe while the other States entertained such unscriptural prejudices against her special weakness in the patriarchal line. Is the only result of our admitting a Territory on Monday to be the giving it a right to steal itself and go out again on Tuesday? Or do only the original thirteen States possess this precious privilege of suicide? We shall need something like a Fugitive Slave Law for runaway republics, and must get a provision inserted in our treaties with foreign powers, that they shall help us catch any delinquent who may take refuge with them, as South Carolina has been trying to do with England and France. It does not matter to the argument, except so far as the good taste of the proceeding is concerned, at what particular time a State may make her territory foreign, thus opening one gate of our national defences and offering a bridge to invasion. The danger of the thing is in her making her territory foreign under any circumstances; and it is a danger which the government must prevent, if only for self-preservation. Within the limits of the constitution two sovereignties cannot exist; and yet what practical odds does it make, if a State may become sovereign by simply declaring herself so? The legitimate consequence of secession is, not that a State becomes sovereign, but that, so far as the general government is concerned, she has outlawed herself, nullified her own existence as a State, and become an aggregate of riotous men who resist the execution of the laws.

We are told that coercion will be civil war; and so is a mob civil war, till it is put down. In the present case, the only coercion called for is the protection of the public property, and the collection of the federal revenues. If it be necessary to send troops to do this, they will not be sectional, as it is the fashion nowadays to call people who insist on their own rights and the maintenance of the laws, but federal troops, representing the will and power of the whole Confederacy. A danger is always great so long as we are afraid of it; and

mischief like that now gathering head in South
Carolina may soon become a danger, if not swiftly
dealt with. Mr. Buchanan seems altogether too
wholesale a disciple of the *laissez-faire* doctrine,
and has allowed activity in mischief the same immunity from interference which is true policy only
in regard to enterprise wisely and profitably directed. He has been naturally reluctant to employ
force, but has overlooked the difference between indecision and moderation, forgetting the lesson of all
experience, that firmness in the beginning saves the
need of force in the end, and that forcible measures applied too late may be made to seem violent
ones, and thus excite a mistaken sympathy with
the sufferers by their own misdoing. The feeling
of the country has been unmistakably expressed in
regard to Major Anderson, and that not merely
because he showed prudence and courage, but because he was the first man holding a position of
trust who did his duty to the nation. Public sentiment unmistakably demands that, in the case of
Anarchy *vs.* America, the cause of the defendant
shall not be suffered to go by default. The proceedings in South Carolina, parodying the sublime
initiative of our own Revolution with a Declaration
of Independence that hangs the franchise of human nature on the kink of a hair, and substitutes
for the visionary right of all men to the pursuit
of happiness the more practical privilege of some
men to pursue their own negro, — these proceedings would be merely ludicrous, were it not for the
danger that the men engaged in them may so far

commit themselves as to find the inconsistency of a return to prudence too galling, and to prefer the safety of their pride to that of their country.

It cannot be too distinctly stated or too often repeated that the discontent of South Carolina is not one to be allayed by any concessions which the Free States can make with dignity or even safety. It is something more radical and of longer standing than distrust of the motives or probable policy of the Republican party. It is neither more nor less than a disbelief in the very principles on which our government is founded. So long as they practically retained the government of the country, and could use its power and patronage to their own advantage, the plotters were willing to wait; but the moment they lost that control, by the breaking up of the Democratic party, and saw that their chance of ever regaining it was hopeless, they declared openly the principles on which they have all along been secretly acting. Denying the constitutionality of special protection to any other species of property or branch of industry, and in 1832 threatening to break up the Union unless their theory of the Constitution in this respect were admitted, they went into the late Presidential contest with a claim for extraordinary protection to a certain kind of property already the only one endowed with special privileges and immunities. Defeated overwhelmingly before the people, they now question the right of the majority to govern, except on their terms, and threaten violence in the hope of extorting from the fears of the Free States what they failed to obtain from their conscience and settled convictions of duty. Their quarrel is not with the Republican party, but with the theory of Democracy.

The South Carolina politicians have hitherto shown themselves adroit managers, shrewd in detecting and profiting by the weaknesses of men; but their experience has not been of a kind to give them practical wisdom in that vastly more important part of government which depends for success on common sense and business habits. The members of the South Carolina Convention have probably less knowledge of political economy than any single average Northern merchant whose success depends on an intimate knowledge of the laws of trade and the world-wide contingencies of profit and loss. Such a man would tell them, as the result of invariable experience, that the prosperity of no community was so precarious as that of one whose very existence was dependent on a single agricultural product. What divinity hedges cotton, that competition may not touch it, — that some disease, like that of the potato and the vine, may not bring it to beggary in a single year, and cure the overweening conceit of prosperity with the sharp medicine of Ireland and Madeira? But these South Carolina economists are better at vaporing than at calculation. They will find to their cost that the figures of statistics have little mercy for the figures of speech, which are so powerful in raising enthusiasm and so helpless in raising money. The eating of one's own words, as they must do, sooner or later, is neither agreeable nor nutritious; but it is better to do it before there is nothing else left to eat. The secessionists are strong in declamation, but they are weak in the multiplication-table and the ledger. They have no notion of any sort of logical connection between treason and taxes. It is all very fine signing Declarations of Independence, and one may thus become a kind of panic-price hero for a week or two, even rising to the effigial martyrdom of the illustrated press; but these gentlemen seem to have forgotten that, if their precious document should lead to anything serious, they have been signing promises to pay for the State of South Carolina to an enormous amount. It is probably far short of the truth to say that the taxes of an autonomous palmetto republic would be three times what they are now. To speak of nothing else, there must be a military force kept constantly on foot; and the ministers of King Cotton will find that the charge made by a standing army on the finances of the new empire is likely to be far more serious and damaging than can be compensated by the glory of a great many such "spirited charges" as that by which Colonel Pettigrew and his gallant rifles took Fort Pinckney, with its garrison of one engineer officer and its armament of no guns. Soldiers are the most costly of all toys or tools. The outgo for the army of the Pope, never amounting to ten thousand effective men, in the cheapest country in the world, has been half a million of dollars a month. Under the present system, it needs no argument to show that the non-slaveholding States, with a free population considerably more than double that of the slaveholding States, and with much more generally distributed wealth and opportunities of spending, pay far more than the proportion predicable on mere preponderance in numbers of the expenses of a government supported mainly by a tariff on importations. And it is not the burden of this difference merely that the new Cotton Republic must assume. They will need as large, probably a larger, army and navy than that of the present Union; as numerous a diplomatic establishment; a postal system whose large yearly deficit they must bear themselves; and they must assume the main charges of the Indian Bureau. If they adopt free trade, they will alienate the Border Slave States, and even Louisiana; if a system of customs, they have cut themselves off from the chief consumers of foreign goods. One of the calculations of the Southern conspirators is to render the Free States tributary to their new republic by adopting free trade and smuggling their imported goods across the border. But this is all moonshine; for, even if smuggling could not be prevented as easily as it now is from the British Provinces, how long would it be before the North would adapt its tariff to the new order of things? And thus thrown back upon direct taxation, how many years would it take to open the eyes of the poorer classes of Secessia to the hardship of their position and its causes? Their ignorance has been trifled with by men who cover treasonable designs with a pretence of local patriotism. Neither they nor their misleaders have any true conception of the people of the Free States, of those "white slaves" who in Massachusetts alone have a deposit in the Savings Banks whose yearly interest would pay seven times over the four hundred thousand dollars which South Carolina cannot raise.

But even if we leave other practical difficulties out of sight, what chance of stability is there for a confederacy whose very foundation is the principle that any member of it may withdraw at the first discontent? If they could contrive to establish a free trade treaty with their chief customer, England, would she consent to gratify Louisiana with an exception in favor of sugar? Some of the leaders of the secession movement have already become aware of this difficulty, and accordingly propose the abolition of all State lines, — the first step toward a military despotism; for, if our present system have one advantage greater than another, it is the neutralization of numberless individual ambitions by adequate opportunities of provincial distinction. Even now the merits of the Napoleonic system are put forward by some of the theorists of Alabama and Mississippi, who doubtless have as good a stomach to be emperors as ever Bottom had to a bottle of hay, when his head was temporarily transformed to the likeness of theirs, — and who, were they subjects of the government that looks so nice across the Atlantic, would, ere this, have been on their way to Cayenne, a spot where such red-peppery temperaments would find themselves at home.

The absurdities with which the telegraphic column of the newspapers has been daily crowded, since the vagaries of South Carolina finally settled down into unmistakable insanity, would give us but a poor opinion of the general intelligence of the country, did we not know that they were due to the necessities of "Our Own Correspondent." At one time, it is Fort Sumter that is to be bombarded with floating batteries mounted on rafts behind a rampart of cotton-bales; at another, it is Mr. Barrett, Mayor of Washington, announcing his intention that the President-elect shall be inaugurated, or Mr. Buchanan declaring that he shall cheerfully assent to it. Indeed! and who gave them any choice in the matter? Yesterday, it was General Scott who would not abandon the flag which he had illustrated with the devotion of a lifetime; to-day, it is General Harney or Commodore Kearney who has concluded to be true to the country whose livery he has worn and whose bread he has eaten for half a century; to-morrow, it will be Ensign Stebbins who has been magnanimous enough not to throw up his commission. What are we to make of the extraordinary confusion of ideas which such things indicate? In what other country would it be considered creditable to an officer that he merely did not turn traitor at the first opportunity? There can be no doubt of the honor both of the army and navy, and of their loyalty to their country. They will do their duty, if we do ours in saving them a country to which they can be loyal.

We have been so long habituated to a kind of
local independence in the management of our affairs,
and the central government has fortunately had so
little occasion for making itself felt at home and in
the domestic concerns of the States, that the idea of
its relation to us as a power, except for protection
from without, has gradually become vague and
alien to our ordinary habits of thought. We have
so long heard the principle admitted, and seen it
acted on with advantage to the general weal, that
the people are sovereign in their own affairs, that
we must recover our presence of mind before we
see the fallacy of the assumption, that the people,
or a bare majority of them, in a single State, can
exercise their right of sovereignty as against the
will of the nation legitimately expressed. When
such a contingency arises, it is for a moment difficult to get rid of our habitual associations, and to
feel that we are not a mere partnership, dissolvable
whether by mutual consent or on the demand of one
or more of its members, but a nation, which can
never abdicate its right, and can never surrender it
while virtue enough is left in the people to make
it worth retaining. It would seem to be the will
of God that from time to time the manhood of
nations, like that of individuals, should be tried by
great dangers or by great opportunities. If the
manhood be there, it makes the great opportunity
out of the great danger ; if it be not there, then
the great danger out of the great opportunity. The
occasion is offered us now of trying whether a conscious nationality and a timely concentration of the

popular will for its maintenance be possible in a democracy, or whether it is only despotisms that are capable of the sudden and selfish energy of protecting themselves from destruction.

The Republican party has thus far borne itself with firmness and moderation, and the great body of the Democratic party in the Free States is gradually being forced into an alliance with it. Let us not be misled by any sophisms about conciliation and compromise. Discontented citizens may be conciliated and compromised with, but never open rebels with arms in their hands. If there be any concessions which justice may demand on the one hand and honor make on the other, let us try if we can adjust them with the Border Slave States; but a government has already signed its own death-warrant, when it consents to make terms with law-breakers. First reestablish the supremacy of order, and then it will be time to discuss terms; but do not call it a compromise, when you give up your purse with a pistol at your head. This is no time for sentimentalisms about the empty chair at the national hearth; all the chairs would be empty soon enough, if one of the children is to amuse itself with setting the house on fire, whenever it can find a match. Since the election of Mr. Lincoln, not one of the arguments has lost its force, not a cipher of the statistics has been proved mistaken, on which the judgment of the people was made up. Nobody proposes, or has proposed, to interfere with any existing rights of property; the majority have not assumed to decide upon any question of the righteousness or policy of certain social arrangements existing in any part of the Confederacy; they have not undertaken to constitute themselves the conscience of their neighbors; they have simply endeavored to do their duty to their own posterity, and to protect them from a system which, as ample experience has shown, and that of our present difficulty were enough to show, fosters a sense of irresponsibleness to all obligation in the governing class, and in the governed an ignorance and a prejudice which may be misled at any moment to the peril of the whole country.

But the present question is one altogether transcending all limits of party and all theories of party policy. It is a question of national existence; it is a question whether Americans shall govern America, or whether a disappointed clique shall nullify all government now, and render a stable government difficult hereafter; it is a question, not whether we shall have civil war under certain contingencies, but whether we shall prevent it under any. It is idle, and worse than idle, to talk about Central Republics that can never be formed. We want neither Central Republics nor Northern Republics, but our own Republic and that of our fathers, destined one day to gather the whole continent under a flag that shall be the most august in the world. Having once known what it was to be members of a grand and peaceful constellation, we shall not believe, without further proof, that the laws of our gravitation are to be abolished, and we flung forth into chaos, a hurlyburly of jostling and splintering stars, whenever Robert Toombs or Robert Rhett, or any other Bob of the secession kite, may give a flirt of self-importance. The first and greatest benefit of government is that it keeps the peace, that it insures every man his right, and not only that, but the permanence of it. In order to this, its first requisite is stability; and this once firmly settled, the greater the extent of conterminous territory that can be subjected to one system and one language and inspired by one patriotism, the better. That there should be some diversity of interests is perhaps an advantage, since the necessity of legislating equitably for all gives legislation its needful safeguards of caution and largeness of view. A single empire embracing the whole world, and controlling, without extinguishing, local organizations and nationalities, has been not only the dream of conquerors, but the ideal of speculative philanthropists. Our own dominion is of such extent and power, that it may, so far as this continent is concerned, be looked upon as something like an approach to the realization of such an ideal. But for slavery, it might have succeeded in realizing it; and in spite of slavery, it may. One language, one law, one citizenship over thousands of miles, and a government on the whole so good that we seem to have forgotten what government means, — these are things not to be spoken of with levity, privileges not to be surrendered without a struggle. And yet while

Germany and Italy, taught by the bloody and bitter and servile experience of centuries, are striving toward unity as the blessing above all others desirable, we are to allow a Union, that for almost eighty years has been the source and the safeguard of incalculable advantages, to be shattered by the caprice of a rabble that has outrun the intention of its leaders, while we are making up our minds what coercion means! Ask the first constable, and he will tell you that it is the force necessary for executing the laws. To avoid the danger of what men who have seized upon forts, arsenals, and other property of the United States, and continue to hold them by military force, may choose to call civil war, we are allowing a state of things to gather head which will make real civil war the occupation of the whole country for years to come, and establish it as a permanent institution. There is no such antipathy between the North and the South as men ambitious of a consideration in the new republic, which their talents and character have failed to secure them in the old, would fain call into existence by asserting that it exists. The misunderstanding and dislike between them is not so great as they were within living memory between England and Scotland, as they are now between England and Ireland. There is no difference of race, language, or religion. Yet, after a dissatisfaction of near a century and two rebellions, there is no part of the British dominion more loyal than Scotland, no British subjects who would be more loath to part with the substantial advantages of their imperial connection than the Scotch ; and even in Ireland, after a longer and more deadly feud, there is no sane man who would consent to see his country irrevocably cut off from power and consideration to obtain an independence which would be nothing but Donnybrook Fair multiplied by every city, town, and village in the island. The same considerations of policy and advantage which render the union of Scotland and Ireland with England a necessity apply with even more force to the several States of our Union. To let one, or two, or half a dozen of them break away in a freak of anger or unjust suspicion, or, still worse, from mistaken notions of sectional advantage, would be to fail in our duty to ourselves and our our country, would be a fatal blindness to the lessons which immemorial history has been tracing on the earth's surface, either with the beneficent furrow of the plough, or, when that was unheeded, the fruitless gash of the cannon ball.

When we speak of coercion, we do not mean violence, but only the assertion of constituted and acknowledged authority. Even if seceding States could be conquered back again, they would not be worth the conquest. We ask only for the assertion of a principle which shall give the friends of order in the discontented quarters a hope to rally round, and the assurance of the support they have a right to expect. There is probably a majority, and certainly a powerful minority, in the seceding States, who are loyal to the Union ; and

these should have that support which the prestige of the General Government can alone give
them. It is not to the North nor to the Republican party that the malcontents are called on
to submit, but to the laws and to the benign intentions of the Constitution, as they were understood by its framers. What the country wants is
a permanent settlement; and it has learned, by
repeated trial, that compromise is not a cement,
but a wedge. The Government did not hesi-
tate to protect the doubtful right of property of
a Virginian in Anthony Burns by the exercise
of coercion, and the loyalty of Massachusetts was
such that her own militia could be used to enforce an obligation abhorrent, and, as there is
reason to believe, made purposely abhorrent, to
her dearest convictions and most venerable traditions; and yet the same Government tampers with
armed treason, and lets *I dare not* wait upon *I
would*, when it is a question of protecting the acknowledged property of the Union, and of sustaining, nay, preserving even, a gallant officer
whose only fault is that he has been too true to
his flag. While we write, the newspapers bring
us the correspondence between Mr. Buchanan
and the South Carolina " Commissioners;" and
surely never did a government stoop so low as
ours has done, not only in consenting to receive
these ambassadors from Nowhere, but in suggesting that a soldier deserves court-martial who has
done all he could to maintain himself in a for-
lorn hope, with rebellion in his front and trea-

chery in his rear. Our Revolutionary heroes had
old-fashioned notions about rebels, suitable to the
straightforward times in which they lived, — times
when blood was as freely shed to secure our national existence as milk-and-water is now to destroy it. Mr. Buchanan might have profited by
the example of men who knew nothing of the
modern arts of Constitutional interpretation, but
saw clearly the distinction between right and
wrong. When a party of the Shays rebels came
to the house of General Pomeroy, in Northamp-
ton, and asked if he could accommodate them, —
the old soldier, seeing the green sprigs in their
hats, the badges of their treason, shouted to his
son, "Fetch me my hanger, and I'll *accommodate* the scoundrels!" General Jackson, we suspect, would have accommodated rebel commissioners in the same peremptory style.

While our Government, like Giles in the old
rhyme, is wondering whether it is a government or
not, emissaries of treason are cunningly working
upon the fears and passions of the Border States,
whose true interests are infinitely more on the side
of the Union than of slavery. They are luring
the ambitious with visionary promises of Southern
grandeur and prosperity, and deceiving the ignorant into the belief that the principles and practice
of the Free States were truly represented by John
Brown. All this might have been prevented, had
Mr. Buchanan in his Message thought of the interests of his country instead of those of his party.
It is not too late to check and neutralize it now.

A decisively national and patriotic policy is all
that can prevent excited men from involving themselves so deeply that they will find "returning as
tedious as go o'er," and be more afraid of cowardice than of consequences.

Slavery is no longer the matter in debate, and
we must beware of being led off upon that side-
issue. The matter now in hand is the reëstablish-
ment of order, the reaffirmation of national unity,
and the settling once for all whether there can be
such a thing as a government without the right
to use its power in self-defence. The Republican
party has done all it could lawfully do in limiting
slavery once more to the States in which it exists,
and in relieving the Free States from forced complicity with an odious system. They can be patient, as Providence is often patient, till natural
causes work that conviction which conscience has
been unable to effect. They believe that the violent abolition of slavery, which would be sure to
follow sooner or later the disruption of our Confederacy, would not compensate for the evil that
would be entailed upon both races by the abolition
of our nationality and the bloody confusion that
would follow it. More than this, they believe that
there can be no permanent settlement except in the
definite establishment of the principle, that this
Government, like all others, rests upon the everlasting foundations of just Authority, — that that authority, once delegated by the people, becomes a
common stock of Power to be wielded for the common protection, and from which no minority or

majority of partners can withdraw its contribution under any conditions, — that this power is what makes us a nation, and implies a corresponding duty of submission, or, if that be refused, then a necessary right of self-vindication. We are citizens, when we make laws; we become subjects, when we attempt to break them after they are made. Lynch-law may be better than no law in new and half-organized communities, but we cannot tolerate its application in the affairs of government. The necessity of suppressing rebellion by force may be a terrible one, but its consequences, whatever they may be, do not weigh a feather in comparison with those that would follow from admitting the principle that there is no social compact binding on any body of men too numerous to be arrested by a United States marshal.

As we are writing these sentences, the news comes to us that South Carolina has taken the initiative, and chosen the arbitrament of war. She has done it because her position was desperate, and because she hoped thereby to unite the Cotton States by a complicity in blood, as they are already committed by a unanimity in bravado. Major Anderson deserves more than ever the thanks of his country for his wise forbearance. The foxes in Charleston, who have already lost their tails in the trap of Secession, wished to throw upon him the responsibility of that second blow which begins a quarrel, and the silence of his guns has balked them. Nothing would have pleased them so much as to have one of his thirty-two-pound shot give a taste of real war to the boys who are playing soldier at Morris's Island. But he has shown the discretion of a brave man. South Carolina will soon learn how much she has undervalued the people of the Free States. Because they prefer law to bowie-knives and revolvers, she has too lightly reckoned on their caution and timidity. She will find that, though slow to kindle, they are as slow to yield, and that they are willing to risk their lives for the defence of law, though not for the breach of it. They are beginning to question the value of a peace that is forced on them at the point of the bayonet, and is to be obtained only by an abandonment of rights and duties.

When we speak of the courage and power of the Free States, we do not wish to be understood as descending to the vulgar level of meeting brag with brag. We speak of them only as among the elements to be gravely considered by the fanatics who may render it necessary for those who value the continued existence of this Confederacy as it deserves to be valued to kindle a back-fire, and to use the desperate means which God has put into their hands to be employed in the last extremity of free institutions. And when we use the term coercion, nothing is farther from our thoughts than the carrying of blood and fire among those whom we still consider our brethren of South Carolina. These civilized communities of ours have interests too serious to be risked on a childish wager of courage, — a quality that can always be bought cheaper than day-labor on a railway-embankment.

We wish to see the Government strong enough for the maintenance of law, and for the protection, if need be, of the unfortunate Governor Pickens from the anarchy he has allowed himself to be made a tool of by evoking. Let the power of the Union be used for any other purpose than that of shutting and barring the door against the return of misguided men to their allegiance. At the same time we think legitimate and responsible force prudently exerted safer than the submission, without a struggle, to unlawful and irresponsible violence.

Peace is the greatest of blessings, when it is won and kept by manhood and wisdom; but it is a blessing that will not long be the housemate of cowardice. It is God alone who is powerful enough to let His authority slumber; it is only His laws that are strong enough to protect and avenge themselves. Every human government is bound to make its laws so far resemble His that they shall be uniform, certain, and unquestionable in their operation; and this it can do only by a timely show of power, and by an appeal to that authority which is of divine right, inasmuch as its office is to maintain that order which is the single attribute of the Infinite Reason that we can clearly apprehend and of which we have hourly example.

THE PICKENS-AND-STEALIN'S REBELLION

1861

HAD any one ventured to prophesy on the Fourth of March that the immediate prospect of Civil War would be hailed by the people of the Free States with a unanimous shout of enthusiasm, he would have been thought a madman. Yet the prophecy would have been verified by what we now see and hear in every city, town, and hamlet from Maine to Kansas. With the advantage of three months' active connivance in the cabinet of Mr. Buchanan, with an empty treasury at Washington, and that reluctance to assume responsibility and to inaugurate a decided policy, the common vice of our politicians, who endeavor to divine and to follow popular sentiment rather than to lead it, it seemed as if Disunion were inevitable, and the only open question were the line of separation. So assured seemed the event that English journalists moralized gravely on the inherent weakness of Democracy. While the leaders of the Southern Rebellion did not dare to expose their treason to the risk of a popular vote in any one of the seceding States, *The Saturday Review*, one of the ablest of British journals, solemnly warned its countrymen to learn by our example the dangers of an extended suffrage.

Meanwhile, the conduct of the people of the Free States, during all these trying and perilous months, had proved, if it proved anything, the essential conservatism of a population in which every grown man has a direct interest in the stability of the national government. So abstinent are they by habit and principle from any abnormal intervention with the machine of administration, so almost superstitious in adherence to constitutional forms, as to be for a moment staggered by the claim to a *right* of secession set up by all the Cotton States, admitted by the Border Slave States, which had the effrontery to deliberate between their plain allegiance and their supposed interest, and but feebly denied by the Administration then in power. The usual panacea of palaver was tried; Congress did its best to add to the general confusion of thought; and, as if that were not enough, a Convention of Notables was called simultaneously to thresh the straw of debate anew, and to convince thoughtful persons that men do not grow wiser as they grow older. So in the two Congresses the notables talked, — in the one those who ought to be shelved, in the other those who were shelved already, — while those who were too thoroughly shelved for a seat in either addressed Great Union Meetings at home. Not a man of them but had a compromise in his pocket, adhesive as Spalding's glue, warranted to stick the shattered Confederacy together so firmly that, if it ever broke again, it

must be in a new place, which was a great con-
solation. If these gentlemen gave nothing very
valuable to the people of the Free States, they
were giving the Secessionists what was of inesti-
mable value to them, — Time. The latter went on
seizing forts, navy-yards, and deposits of Federal
money, erecting batteries, and raising and arming
men at their leisure; above all, they acquired a
prestige, and accustomed men's minds to the thought
of disunion, not only as possible, but actual. They
began to grow insolent, and, while compelling
absolute submission to their rebellious usurpation
at home, decried any exercise of legitimate authority on the part of the General Government as
Coercion, — a new term, by which it was sought
to be established as a principle of constitutional
law, that it is always the Northern bull that has
gored the Southern ox.

During all this time, the Border Slave States,
and especially Virginia, were playing a part at
once cowardly and selfish. They assumed the right
to stand neutral between the government and rebellion, to contract a kind of morganatic marriage
with Treason, by which they could enjoy the pleasant sin without the tedious responsibility, and to
be traitors in everything but the vulgar contingency
of hemp. Doubtless the aim of the political managers in these States was to keep the North amused
with schemes of arbitration, reconstruction, and
whatever other fine words would serve the purpose
of hiding the real issue, till the new government
of Secessia should have so far consolidated itself

as to be able to demand with some show of reason a recognition from foreign powers, and to render it politic for the United States to consent to peaceable separation. They counted on the self-interest of England and the supineness of the North. As to the former, they were not wholly without justification, — for nearly all the English discussions of the "American Crisis" which we have seen have shown far more of the shop-keeping spirit than of interest in the maintenance of free institutions; but in regard to the latter they made the fatal mistake of believing our Buchanans, Cushings, and Touceys to be representative men. They were not aware how utterly the Democratic party had divorced itself from the moral sense of the Free States, nor had they any conception of the tremendous recoil of which the long-repressed convictions, traditions, and instincts of a people are capable.

Never was a nation so in want of a leader; never was it more plain that, without a head, the people "bluster abroad as beasts," with plenty of the iron of purpose, but purpose without coherence, and with no cunning smith of circumstance to edge it with plan and helve it with direction. What the country was waiting for showed itself in the universal thrill of satisfaction when Major Anderson took the extraordinary responsibility of doing his duty. But such was the general uncertainty, so doubtful seemed the loyalty of the Democratic party as represented by its spokesmen at the North, so irresolute was the tone of many

Republican leaders and journals, that a powerful and wealthy community of twenty millions of people gave a sigh of relief when they had been permitted to install the Chief Magistrate of their choice in their own National Capital. Even after the inauguration of Mr. Lincoln, it was confidently announced that Jefferson Davis, the Burr of the Southern conspiracy, would be in Washington before the month was out; and so great was the Northern despondency that the chances of such an event were seriously discussed. While the nation was falling to pieces, there were newspapers and "distinguished statesmen" of the party so lately and so long in power base enough to be willing to make political capital out of the common danger, and to lose their country, if they could only find their profit. There was even one man found in Massachusetts, who, measuring the moral standard of his party by his own, had the unhappy audacity to declare publicly that there were friends enough of the South in his native State to prevent the march of any troops thence to sustain that Constitution to which he had sworn fealty in Heaven knows how many offices, the rewards of almost as many turnings of his political coat. There was one journal in New York which had the insolence to speak of *President* Davis and *Mister* Lincoln in the same paragraph. No wonder the "dirt-eaters" of the Carolinas could be taught to despise a race among whom creatures might be found to do that by choice which they themselves were driven to do by misery.

Thus far the Secessionists had the game all their own way, for their dice were loaded with Northern lead. They framed their sham constitution, appointed themselves to their sham offices, issued their sham commissions, endeavored to bribe England with a sham offer of low duties and Virginia with a sham prohibition of the slave-trade, advertised their proposals for a sham loan which was to be taken up under intimidation, and levied real taxes on the people in the name of the people whom they had never allowed to vote directly on their enormous swindle. With money stolen from the Government, they raised troops whom they equipped with stolen arms, and beleaguered national fortresses with cannon stolen from national arsenals. They sent out secret agents to Europe, they had their secret allies in the Free States, their conventions transacted all important business in secret session ; — there was but one exception to the shrinking delicacy becoming a maiden government, and that was the openness of the stealing. We had always thought a high sense of personal honor an essential element of chivalry; but among the *Romanic* races, by which, as the wonderful ethnologist of *De Bow's Review* tells us, the Southern States where settled, and from which they derive a close entail of chivalric characteristics, to the exclusion of the vulgar Saxons of the North, such is by no means the case. For the first time in history the deliberate treachery of a general is deemed worthy of a civic ovation, and Virginia has the honor of being the first State claiming to be civilized that has decreed the honors of a triumph to a cabinet officer who had contrived to gild a treason that did not endanger his life with a peculation that could not further damage his reputation. Rebellion, even in a bad cause, may have its romantic side; treason, which had not been such but for being on the losing side, may challenge admiration; but nothing can sweeten larceny or disinfect perjury. A rebellion inaugurated with theft, and which has effected its entry into national fortresses, not over broken walls, but by breaches of trust, should take Jonathan Wild for its patron saint, with the run of Mr. Buchanan's cabinet for a choice of sponsors, — godfathers we should not dare to call them.

Mr. Lincoln's Inaugural Speech was of the kind usually called "firm, but conciliatory," — a policy doubtful in troublous times, since it commonly argues weakness, and more than doubtful in a crisis like ours, since it left the course which the Administration meant to take ambiguous, and, while it weakened the Government by exciting the distrust of all who wished for vigorous measures, really strengthened the enemy by encouraging the conspirators in the Border States. There might be a question as to whether this or that attitude were expedient for the Republican party; there could be none as to the only safe and dignified one for the Government of the Nation. Treason was as much treason in the beginning of March as in the middle of April; and it seems certain now, as it seemed probable to many then, that the country

would have sooner rallied to the support of the
Government, if the Government had shown an
earlier confidence in the loyalty of the people.
Though the President talked of "repossessing"
the stolen forts, arsenals, and custom-houses, yet
close upon this declaration followed the disheartening intelligence that the cabinet were discussing
the propriety of evacuating not only Fort Sumter,
which was of no strategic importance, but Fort
Pickens, which was the key to the Gulf of Mexico,
and to abandon which was almost to acknowledge
the independence of the Rebel States. Thus far
the Free States had waited with commendable
patience for some symptom of vitality in the new
Administration, something that should distinguish
it from the piteous helplessness of its predecessor.
But now their pride was too deeply outraged for
endurance; indignant remonstrances were heard
from all quarters, and the Government seemed for
the first time fairly to comprehend that it had
twenty millions of freemen at its back, and that
forts might be taken and held by honest men as
well as by knaves and traitors. The nettle had
been stroked long enough; it was time to try a firm
grip. Still the Administration seemed inclined to
temporize, so thoroughly was it possessed by the
notion of conciliating the Border States. In point
of fact, the side which those States might take in
the struggle between Law and Anarchy was of
vastly more import to them than to us. They
could bring no considerable reinforcement of
money, credit, or arms to the rebels; they could at

best but add so many mouths to an army whose
commissariat was already dangerously embarrassed.
They could not even, except temporarily, keep the
war away from the territory of the seceding States,
every one of which had a sea-door open to the
invasion of an enemy who controlled the entire
navy and shipping of the country. The position
assumed by Eastern Virginia and Maryland was
of consequence only so far as it might facilitate
a sudden raid on Washington, and the policy of
both these States was to amuse the Government
by imaginary negotiations till the plans of the conspirators were ripe. In both States men were
actively recruited and enrolled to assist in attacking the capital. With them, as with the more
openly rebellious States, the new theory of "Coercion" was ingeniously arranged like a valve, yielding at the slightest impulse to the passage of forces
for the subversion of legitimate authority, closing
imperviously, so that no drop of power could ooze
through in the opposite direction. Lord De Roos,
long suspected of cheating at cards, would never
have been convicted but for the resolution of an
adversary, who, pinning his hand to the table with
a fork, said to him blandly, "My Lord, if the ace
of spades is not under your Lordship's hand, why,
then, I beg your pardon!" It seems to us that a
timely treatment of Governor Letcher in the same
energetic way would have saved the disasters of
Harper's Ferry and Norfolk, — for disasters they
were, though six months of temporizing had so
lowered the public sense of what was due to the

national dignity that people were glad to see the Government active at length, even if only in setting fire to its own house.

We are by no means inclined to criticise the Administration, even if this were the proper time for it; but we cannot help thinking that there was great wisdom in Napoleon's recipe for saving life in dealing with a mob, — "First fire grape-shot *into* them; after that, over their heads as much as you like." The position of Mr. Lincoln was already embarrassed when he entered upon office, by what we believe to have been a political blunder in the leaders of the Republican party. Instead of keeping closely to the real point, and the only point, at issue, namely, the claim of a minority to a right of rebellion when displeased with the result of an election, the bare question of Secession, pure and simple, they allowed their party to become divided, and to waste themselves in discussing terms of compromise and guaranties of slavery which had nothing to do with the business in hand. Unless they were ready to admit that popular government was at an end, those were matters already settled by the Constitution and the last election. Compromise was out of the question with men who had gone through the motions, at least, of establishing a government and electing an anti-president. The way to insure the loyalty of the Border States, as the event has shown, was to convince them that disloyalty was dangerous. That revolutions never go backward is one of those compact generalizations which the world is so ready to accept because they save the trouble of thinking; but, however it may be with revolutions, it is certain that rebellions most commonly go backward with disastrous rapidity, and it was of the gravest moment, as respected its moral influence, that Secession should not have time allowed it to assume the proportions and the dignity of revolution; in other words, of a rebellion too powerful to be crushed. The secret friends of the secession treason in the Free States have done their best to bewilder the public mind and to give factitious prestige to a conspiracy against free government and civilization by talking about the *right* of revolution, as if it were some acknowledged principle of the Law of Nations. There is a right and sometimes a duty of rebellion, as there is also a right and sometimes a duty of hanging men for it; but rebellion continues to be rebellion until it has accomplished its object and secured the acknowledgment of it from the other party to the quarrel, and from the world at large. The Republican Party in the November elections had really effected a peaceful revolution, had emancipated the country from the tyranny of an oligarchy which had abused the functions of the Government almost from the time of its establishment, to the advancement of their own selfish aims and interests; and it was this legitimate change of rulers and of national policy by constitutional means which the Secessionists intended to prevent. To put the matter in plain English, they resolved to treat the people of the United States, in the exercise of their un-

doubted and lawful authority, as rebels, and resorted to their usual policy of intimidation in order
to subdue them.   Either this magnificent empire
should be their plantation, or it should perish.
This was the view even of what were called the
moderate slaveholders of the Border States; and
all the so-called compromises and plans of reconstruction that were thrown into the caldron where
the hell-broth of anarchy was brewing had this
extent, no more, — What terms of *submission*
would the people make with their natural masters?
Whatever other result may have come of the long
debates in Congress and elsewhere, they have at
least convinced the people of the Free States that
there can be no such thing as a moderate slaveholder, — that moderation and slavery can no more
coexist than Floyd and honesty, or Anderson and
treason.

We believe, then, that conciliation was from the
first impossible, — that to attempt it was unwise,
because it put the party of law and loyalty in the
wrong, — and that, if it was done as a mere matter
of policy in order to gain time, it was a still
greater mistake, because it was the rebels only who
could profit by it in consolidating their organization, while the seeming gain of a few days or weeks
was a loss to the Government, whose great advantage was in an administrative system thoroughly
established, and, above all, in the vast power of
the national idea, a power weakened by every day's
delay.   This is so true that already men began to
talk of the rival governments at Montgomery and

Washington, and Canadian journals to recommend a strict neutrality, as if the independence and legitimacy of the mushroom despotism of New Ashantee were an acknowledged fact, and the name of the United States of America had no more authority than that of Jefferson Davis and Company, dealers in all kinds of repudiation and anarchy. For more than a month after the inauguration of President Lincoln there seemed to be a kind of interregnum, during which the confusion of ideas in the Border States as to their rights and duties as members of the " old " Union, as it began to be called, became positively chaotic. Virginia, still professing neutrality, prepared to seize the arsenal at Harper's Ferry and the navy-yard at Norfolk; she would prevent the passage of the United States' forces " with a serried phalanx of her gallant sons," two regiments of whom stood looking on while a file of marines took seven wounded men in an engine-house for them; she would do everything but her duty, — the gallant Ancient Pistol of a commonwealth. She " resumed her sovereignty," whatever that meant; her Convention passed an ordinance of secession, concluded a league offensive and defensive with the rebel Confederacy, appointed Jefferson Davis commander-in-chief of her land-forces and somebody else of the fleet she meant to steal at Norfolk, and then coolly referred the whole matter back to the people to vote three weeks afterwards whether they *would* secede three weeks before. Wherever the doctrine of Secession has penetrated, it seems to have obliterated every notion of law and precedent.

The country had come to the conclusion that Mr. Lincoln and his cabinet were mainly employed in packing their trunks to leave Washington, when the "venerable Edward Ruffin of Virginia" fired that first gun at Fort Sumter which brought all the Free States to their feet as one man. That shot is destined to be the most memorable one ever fired on this continent since the Concord fowling-pieces said, "That bridge is ours, and we mean to go across it," eighty-seven Aprils ago. As these began a conflict which gave us independence, so that began another which is to give us nationality. It was certainly a great piece of good-luck for the Government that they had a fort which it was so profitable to lose. The people were weary of a masterly inactivity which seemed to consist mainly in submitting to be kicked. We know very well the difficulties that surrounded the new Administration; we appreciate their reluctance to begin a war the responsibility of which was as great as its consequences seemed doubtful; but we cannot understand how it was hoped to evade war, except by concessions vastly more disastrous than war itself. War has no evil comparable in its effect on national character to that of a craven submission to manifest wrong, the postponement of moral to material interests. There is no prosperity so great as courage. We do not believe that any amount of forbearance would have conciliated the South so long as they thought us pusillanimous. The only way to retain the Border States was by showing that we had the will and the power to do without them. The little Bopeep policy of

" Let them alone, and they 'll all come home
   Wagging their tails behind them "

was certainly tried long enough with conspirators
who had shown unmistakably that they desired
nothing so much as the continuance of peace, especially when it was all on one side, and who would
never have given the Government the great advantage of being attacked in Fort Sumter, had they
not supposed they were dealing with men who
could not be cuffed into resistance. The lesson we
have to teach them now is, that we are thoroughly
and terribly in earnest. Mr. Stephens's theories
are to be put to a speedier and sterner test than he
expected, and we are to prove which is stronger,
— an oligarchy built *on* men, or a commonwealth
built *of* them. Our structure is alive in every part
with defensive and recuperative energies ; woe to
theirs, if that vaunted corner-stone which they believe patient and enduring as marble should begin
to writhe with intelligent life !

We have no doubt of the issue. We believe
that the strongest battalions are always on the side
of God. The Southern army will be fighting for
Jefferson Davis, or at most for the liberty of self-
misgovernment, while we go forth for the defence
of principles which alone make government august
and civil society possible. It is the very life of the
nation that is at stake. There is no question here
of dynasties, races, religions, but simply whether
we will consent to include in our Bill of Rights —
not merely as of equal validity with all other rights,
whether natural or acquired, but by its very nature

transcending and abrogating them all — the Right of Anarchy. We must convince men that treason against the ballot-box is as dangerous as treason against a throne, and that, if they play so desperate a game, they must stake their lives on the hazard. The one lesson that remained for us to teach the political theorists of the Old World was, that we are as strong to suppress intestine disorder as foreign aggression, and we must teach it decisively and thoroughly. The economy of war is to be tested by the value of the object to be gained by it. A ten years' war would be cheap that gave us a country to be proud of, and a flag that should command the respect of the world because it was the symbol of the enthusiastic unity of a great nation.

The Government, however slow it may have been to accept the war which Mr. Buchanan's supineness left them, is acting now with all energy and determination. What they have a right to claim is the confidence of the people, and that depends in good measure on the discretion of the press. Only let us have no more weakness under the plausible name of Conciliation. We need not discuss the probabilities of an acknowledgment of the Confederated States by England and France; we have only to say, "Acknowledge them at your peril." But there is no chance of the recognition of the Confederacy by any foreign governments, so long as it is without the confidence of the brokers. There is no question on which side the strength lies. The whole tone of the Southern journals, so far as we are able to judge, shows the inherent folly and weakness of the secession movement. Men who feel strong in the justice of their cause, or confident in their powers, do not waste breath in childish boasts of their own superiority and querulous depreciation of their antagonists. They are weak, and they know it. And not only are they weak in comparison with the Free States, but we believe they are without the moral support of whatever deserves the name of public opinion at home. If not, why does their Congress, as they call it, hold council always with closed doors, like a knot of conspirators? The first tap of the Northern drum dispelled many illusions, and we need no better proof of which ship is sinking than that Mr. Caleb Cushing should have made such haste to come over to the old Constitution, with the stars and stripes at her mast-head.

We cannot think that the war we are entering on can end without some radical change in the system of African slavery. Whether it be doomed to a sudden extinction, or to a gradual abolition through economical causes, this war will not leave it where it was before. As a power in the state, its reign is already over. The fiery tongues of the batteries in Charleston harbor accomplished in one day a conversion which the constancy of Garrison and the eloquence of Phillips had failed to bring about in thirty years. And whatever other result this war is destined to produce, it has already won for us a blessing worth everything to us as a nation in emancipating the public opinion of the North.

GENERAL McCLELLAN'S REPORT

1864

WE can conceive of no object capable of rousing deeper sympathy than a defeated commander. Though the first movement of popular feeling may be one of wrathful injustice, yet, when the ebb of depression has once fairly run out, and confidence begins to set back, hiding again that muddy bed of human nature which such neap-tides are apt to lay bare, there is a kindly instinct which leads all generous minds to seek every possible ground of extenuation, to look for excuses in misfortune rather than incapacity, and to allow personal gallantry to make up, as far as may be, for want of military genius. There is no other kind of failure which comes so directly home to us, none which appeals to so many of the most deeply rooted sentiments at once. Want of success in any other shape is comparatively a personal misfortune to the man himself who fails; but how many hopes, prides, sacrifices, and heroisms are centred in him who wields the embattled manhood of his country! An army is too multitudinous to call forth that personal enthusiasm which is a necessity of the heart. The imagination needs a single figure which it can invest with all those attributes of admiration that become vague and pointless when divided among a host. Accordingly, we impersonate in the general, not only the army he leads, but whatever qualities we are proud of in the nation itself. He becomes for the moment the ideal of all masculine virtues, and the people are eager to lavish their admiration on him. His position gives him at a bound what other men must spend their lives in winning or vainly striving to win. If he gain a battle, he flatters that pride of prowess which, though it may be a fault of character in the individual man, is the noblest of passions in a people. If he lose one, we are all beaten with him, we all fall down with our Cæsar, and the grief glistens in every eye, the shame burns on every cheek. Moralize as we may about the victories of peace and the superiority of the goose-quill over the sword, there is no achievement of human genius on which a country so prides itself as on success in war, no disgrace over which it broods so inconsolably as military disaster.

There is nothing more touching than the sight of a nation in search of its great man, nothing more beautiful than its readiness to accept a hero on trust. Nor is this a feeble sentimentality. It is much rather a noble yearning of what is best in us, for it is only in these splendid figures which now and then sum up all the higher attributes of character that the multitude of men can ever hope to find their blind instinct of excellence realized and satisfied. Not without reason are nations always symbolized as women, for there is some-

thing truly feminine in the devotion with which
they are willing to give all for and to their ideal
man, and the zeal with which they drape some
improvised Agamemnon with all the outward shows
of royalty from the property-room of imagination.
This eagerness of loyalty toward first-rate character is one of the conditions of mastery in every
sphere of human activity, for it is the stuff that
genius works in.   Heroes, to be sure, cannot be
made to order, yet with a man of the right fibre,
who has the stuff for greatness in him, the popular
enthusiasm would go far toward making him in
fact what he is in fancy.   No commander ever had
more of this paid-up capital of fortune, this fame
in advance, this success before succeeding, than
General McClellan.   That dear old domestic bird,
the Public, which lays the golden eggs out of
which greenbacks are hatched, was sure she had
brooded out an eagle-chick at last.   How we all
waited to see him stoop on the dove-cote of Richmond!   Never did nation give such an example of
faith and patience as while the Army of the Potomac lay during all those weary months before
Washington.   Every excuse was invented, every
palliation suggested, except the true one, that our
chicken was no eagle, after all.   He was hardening
his seres, he was waiting for his wings to grow, he
was whetting his beak; we should see him soar at
last and shake the thunder from his wings.   But
do what we could, hope what we might, it became
daily clearer that, whatever other excellent qualities
he might have, this of being aquiline was wanting.

Disguise and soften it as we may, the campaign of the Peninsula was a disastrous failure, — a failure months long, like a bad novel in weekly instalments, with "To be continued" grimly ominous at the end of every part. So far was it from ending in the capture of Richmond that nothing but the gallantry of General Pope and his little army hindered the Rebels from taking Washington. And now comes Major-General George B. McClellan, and makes affidavit in one volume [1] octavo that he is a great military genius, after all. It should seem that this genius is of two varieties. The first finds the enemy, and beats him; the second finds him, and succeeds in getting away. General McClellan is now attempting a change of base in the face of public opinion, and is endeavoring to escape the consequences of having escaped from the Peninsula. For a year his reputation flared upward like a rocket, culminated, burst, and now, after as long an interval, the burnt-out case comes down to us in this Report.

There is something ludicrously tragic, as our politics are managed, in seeing an Administration compelled to print a campaign document (for such is General McClellan's Report in a double sense) directed against itself. Yet in the present case, had it been possible to escape the penance, it had

---

[1] *Letter of the Secretary of War, transmitting Report on the Organization of the Army of the Potomac, and of the Campaigns in Virginia and Maryland under the Command of Major-General George B. McClellan, from July 26, 1861, to November 7, 1862.* Washington: Government Printing-Office. 1864. 8vo, pp. 242.

been unwise, for we think that no unprejudiced person can read the volume without a melancholy feeling that General McClellan has foiled himself even
more completely than the Rebels were able to do.
He should have been more careful of his communications, for a line two hundred and forty-two pages
long is likely to have its weak points. The volume
before us is rather the plea of an advocate retained
to defend the General's professional character and
expound his political opinions than the curt, color-
less, unimpassioned statement of facts which is
usually so refreshing in the official papers of military men, and has much more the air of being
addressed to a jury than to the War Department
at Washington. It is, in short, a letter to the
people of the United States, under cover to the
Secretary of War. General McClellan puts himself upon the country, and, after taking as much
time to make up his mind as when he wearied and
imperilled the nation in his camp on the Potomac,
endeavors to win back from public opinion the
victory which nothing but his own over-caution
enabled the Rebels to snatch from him before
Richmond. He cannot give us back our lost time
or our squandered legions; but how nice it would
be if we would give him back his reputation, which
has never been of any great use to us, and yet
would be so convenient for him! It was made for
him, and accordingly fits him better than it would
any one else. But it is altogether too late. There
is no argument for the soldier but success, no wisdom for the man but to acknowledge defeat and be

silent under it. The Great Captain on his sofa at Longwood may demonstrate how the Russian expedition might, could, would, and should have ended otherwise; but meanwhile its results are not to be reasoned with, — the Bourbons are at the Tuileries, and he at St. Helena. There is hardly anything that may not be made out of history by a skilful manipulator. Characters may be white-washed, bigotry made over into zeal, timidity into prudence, want of conviction into toleration, obstinacy into firmness; but the one thing that cannot be theorized out of existence, or made to look like anything else, is a lost campaign.

We have had other unsuccessful generals, but not one of them has ever been tempted into the indecorum of endeavoring to turn a defeat in the field to political advantage. Not one has thought of defending himself by imputations on his superiors. Early in the war General McDowell set an example of silence under slanderous reproach that won for him the sympathy and respect of whoever could be touched by self-reliant manliness. It is because General McClellan has seen fit to overstep the bounds of a proper official reserve, because, after more than a year for reflection, he has repeated charges of the grossest kind against those under whose orders he was acting, and all this from a political motive, that we think his Report deserving of more than usual attention. It will be no fault of his if he be not put in nomination for the Presidency, and accordingly it becomes worth our while to consider such evidences of character and capacity as his words and deeds afford us.

We believe that General McClellan has been ruined, like another general whose name began with Mac, by the "All hail hereafter" of certain political witches, who took his fortunes into their keeping after his campaign in Western Virginia. He had shown both ability and decision in handling a small force, and he might with experience have shown similar qualities in directing the operations of a great army, had not the promise of the Presidency made him responsible to other masters than military duty and unselfish patriotism. Thenceforward the soldier was lost in the politician. He thought more of the effect to be produced by his strategy on the voters behind him than on the enemy in his front. What should have been his single object — the suppression of the rebellion for the sake of the country — was now divided with the desire of merely ending it by some plan that should be wholly of his own contrivance, and should redound solely to his own credit and advancement. He became giddy and presumptuous, and lost that sense of present realities, so essential to a commander, in contemplating the mirage that floated the White House before his eyes. At an age considerably beyond that of General Bonaparte when he had triumphantly closed his first Italian campaign, he was nick-named "the *young* Napoleon," and from that time forth seems honestly to have endeavored, like Toepffer's Albert, to resemble the ideal portrait which had been drawn for him by those who put him forward as their stalking-horse. And it must be admitted that these last managed matters cleverly, if a little coarsely. They went to work deliberately to Barnumize their prospective candidate. No *prima donna* was ever more thoroughly exploited by her Hebrew *impresario*. The papers swarmed with anecdotes, incidents, sayings. Nothing was too unimportant, and the new commander-in-chief pulled on his boots by telegram from Maine to California, and picked his teeth by special despatch to the Associated Press. We had him warm for supper in *the very latest* with three exclamation marks, and cold for breakfast in *last evening's telegraphic news* with none. Nothing but a patent pill was ever so suddenly famous.

We are far from blaming General McClellan for all this. He probably looked upon it as one of the inevitable discomforts of distinction in America. But we think that it insensibly affected his judgment, led him to regard himself as the representative of certain opinions, rather than as a general whose whole duty was limited to the army under his command, and brought him at last to a temper of mind most unfortunate for the public interests, in which he could believe the administration personally hostile to himself because opposed to the political principles of those who wished to profit by his "availability." It was only natural, too, that he should gradually come to think himself what his partisans constantly affirmed that he was, — the sole depositary of the country's destiny. We form our judgment of General McClellan solely from his own Report; we believe him to be honest in his opinions, and patriotic so far as those opinions will allow him to be ; we know him to be capable of attaching those about him in a warm personal friendship, and we reject with the contempt they deserve the imputations on his courage and his military honor ; but at the same time we consider him a man like other men, with a head liable to be turned by a fame too easily won. His great misfortune was that he began his first important campaign with a reputation to save instead of to earn, so that he was hampered by the crowning disadvantage of age in a general without the experience which might neutralize it. Nay, what was still worse, he had two reputations to keep from damage, the one as soldier, the other as politician.

He seems very early to have misapprehended the true relation in which he stood to the government. By the operation of natural causes, as politicians would call them, he had become heir presumptive to the chair of state, and felt called on to exert an influence on the policy of the war, or at least to express an opinion that might go upon record for future convenience. He plunged into that Dismal Swamp of constitutional hermeneutics, in which the wheels of government were stalled at the outbreak of our rebellion, and from which every untrained explorer rises with a mouth too full of mud to be intelligible to Christian men. He appears to have thought it within the sphere of his duty to take charge of the statesmanship of the President no less than of the movements of the army, nor was it long before there were unmistakable symptoms that he began to consider himself quite as much the chief of an opposition who could dictate terms as the military subordinate who was to obey orders. Whatever might have been his capacity as a soldier, this divided allegiance could not fail of disastrous consequences to the public service, for no mistress exacts so jealously the entire devotion of her servants as war. A mind distracted with calculations of future political contingencies was not to be relied on in the conduct of movements which above all others demand the constant presence, the undivided energy, of all the faculties, and the concentration of every personal interest on the one object of immediate success. A general who is conscious that he has an army of one hundred and fifty thousand voters at his back will be always weakened by those personal considerations which are the worst consequence of the elective system. General McClellan's motions were encumbered in every direction by a huge train of political baggage. This misconception of his own position, or rather his confounding the two characters of possible candidate and actual general, forced the growth of whatever egotism was latent in his nature. He began erelong to look at everything from a personal point of view, to judge men and measures by their presumed relation to his own interests, and at length fairly persuaded himself that the inevitable results of his own want of initiative were due to the hostile combination against him of Mr. Lincoln, Mr. Stanton, and General

Halleck. Regarding himself too much in considering the advantages of success, he regards others too little in awarding the responsibility of failure.

The intense self-consciousness of General McClellan and a certain aim at effect for ulterior and unmilitary purposes show themselves early. In October, 1861, addressing a memorial to Mr. Cameron, then Secretary of War, he does not forget the important constituency of Buncombe. " The unity of this nation," he says, " the preservation of our institutions, are so dear to me that I have willingly sacrificed my private happiness with the single object of doing my duty to my country. When the task is accomplished, I shall be glad to retire to the obscurity from which events have drawn me. Whatever the determination of the government may be, I will do the best I can with the Army of the Potomac, and will share its fate, whatever may be the task imposed upon me." Not to speak of taste, the utter blindness to the true relations of things shown in such language is startling. What sacrifice had General McClellan made which had not been equally made by every one of the hundred and fifty thousand men of his army? Educated at the expense of the country, his services were a debt due on demand. And what was the sacrifice of which a soldier speaks so pathetically? To be raised from the management of a railway to one of the most conspicuous and inspiring positions of modern times, to an opportunity such as comes rarely to any man, and then only as the reward of transcendent ability transcendently displayed! To step from a captaincy of engineers to the command in chief of a great nation on fire with angry enthusiasm, spendthrift of men, money, devotion, to be the chosen champion of order, freedom, and civilization, — this is indeed a sacrifice such as few men have been called upon to make by their native land! And of what is General McClellan thinking when he talks of returning to obscurity? Of what are men commonly thinking when they talk thus? The newspapers would soon grow rich, if everybody should take to advertising what he did not want. And, moreover, to what kind of obscurity can a successful general return? An obscurity made up of the gratitude and admiration of his countrymen, a strange obscurity of glory! Nor is this the only occasion on which the General speaks of his willingness to share the fate of his army. What corporal could do less? No man thoroughly in earnest, and with the fate of his country in his hands and no thought but of that, could have any place in his mind for such footlight phrases as these.

General McClellan's theory from the first seems to have been that a large army would make a great general, though all history shows that the genius, decision, and confidence of a leader are the most powerful reinforcement of the troops under his command, and that an able captain makes a small army powerful by recruiting it with his own vigor and enthusiasm. From the time of his taking the command till his removal, he was constantly asking for more men, constantly receiving

them, and constantly unable to begin anything
with them after he got them. He could not move
without one hundred and fifty thousand pairs of
legs, and when his force had long reached that
number, the President was obliged by the over-
taxed impatience of the country to pry him up
from his encampment on the Potomac with a special order. What the army really needed was an
addition of one man, and that at the head of it;
for a general, like an orator, must be moved himself before he can move others. The larger his
army, the more helpless was General McClellan.
Like the magician's *famulus*, who rashly under-
took to play the part of master, and who could
evoke powers that he could not control, he was
swamped in his own supplies. With every reinforcement sent him on the Peninsula, his estimate
of the numbers opposed to him increased. His
own imagination faced him in superior numbers at
every turn. Since Don Quixote's enumeration of
the armies of the Emperor Alifanfaron and King
Pentapolin of the Naked Arm, there has been
nothing like our General's vision of the Rebel
forces, with their ever-lengthening list of leaders,
gathered for the defence of Richmond. His anxiety swells their muster-roll at last to two hundred
thousand. We say his anxiety, for no man of ordinary judgment can believe that with that number
of men the Rebel leaders would not have divided
their forces, with one army occupying General
McClellan, while they attempted the capital he
had left uncovered with the other.

The first plan proposed by General McClellan covered operations extending from Virginia to Texas. With a main army of two hundred and seventy-three thousand he proposes "not only to drive the enemy out of Virginia and occupy Richmond, but to occupy Charleston, Savannah, Montgomery, Pensacola, Mobile, and New Orleans; in other words, to move into the heart of the enemy's country and crush the rebellion in its very heart." We do not say that General McClellan's ambition to be the one man who should crush the rebellion was an unworthy one, but that his theory that this was possible, and in the way he proposed, shows him better fitted to state the abstract problems than to apprehend the complex details of their solution when they lie before him as practical difficulties. For when we consider the necessary detachments from this force to guard his communications through an enemy's country, as he wishes the President to do, in order to justify the largeness of the force required, we cannot help asking how soon the army for active operations would be reduced to a hundred and fifty thousand. And how long would a general be in reaching New Orleans, if he is six months in making up his mind to advance with an army of that strength on the insignificant fortifications of Manassas, manned, according to the best information, with forty thousand troops? At the same time General McClellan assigns twenty thousand as a force adequate for opening the Mississippi. This plan, to be sure, was soon abandoned, but it is an illustration of the

want of precision and forethought which charac-
terizes the mind of its author.   A man so vague in
his conceptions is apt to be timid in action, for the
same haziness of mind may, according to circumstances, either soften and obscure the objects of
thought, or make them loom with purely fantastic
exaggeration.   There is a vast difference between
clearness of head on demand and the power of
framing abstract schemes of action, beautiful in
their correctness of outline and apparent simplicity.
It is a perception of this truth, we believe, which
leads practical men always to suspect plans supported by statistics too exquisitely conclusive.

It was on precisely such a specious basis of definite misinformation that General McClellan's next
proposal for the campaign by way of the Peninsula
rested, — precise facts before he sets out turning
to something like precise no-facts when he gets
there, — beautiful completeness of conception ending in hesitation, confusion, and failure.   Before
starting, "the roads are passable at all seasons of
the year, the country much more favorable for
offensive operations than that in front of Washington, much more level, the woods less dense, the soil
more sandy" (p. 47).   After arriving, we find
"the roads impassable," "very dense and extensive
forests, the clearings being small and few;" and
"the comparative flatness of the country and the
alertness of the enemy, everywhere in force, rendered thorough reconnoissances slow, dangerous,
and difficult" (p. 79).   General McClellan's mental constitution would seem to be one of those, easily

elated and easily depressed, that exaggerate distant advantages and dangers near at hand, — minds stronger in conception than perception, and accordingly, as such always are, wanting that faculty of swift decision which, catching inspiration from danger, makes opportunity success. Add to this a kind of adhesiveness (we can hardly call it obstinacy or pertinacity) of temper, which can make no allowance for change of circumstances, and we think we have a tolerably clear notion of the causes of General McClellan's disasters. He can compose a good campaign beforehand, but he cannot improvise one out of the events of the moment, as is the wont of great generals. Occasion seldom offers her forelock twice to the grasp of the same man, and yet General McClellan, by the admission of the Rebels themselves, had Richmond at his mercy more than once.

He seems to attribute his misfortunes mainly to the withdrawal of General McDowell's division, and its consequent failure to coöperate with his own forces. But the fact is patent that the campaign was lost by his sitting down in front of Yorktown, and wasting a whole month in a series of approaches whose scientific propriety would have delighted Uncle Toby, to reduce a garrison of eight thousand men. Without that delay, which gave the Rebels time to send Jackson into the Shenandoah valley, General McDowell's army would have been enabled to come to his assistance. General McClellan, it is true, complains that it was not sent round by water, as he wished; but even if it had been, it could only have been an addition of helplessness to an army already too unwieldy for its commander; for he really made the Rebel force double his own (as he always fancied it) by never bringing more than a quarter of his army into action at once. Yet during the whole campaign he was calling for more men, and getting them, till his force reached the highest limit he himself had ever set. When every available man, and more, had been sent him, he writes from Harrison's Bar to Mr. Stanton, "To accomplish the great task of capturing Richmond and putting an end to this rebellion, reinforcements should be sent to me *rather much over than less than one hundred thousand men.*" This letter General McClellan has not seen fit to include in his Report. Was the government to be blamed for pouring no more water into a sieve like this?

It certainly was a great mistake on Mr. Lincoln's part to order General McDowell off on a wild-goose chase after Jackson. The coöperation of this force might have enabled General McClellan even then to retrieve his campaign, and we do not in the least blame him for feeling bitterly the disappointment of wanting it. But it seems to us that it was mainly his own fault that there was anything to retrieve, and the true occasion to recover his lost ground was offered him after his bloody repulse of the enemy at Malvern Hill, though he did not turn it to account. For his retreat we think he would deserve all credit, had he not been under the necessity of making it. It was conducted with great judgment and ability, and we do not love that partisan narrowness of mind that would grudge him the praise so fairly earned. But at the same time it is not ungenerous to say that the obstinate valor shown by his army under all the depression of a backward movement, while it proves how much General McClellan had done to make it an effective force, makes us regret all the more that he should have wanted the decision to try its quality under the inspiration of attack. It is impossible that the spirit of the army should not have been affected by the doubt and indecision of their general. They fought nobly, but they were always on the defensive. Had General McClellan put them at once on the aggressive, we believe his campaign would have been a triumphant one. With truly great generals resolve is instinctive, a deduction from premises supplied by the eye, not the memory, and men find out the science of their achievements afterwards, like the mathematical law in the Greek column. The stiffness rather than firmness of mind, the surrender of all spontaneous action in the strait-waistcoat of a preconceived plan, to which we have before alluded, unfitted him for that rapid change of combinations on the great chess-board of battle which enabled General Rosecrans at Murfreesboro to turn defeat into victory, an achievement without parallel in the history of the war.

General McClellan seems to have considered the President too careful of the safety of the capital; but he should measure the value of Washington by what he himself thought of the importance of taking Richmond. That, no doubt, would be a great advantage, but the loss of a recognized seat of government, with its diplomatic and other traditions, would have been of vastly more fatal consequence to us than the capture of their provisional perch in Virginia would have been to the Rebel authorities. It would have brought foreign recognition to the Rebels, and thrown Maryland certainly, and probably Kentucky, into the scale against us. So long as we held Washington, we had on our side the two powerful sentiments of permanence and tradition, some insensible portions of which the Rebels were winning from us with every day of repose allowed them by General McClellan. It was a clear sense of this that both excited and justified the impatience of the people, who saw that the insurrection was gaining the coherence and prestige of an established power, — an element of much strength at home and abroad. That this popular instinct was not at fault, we have the witness of General Kirby Smith, who told Colonel Fremantle "that McClellan might probably have destroyed the Southern army with the greatest ease during the first winter, and without much risk to himself, as the Southerners were so much over-elated by their easy triumph at Manassas, and their army had dwindled away."

We have said that General McClellan's volume is rather a plea in abatement of judgment than a report. It was perfectly proper that he should endeavor to put everything in its true light, and he would be sure of the sympathy of all right-minded men in so doing; but an *ex parte* statement at once rouses and justifies adverse criticism. He has omitted many documents essential to the formation of a just opinion; and it is only when we have read these also, in the Report of the Committee on the Conduct of the War, that we feel the full weight of the cumulative evidence going to show the hearty support in men and confidence that he received from the Administration, and, when there were no more men to be sent, and confidence began to yield before irresistible facts, the prolonged forbearance with which he was still favored. Nothing can be kinder or more cordial than the despatches and letters both of the President and Mr. Stanton, down to the time when General McClellan wrote the following sentences at the end of an official communication addressed to the latter: "If I save this army now, I tell you plainly that I owe no thanks to you, or to any other persons in Washington. You have done your best to sacrifice this army." (28th June, 1862.) We shall seek no epithet to characterize language like this. All but the most bigoted partisans will qualify it as it deserves. We have here a glaring example of that warping of good sense and good feeling which the consciousness of having a political stake at risk will produce in a gallant soldier and a courteous gentleman. Can General McClellan, after a year to grow cool in, either himself believe, or expect any one else to believe, that the President and the Secretary of War would "do their best to sacrifice" an army of a hundred and fifty thousand brave men, in order to lessen his possible chances as a candidate for the Presidency? It was of vastly more importance to them than to him that he should succeed. The dignified good temper of Mr. Lincoln's answer to this wanton insult does him honor: "I have not said you were ungenerous for saying you needed reinforcements; I thought you were ungenerous in assuming that I did not send them as fast as I could. I feel any misfortune to you and your army quite as keenly as you feel it yourself." Mr. Stanton could only be silent; and whatever criticisms may be made on some traits of his character, he is quite safe in leaving the rebuke of such an imputation to whoever feels that earnestness, devotion, and unflagging purpose are high qualities in a public officer.

If General McClellan had been as prompt in attacking the enemy as he showed himself in this assault on his superiors, we think his campaign in the Peninsula would have ended more satisfactorily. We have no doubt that he would conduct a siege or a defence with all the science and all the proprieties of warfare, but we think he has proved himself singularly wanting in the qualities which distinguish the natural leaders of men. He had every theoretic qualification, but no ardor, no leap, no inspiration. A defensive general is an earthen redoubt, not an ensign to rally enthusiasm and inspire devotion. Caution will never make an army, though it may sometimes save one. We

think General McClellan reduced the efficiency
and lowered the tone of his soldiers by his six
months' dose of prudence. With every day he
gave the enemy, he lessened his chances of success,
and added months to the duration of the war. He
never knew how to find opportunity, much less to
make it. He was an accomplished soldier, but
lacked that downright common sense which is only
another name for genius with its coat off for actual
work in hand.

Were General McClellan's Report nothing more
than a report, were the General himself nothing
more than an officer endeavoring to palliate a failure, we should not have felt called on to notice his
plea, unless to add publicity to any new facts he
might be able to bring forward. But the Report
is a political manifesto, and not only that, but an
attack on the administration which appointed him
to the command, supported him with all its resources, and whose only fault it was not sooner to
discover his incapacity to conduct aggressive movements. General McClellan is a candidate for the
Presidency, and as he has had no opportunity to
show his capacity in any civil function, his claim
must rest on one of two grounds, — either the ability he has shown as a general, or the specific principles of policy he is supposed to represent. Whatever may be the success of our operations in the
field, our Chief Magistracy for the next four years
will demand a person of great experience and ability. Questions cannot fail to arise taxing prudence of the longest forecast and decision of the

firmest quality. How far is General McClellan likely to fulfill these conditions? What are the qualities of mind of which both his career and his Report give the most irrefragable evidence?

General McClellan's mind seems to be equally incapable of appreciating the value of time as the material of action, and its power in changing the relations of facts, and thus modifying the basis of opinion. He is a good maker of almanacs, but no good judge of the weather. Judging by the political counsel which he more than once felt called upon to offer the President, and which, as he has included it in his Report, we must presume to represent his present opinions, he does not seem even yet to appreciate the fact that this is not a war between two nations, but an attempt at revolution within ourselves, which can be adequately met only by revolutionary measures. And yet, if he were at this moment elevated to the conduct of our affairs, he would find himself controlled by the same necessities which have guided Mr. Lincoln, and must either adopt his measures, or submit to a peace dictated by the South. No side issue as to how the war shall be conducted is any longer possible. The naked question is one of war or submission, for compromise means surrender; and if the choice be war, we cannot afford to give the enemy fifty in the game, by standing upon scruples which he would be the last to appreciate or to act upon. It is one of the most terrible features of war that it must be inexorable by its very nature.

Great statesmanship and great generalship have

been more than once shown by the same man, and, naturally enough, because they both result from the same qualities of mind, an instant apprehension of the demand of the moment, and a self-confidence that can as instantly meet it, so that every energy of the man is gathered to one intense focus. It is the faculty of being a present man, instead of a prospective one; of being ready, instead of getting ready. Though we think great injustice has been done by the public to General McClellan's really high merits as an officer, yet it seems to us that those very merits show precisely the character of intellect to unfit him for the task just now demanded of a statesman. His capacity for organization may be conspicuous; but, be it what it may, it is one thing to bring order out of the confusion of mere inexperience, and quite another to retrieve it from a chaos of elements mutually hostile, which is the problem sure to present itself to the next administration. This will constantly require precisely that judgment on the nail, and not to be drawn for at three days' sight, of which General McClellan has shown least.

Is our path to be so smooth for the next four years that a man whose leading characteristic is an exaggeration of difficulties is likely to be our surest guide? If the war is still to be carried on, — and surely the nation has shown no symptoms of slackening in its purpose, — what modifications of it would General McClellan introduce? The only information that is vouchsafed us is, that he is to be the " conservative " candidate, a phrase that may mean too little or too much. As well as we can understand it, it is the convenient formula by which to express the average want of opinions of all who are out of place, out of humor, or dislike the dust which blinds and chokes whoever is behind the times. Sometimes it is used as the rallying-cry of an amiable class of men, who still believe, in a vague sort of way, that the rebels can be conciliated by offering them a ruler more *comme il faut* than Mr. Lincoln, a country where a flatboatman may rise to the top, by virtue of mere manhood, being hardly the place for people of truly refined sensibilities. Or does it really mean nothing more nor less than that we are to try to put slavery back again where it was before (only that it is not quite convenient just now to say so), on the theory that teleologically the pot of ointment was made to conserve the dead fly?

In the providence of God the first thoughtless enthusiasm of the nation has settled to deep purpose, their anger has been purified by trial into a conviction of duty, and they are face to face with one of those rare occasions where duty and advantage are identical. The man who is fit for the office of President in these times should be one who knows how to advance, an art which General McClellan has never learned. He must be one who comprehends that three years of war have made vast changes in the relative values of things. He must be one who feels to the very marrow of his bones that this is a war, not to conserve the forms, but the essence, of free institutions. He must be willing to sacrifice everything to the single consideration of success, because success means truth and honor; to use every means, though they may alarm the fears of men who are loyal with a reservation, or shock the prejudices of would-be traitors. No middle course is safe in troubled times, and the only way to escape the dangers of revolution is by directing its forces and giving it useful work to do.

THE REBELLION: ITS CAUSES AND CONSEQUENCES

1864

In spite of the popular theory that nothing is so fallacious as circumstantial evidence, there is no man of observation who would not deem it more trustworthy than any human testimony, however honest, which was made up from personal recollection. The actors in great affairs are seldom to be depended on as witnesses, either to the order of events or their bearing upon results; for even where selfish interest is not to be taken into account, the mythic instinct erelong begins to shape things as they ought to have been, rather than as they were. This is true even of subjects in which we have no personal interest, and not only do no two men describe the same street-scene in the same way, but the same man, unless prosaic to a degree below the freezing-point of Tupper, will never do it twice in the same way. Few men, looking into their old diaries, but are astonished at the contrast, sometimes even the absolute unlikeness, between the matters of fact recorded there and their own recollection of them. Shortly after the battle of Lexington it was the interest of the Colonies to make the British troops not only wanton, but unresisted, aggressors; and if primitive Christians could be manufactured by affidavit, so large a body of them ready to turn the other cheek also was never gathered as in the minutemen before the meeting-house on the 19th of April, 1775. The Anglo-Saxon could not fight comfortably without the law on his side. But later, when the battle became a matter of local pride, the muskets that had been fired at the Redcoats under Pitcairn almost rivalled in number the pieces of furniture that came over in the Mayflower. Indeed, whoever has talked much with Revolutionary pensioners knows that those honored veterans were no less remarkable for imagination than for patriotism. It should seem that there is, perhaps, nothing on which so little reliance is to be placed as facts, especially when related by one who saw them. It is no slight help to our charity to recollect that, in disputable matters, every man sees according to his prejudices, and is stone-blind to whatever he did not expect or did not mean to see. Even where no personal bias can be suspected, contemporary and popular evidence is to be taken with great caution, so exceedingly careless are men as to exact truth, and such poor observers, for the most part, of what goes on under their eyes. The ballad which was hawked about the streets at the execution of Captain Kidd, and which was still to be bought at street-stalls within a few years, affirms three times in a single stanza that the pirate's name was Robert. Yet he was commissioned, indicted, convicted, and hanged as William Kidd. Nor was he, as is generally supposed, convicted of piracy, but of murder. The marvels of Spiritualism are supernatural to the average observer, who is willing to pay for that dulness from another world which he might have for nothing in this, while they seem mere legerdemain, and not of the highest quality, to the trained organs of scientific men.

History, we are told, is philosophy teaching by example. But how if the example does not apply? Le Verrier discovers Neptune when, according to his own calculations, the planet should not have been in the place where his telescope found it. Does the example redound to the credit of luck or of mathematics? The historian may give a thoroughly false view of an event by simply assuming that *after* means *in consequence of*, or even by the felicitous turn of a sentence. Style will find readers and shape convictions, while mere truth only gathers dust on the shelf. The memory first, and by degrees the judgment, is enslaved by the epigrams of Tacitus or Michelet. Our conception of scenes and men is outlined and colored for us by the pictorial imagination of Carlyle. Indeed, after reading history, one can only turn round, with Montaigne, and say, *What know I?* There was a time when the reputation of Judas might have been thought past mending, but a German has whitewashed him as thoroughly as Malone did Shakespeare's bust, and an English poet made him the hero of a tragedy, as the one among the disciples who believed too much. Call no one happy till he is dead? Rather call no one safe, whether in good repute or evil, after he has been dead long enough to have his effigy done in historical wax-work. Only get the real clothes, that is, only be careful to envelop him in a sufficiently probable dressing of facts, and the public will be entirely satisfied. What's Hecuba to us, or we to Hecuba? Or is Thackeray's way any nearer the truth, who strips Louis the Great of all his stage-properties, and shows him to us the miserable forked radish of decrepitude?

There are many ways of writing what is called history. The earliest and simplest was to record in the form of annals, without investigating, whatever the writer could lay hold of, the only thread of connection being the order of time, so that events have no more relation to each other than so many beads on a string. Higher then this, because more picturesque, and because living men take the place of mere names, are the better class of chronicles, like Froissart's, in which the scenes sometimes have the minute vividness of illumination, and the page seems to take life and motion as we read. The annalist still survives, a kind of literary dodo, in the "standard" historian, respectable, immitigable, — with his philosophy of history, and his stereotyped phrase, his one Amurath succeeding another, so very dead, so unlike anything but historical characters, that we can scarce believe they

ever lived, — and only differing from his ancient
congener of the monastery by his skill in making
ten words do the duty of one. His are the fatal
books without which no gentleman's library can be
complete; his the storied pages which ingenuous
youth is invited to turn, and is apt to turn four or
five together. With him something is still always
sure to transpire in the course of these negotiations, still the traditional door is opened to the
inroad of democratic innovation, still it is impossible to interpret the motives which inspired
the conduct of so-and-so in this particular emergency. So little does he himself conceive of any
possible past or future life in his characters that
he periphrases death into a disappearance from the
page of history, as if they were bodiless and soul-
less creatures of pen and ink; mere names, not
things. Picturesqueness he sternly avoids as the
Delilah of the philosophic mind, liveliness as a
snare of the careless investigator; and so, stopping both ears, he slips safely by those Sirens,
keeping safe that sobriety of style which his fellow-men call by another name. Unhappy books,
which we know by heart before we read them, and
which a mysterious superstition yet compels many
unoffending persons to read! What has not the
benevolent reader had to suffer at the hands of
the so-called impartial historian, who, wholly disinterested and disinteresting, writes with as me-
chanic an industry and as little emotion as he
would have brought to the weaving of calico or
the digging of potatoes, under other circum-

stances! Far truer, at least to nature and to
some conceivable theory of an immortal soul in
man, is the method of the poet, who makes his
personages luminous from within by an instinctive sympathy with human motives of action, and
a conception of the essential unity of character
through every change of fate.

Of late years men have begun to question the
prescriptive right of this "great gyant Asdryas-
dust, who has choked many men," to choke them
also because he had worked his wicked will on their
fathers. It occurred to an inquiring mind here and
there that if the representation of men's action
and passion on the theatre could be made interesting, there was no good reason why the great drama
of history should be dull as a miracle-play. Need
philosophy teaching by example be so tiresome that
the pupils would rather burst in ignorance than go
within earshot of the pedagogue? Hence the historical romance, sometimes honestly called so, and
limited by custom in number of volumes; sometimes
not called so, and without any such limitation.
This latter variety admits several styles of treatment. Sometimes a special epoch is chosen, where
one heroic figure may serve as a centre round which
events and subordinate characters group themselves,
with no more sacrifice of truth than is absolutely
demanded by artistic keeping. This may be called
the epic style, of which Carlyle is the acknowledged
master. Sometimes a period is selected, where the
facts, by coloring and arrangement, may be made
to support the views of a party, and history becomes

a political pamphlet indefinitely prolonged. Here
point is the one thing needful, — to be attained at
all hazards, whether by the turn of a sentence or
the twisting of a motive. Macaulay is preëminent
in this kind, and woe to the party or the man that
comes between him and his epigrammatic necessity! Again, there is the new light, or perhaps,
more properly, the forlorn-hope method, where the
author accepts a brief against the *advocatus diaboli*, and strives to win a reverse of judgment, as
Mr. Froude has done in the case of Henry VIII.
The latest fashion of all is the *a priori*, in which
a certain dominant principle is taken for granted,
and everything is deduced from x, instead of serv-
ing to prove what x may really be. The weakness
of this heroic treatment, it seems to us, is in allowing too little to human nature as an element in the
problem. This would be a fine world, if facts
would only be as subservient to theory in real life
as in the author's inkstand. Mr. Buckle stands at
the head of this school, and has just found a worthy
disciple in M. Taine, who, in his *Histoire de la
Littérature Anglaise*, having first assumed certain
ethnological postulates, seems rather to shape the
character of the literature to the race than to illus-
trate that of the race by the literature.

In short, whether we consider the incompetence
of men in general as observers, their carelessness
about things at the moment indifferent, but which
may become of consequence hereafter (as, for
example, in the dating of letters), their want of
impartiality, both in seeing and stating occurrences

and in tracing or attributing motives, it is plain
that history is not to be depended on in any absolute sense. That smooth and indifferent quality
of mind, without a flaw of prejudice or a blur of
theory, which can reflect passing events as they
truly are, is as rare, if not so precious, as that
artistic sense which can hold the mirror up to
nature. The fact that there is so little historical
or political prescience, that no man of experience
ventures to prophesy, is enough to prove, either
that it is impossible to know all the terms of our
problem, or that history does not repeat itself with
anything like the exactness of coincidence which is
so pleasing to the imagination. Six months *after*
the *coup d'état* of December, 1851, Mr. Savage
Landor, who knew him well, said to us that Louis
Napoleon had ten times the political sagacity of
his uncle; but who foresaw or foretold an Augustus
in the dull-eyed frequenter of Lady Blessington's,
the melodramatic hero of Strasburg and Bologne,
with his cocked hat and his eagle from Astley's?
What insurance company would have taken the
risk of his hare-brained adventure? Coleridge
used to take credit to himself for certain lucky
vaticinations, but his memory was always inexact,
his confounding of what he did and what he
thought he meant to do always to be suspected,
and his prophecies, when examined, are hardly
more precise than an ancient oracle or a couplet
of Nostradamus. The almanac-makers took the
wisest course, stretching through a whole month
their "about this time expect a change of weather."

That history repeats itself has become a kind of truism, but of as little practical value in helping us to form our opinions as other similar labor-saving expedients to escape thought. Sceptical minds see in human affairs a regular oscillation, hopeful ones a continual progress, and both can support their creeds with abundance of pertinent example. Both seem to admit a law of recurrence, but the former make it act in a circle, the latter in a spiral. There is, no doubt, one constant element in the reckoning, namely, human nature, and perhaps another in human nature itself, — the tendency to reaction from all extremes; but the way in which these shall operate, and the force they shall exert, are dependent on a multitude of new and impredicable circumstances. Coincidences there certainly are, but our records are hardly yet long enough to furnish the basis for secure induction. Such parallelisms are merely curious, and entertain the fancy rather than supply precedent for the judgment. When Tacitus tells us that gladiators have not so much stomach for fighting as soldiers, we remember our own roughs and shoulder-hitters at the beginning of the war, and are inclined to think that Macer and Billy Wilson illustrated a general truth. But, unfortunately, Octavius found prize-fighters of another metal, not to speak of Spartacus. Perhaps the objections to our making use of colored soldiers (*hic niger est, hunc tu, Romane, caveto*) will seem as absurd one of these days as the outcry that Cæsar was degrading the service by enlisting Gauls; but we will not hazard a prophecy. In the alarm of the Pannonian revolt, his nephew recruited the army of Italy by a conscription of slaves, who thereby became free, and this measure seems to have been acquiesced in by the unwarlike citizens, who preferred that the experiment of death should be made *in corpore vili* rather than in their own persons.

If the analogies between past and present were as precise as they are sometimes represented to be, if Time really dotes and repeats his old stories, then ought students of history to be the best statesmen. Yet, with Guizot for an adviser, Louis Philippe, himself the eyewitness of two revolutions, became the easy victim of a third. Reasoning from what has been to what will be is apt to be paralogistic at the best. Much influence must still be left to chance, much accounted for by what pagans called Fate, and we Providence. We can only say, *Victrix causa diis placuit*, and Cato must make the best of it. What is called poetical justice, that is, an exact subservience of human fortunes to moral laws, so that the actual becomes the liege vassal of the ideal, is so seldom seen in the events of real life that even the gentile world felt the need of a future state of rewards and punishments to make the scale of Divine justice even, and satisfy the cravings of the soul. Our sense of right, or of what we believe to be right, is so pleased with an example of retribution that a single instance is allowed to outweigh the many in which wrong escapes unwhipped. It was remarked that sudden death overtook the purchasers of certain property bequeathed for pious uses in England, and sequestered at the Reformation. Fuller tells of a Sir Miles Pateridge, who threw dice with the king for Jesus' bells, and how " the ropes after catched about his neck," he being hanged in the reign of Edward VI. But at least a fifth of the land in England was held by suppressed monasteries, and the metal for the victorious cannon of revolutionary France once called to the service of the Prince of Peace from consecrated spires. We err in looking for a visible and material penalty, as if God imposed a fine of mishap for the breach of his statutes. Seldom, says Horace, has penalty lost the scent of crime, yet, on second thought, he makes the sleuth-hound lame. Slow seems the sword of Divine justice, adds Dante, to him who longs to see it smite. The cry of all generations has been, " How long, O Lord ? " Where crime has its root in weakness of character, that same weakness is likely to play the avenger ; but where it springs from that indifference as to means and that contempt of consequences which are likely to be felt by a strong nature, intent upon its end, it would be hardy to reckon on the same dramatic result. And if we find this difficulty in the cases of individual men, it is even more rash to personify nations, and deal out to them our little vials of Divine retribution, as if we were the general dispensaries of doom. Shall we lay to a nation the sins of a line of despots whom it cannot shake off ? If we accept too blindly the theory of national responsibility, we ought, by parity of reason, to admit success as a valid proof of right. The moralists of fifty years ago, who saw the democratic orgies of France punished with Napoleon, whose own crimes brought him in turn to the rock of Prometheus, how would they explain the phenomenon of Napoleon III. ? The readiness to trace a too close and consequent relation between public delinquencies and temporal judgments seems to us a superstition holding over from the time when each race, each family even, had its private and tutelary divinity, — a mere refinement of fetichism. The world has too often seen "captive good attending captain ill " to believe in a providence that sets man-traps and spring-guns for the trespassers on its domain, and Christianity, perhaps, elevated man in no way so much as in making every one personally, not gregariously, answerable for his doings or not-doings, and thus inventing conscience, as we understand its meaning. But just in proportion as the private citizen is enlightened does he become capable of an influence on that manifold result of thought, sentiment, reason, impulse, magnanimity, and meanness which, as Public Opinion, has now so great a share in shaping the destiny of nations. And in this sense does he become responsible, and out of the aggregate of such individual responsibilities we can assume a common complicity in the guilt of common wrongdoing.

But surely the Lord God Omnipotent reigneth ; and though we do not believe in his so immediate interference in events as would satisfy our impatience of injustice, yet he achieves his ends and brings about his compensations by having made Good infinitely and eternally lovely to the soul of man, while the beauty of Evil is but a brief cheat, which their own lusts put upon the senses of her victims. And it is surely fixed as the foundations of the earth that faithfulness to right and duty, self-sacrifice, loyalty to that service whose visible reward is often but suffering and baffled hope, draw strength and succor from exhaustless springs far up in those Delectable Mountains of trial which the All-knowing has set between us and the achievement of every noble purpose. History teaches, at least, that wrong can reckon on no alliance with the diviner part of man, while every high example of virtue, though it led to the stake or the scaffold, becomes a part of the reserved force of humanity, and from generation to generation summons kindred natures to the standard of righteousness as with the sound of a trumpet. There is no such reinforcement as faith in God, and that faith is impossible till we have squared our policy and conduct with our highest instincts. In the loom of time, though the woof be divinely foreordained, yet man supplies the weft, and the figures of the endless web are shaped and colored by our own wisdom or folly. Let no nation think itself safe in being merely right, unless its captains are inspired and sustained by a sense thereof.

We do not believe that history supplies any trustworthy data for casting the horoscope of our war. America is something without precedent.

Moreover, such changes have been going on in the social and moral condition of nations as to make the lessons of even comparatively recent times of little import in forming conclusions on contemporary affairs. Formerly a fact, not yet forgetful of its etymology, was a thing done, a deed, and in a certain sense implied, truly enough, the predominance of individual actors and prevailing characters. But powerful personalities are becoming of less and less account, when facility of communication has given both force and the means of exerting it to the sentiment of civilized mankind, and when commerce has made the banker's strong-box a true temple of Janus, the shutting or opening of which means peace or war. Battles are decisive now not so much by the destruction of armies as by the defeat of public spirit, and a something that has actually happened may be a less important fact, either in conjecturing probabilities or determining policy, than the indefinable progress of change, not marked on any dial, but instinctively divined, that is taking place in the general thought.

The history of no civil war can be written without bias, scarcely without passionate prejudice. It is always hard for men to conceive the honesty or intelligence of those who hold other opinions, or indeed to allow them the *right* to think for themselves; but in troubled times the blood mounts to the head, and colors the judgment, giving to suspicions and fancies the force of realities, and intensifying personal predilections, till they seem the

pith and substance of national duties. Even where
the office of historian is assumed in the fairest
temper, it is impossible that the narrative of events
whose bearing is so momentous should not insensibly take somewhat the form of an argument, —
that the political sympathies of the author should
not affect his judgment of men and measures. And
in such conflicts, far more than in ordinary times,
as the stake at issue is more absorbing and appeals
more directly to every private interest and patriotic
sentiment, so men, as they become prominent, and
more or less identified with this or that policy, at
. last take the place of principles with the majority
of minds. To agree with us is to be a great commander, a prudent administrator, a politician without private ends.

The contrast between the works of Mr. Pollard [1]
and Mr. Greeley [2] is very striking. Though coin-
cident in design, they are the antipodes of each
other in treatment. Mr. Greeley, finding a country beyond measure prosperous suddenly assailed
by rebellion, is naturally led to seek an adequate
cause for so abnormal an effect. Mr. Pollard,
formerly an office-holder under the United States,
and now the editor of a Richmond newspaper, is
struck by the same reflection, and, unwilling to
state the true cause, or unable to find a plausible
reason, is driven to hunt up an excuse for what
strikes ordinary people as one of the greatest crimes
in history. The difference is instructive.

[1] *The Southern History of the War. The First Year of the War.*
By Edward A. Pollard.

[2] *The American Conflict.* By Horace Greeley. Vol. I.

Mr. Pollard's book, however, is well worth reading by those who wish to learn something of the motives which originally led the Southern States into rebellion, and still actuate them in their obstinate resistance. To any one familiar with the history of the last thirty years, it would almost seem that Mr. Pollard's object had been to expose the futility of the pretences set up by the originators of Secession, so utterly does he fail in showing any adequate grounds for that desperate measure. As a history, the book is of little value, except as giving us here and there a hint by which we can guess something of the state of mind prevailing at the South. In point of style it is a curious jumble of American sense and Southern *highfaluting.* One might fancy it written by a schoolmaster, whose boys had got hold of the manuscript, and inserted here and there passages taken at random from the *Gems of Irish Oratory.* Mr. Pollard's notions of the "Yankees," and the condition of things among them, would be creditable to a Chinaman from pretty well up in the back country. No society could hold together for a moment in the condition of moral decay which he attributes to the Northern States. Before writing his next volume he should read Charles Lamb's advice " to those who have the framing of advertisements for the apprehension of offenders." We must do him the justice to say, however, that he writes no nonsense about difference of races, and that, of all "Yankees," he most thoroughly despises the Northern snob who professes a sympathy for " Southern institutions " because he believes that a slaveholder is a better man than himself.

In narrating the causes which brought about the present state of things, Mr. Pollard arranges matters to suit his own convenience, constantly reversing the relations of cause and effect, and forgetting that the order of events is of every importance in estimating their moral bearing. The only theoretic reason he gives for Secession is the desire to escape from the tyranny of a " numerical majority." Yet it was by precisely such a majority, and that attained by force or fraud, that the seceding States were taken out of the Union. We entirely agree with Mr. Pollard that a show of hands is no test of truth; but he seems to forget that, except under a despotism, a numerical majority of some sort or other is sure to govern. No man capable of thought, as Mr. Pollard certainly is, would admit that a majority was any more likely to be right under a system of limited than under one of universal suffrage, always provided the said majority did not express his own opinions. The majority always governs in the long run, because it comes gradually round to the side of what is just and for the common interest, and the only dangerous majority is that of a mob unchecked by the delay for reflection which all constitutional government interposes. The constitutions of most of the Slave States, so far as white men are concerned, are of the most intensely democratic type. Would Mr. Pollard consolidate them all under one strong government, or does he believe that to be good for

a single State which is bad for many united? It
is curious to see, in his own intense antipathy to a
slaveholding aristocracy, how purely American he
is in spite of his theories; and, bitterly hostile as
he is to the Davis administration, he may chance
on the reflection that a majority is pretty much
the same thing in one parallel of latitude as another. Of one thing he may be assured, — that
we of the North do not understand by republic a
government of the better and more intelligent class
by the worse and more ignorant, and accordingly
are doing our best by education to abolish the distinction between the two.

The fact that no adequate reasons for Secession
have ever been brought forward, either by the
seceding States at the time, or by their apologists
since, can only be explained on the theory that
nothing more than a *coup d'état* was intended,
which should put the South in possession of the
government. Owing to the wretched policy (if
supineness deserve the name) largely prevalent in
the North, of sending to the lower house of Congress the men who needed rather than those who
ought to go there, — men without the responsibility
or the independence which only established reputation, social position, long converse with great
questions, or native strength of character can give,
— and to the habit of looking on a seat in the
national legislature more as the reward for partisan
activity than as imposing a service of the highest
nature, so that representatives were changed as
often as there were new political debts to pay or

cliques to be conciliated, — owing to these things,
the South maintained an easy superiority at Washington, and learned to measure the Free States by
men who represented their weakest, and sometimes
their least honorable, characteristics. We doubt if
the Slave States have sent many men to the Capi-
tol who could be bought, while it is notorious that
from the north of Mason and Dixon's line many
an M. C. has cleared, like a ship, for Washington
and a market. Southern politicians judge the
North by men without courage and without principle, who would consent to any measure if it could
be becomingly draped in generalities, or if they
could evade the pillory of the yeas and nays. The
increasing drain of forensic ability toward the large
cities, with the mistaken theory that residence in
the district was a necessary qualification in candidates, tended still more to bring down the average
of Northern representation. The "claims" of a
section of the State, or even part of a district,
have been allowed to have weight, as if square
miles or acres were to be weighed against capacity
and experience. We attached too little importance
to the social prestige which the South acquired and
maintained at the seat of government, forgetting
the necessary influence it would exert upon the independence of many of our own members. These
in turn brought home the new impressions they had
acquired, till the fallacy gradually became conviction of a general superiority in the South,
though it had only so much truth in it as this,
that the people of that section sent their men of

character and position to Washington, and kept them there till every year of experience added an efficiency which more than made up for their numerical inferiority. Meanwhile, our thinking men allowed, whether from timidity or contempt, certain demagogic fallacies to become axioms by dint of repetition, chief among which was the notion that a man was the better representative of the democratic principle who had contrived to push himself forward to popularity by whatever means, and who represented the average instead of the highest culture of the community, thus establishing an aristocracy of mediocrity, nay, even of vulgarity, in some less intelligent constituencies. The one great strength of democracy is, that it opens all the highways of power and station to the better man, that it gives every man the chance of rising to his natural level; and its great weakness is in its tendency to urge this principle to a vicious excess, by pushing men forward into positions for which they are unfit, not so much because they deserve to rise, or because they have risen by great qualities, as because they began low. Our quadrennial change of offices, which turns public service into a matter of bargain and sale instead of the reward of merit and capacity, which sends men to Congress to represent private interests in the sharing of plunder, without regard to any claims of statesmanship or questions of national policy, as if the ship of state were periodically captured by privateers, has hastened our downward progress in the evil way. By making the administration promi-

nent at the cost of the government, and by its
constant lesson of scramble and vicissitude, almost
obliterating the idea of orderly permanence, it has
tended in no small measure to make disruption
possible, for Mr. Lincoln's election threw the
weight of every office-holder in the South into the
scale of Secession. The war, however, has proved
that the core of Democracy was sound; that the
people, if they had been neglectful of their duties,
or had misapprehended them, had not become
corrupt.

Mr. Greeley's volume is a valuable contribution
to our political history. Though for many years
well known as an ardent politician, and associated
by popular prejudice with that class of untried
social theories which are known by the name of
isms, his tone is singularly calm and dispassionate.
Disfigured here and there by a vulgarism which
adds nothing to its point, while it detracts from
its purity, his style is clear, straightforward,
and masculine, — a good business style, at once
bare of ornament and undiluted with eloquence.
Mr. Greeley's intimate knowledge of our politics
and instinctive sympathy with the far-reaching
scope of our institutions (for, as Béranger said of
himself, he is *tout peuple*) admirably fitted him
for his task. He is clear, concise, and accurate,
honestly striving after the truth, while his judi-
cious Preface shows that he appreciates fully the
difficulties that beset whoever seeks to find it. If
none of his readers will be surprised to find his
work that of an able man, there are many who

would not expect it to be, as it is, that of a fair-minded one. He writes without passion, making due allowance for human nature in the South as well as the North, and does not waste his strength, as is the manner of fanatics, in fighting imaginary giants while a real enemy is in the field. Tracing Secession to its twin sources in slavery and the doctrine of State Rights, and amply sustaining his statements of fact by citations from contemporary documents and speeches, he has made the plainest, and for that very reason, we think, the strongest, argument that has been put forth on the national side of the question at issue in our civil war. Above all, he is ready to allow those virtues in the character of the Southern people whose existence alone makes reunion desirable or possible. We should not forget that the Negro is at least no more our brother than they, for if he have fallen among thieves who have robbed him of his manhood, they have been equally enslaved by prejudice, ignorance, and social inferiority.

It is not a little singular that, while slavery has been for nearly eighty years the one root of bitterness in our politics, the general knowledge of its history should be so superficial. Abolitionism has been so persistently represented as the disturbing element which threatened the permanence of our Union, that mere repetition has at last become conviction with that large class of minds with which a conclusion is valuable exactly in proportion as it saves mental labor. Mr. Greeley's chronological narrative is an excellent corrective of this delusion, and his tough little facts, driven firmly home, will serve to spike this parrot battery, and render it harmless for the future. A consecutive statement of such of the events in our history as bear directly on the question of slavery, separated from all secondary circumstances, shows two things clearly : first, that the doctrine that there was any national obligation to consider slaves as merely property, or to hold our tongues about slavery, is of comparatively recent origin; and, second, that there was a pretty uniform ebb of anti-slavery sentiment for nearly sixty years after the adoption of the Constitution, the young flood beginning to set strongly in again after the full meaning of the annexation of Texas began to be understood at the North, but not fairly filling up again even its own deserted channels till the Southern party succeeded in cutting the embankment of the Missouri Compromise. Then at last it became evident that the real danger to be guarded against was the abolition of Freedom, and the reaction was as violent as it was sudden.

In the early days of the Republic, slavery was admitted to be a social and moral evil, only to be justified by necessity; and we think it more than doubtful if South Carolina and Georgia could have procured an extension of the slave-trade, had there not been a general persuasion that the whole system could not long maintain itself against the growth of intelligence and humanity. As early as 1786 a resident of South Carolina wrote : " In countries where slavery is encouraged, the ideas of the people are of a peculiar cast; the soul becomes dark and narrow, and assumes a tone of savage brutality. . . . The most elevated and liberal Carolinians abhor slavery; they will not debase themselves by attempting to vindicate it." In 1789 William Pinckney said, in the Maryland Assembly: " Sir, by the eternal principles of natural justice, no master in the State has a right to hold his slave in bondage for a single hour." And he went on to speak of slavery in a way which, fifty years later, would have earned him a coat of tar and feathers, if not a halter, in any of the Slave States, and in some of the Free. In 1787 Delaware passed an act forbidding the importation of "negro or mulatto slaves into the State for sale or otherwise;" and three years later her courts declared a slave, hired in Maryland and brought over the border, free under this statute. In 1790 there were Abolition societies in Maryland and Virginia. In 1787 the Synod of the Presbyterian Church (since called the General Assembly), in their pastoral letter, "strongly recommended the abolition of slavery, with the instruction of the negroes in literature and religion." We cite these instances to show that the sacredness of slavery from discussion was a discovery of much later date. So also was the theory of its divine origin, — a theological slough in which, we are sorry to say, Northern men have shown themselves readiest to bemire themselves. It was when slave labor and slave breeding began to bring large and rapid profits, by the extension of cotton-culture consequent on the in-

vention of Whitney's gin, and the purchase of
Louisiana, that slavery was found to be identical
with religion, and, like Duty, a " daughter of the
voice of God." Till it became rich, it had been
content with claiming the municipal law for its
parent, but now it was easy to find heralds who
could blazon for it a nobler pedigree. Men who
looked upon dancing as sinful could see the very
beauty of holiness in a system like this! It is
consoling to think that, even in England, it is little
more than a century since the divine right of kings
ceased to be defended in the same way, by making the narrative portions of Scripture doctrinal.
Such strange things have been found in the Bible
that we are not without hope of the discovery of
Christianity there, one of these days.

The influence of the Southern States in the national politics was due mainly to the fact of their
having a single interest on which they were all
united, and, though fond of contrasting their more
chivalric character with the commercial spirit of
the North, it will be found that profit has been the
motive to all the encroachments of slavery. These
encroachments first assumed the offensive with the
annexation of Texas. In the admission of Missouri, though the Free States might justly claim a
right to fix the political destiny of half the territory, bought with the common money of the nation,
and though events have since proved that the compromise of 1820 was a fatal mistake, yet, as slavery was already established there, the South might,
with some show of reason, claim to be on the

defensive. In one sense, it is true, every enlarge-
ment of the boundaries of slavery has been an
aggression. For it cannot with any fairness be
assumed that the framers of the Constitution intended to foreordain a perpetual balance of power
between the Free and the Slave States. If they
had, it is morally certain that they would not so
have arranged the basis of representation as to secure to the South an unfair preponderance, to be
increased with every addition of territory. It is
much more probable that they expected the Southern States to fall more and more into a minority
of population and wealth, and were willing to
strengthen this minority by yielding it somewhat
more than its just share of power in Congress. Indeed, it was mainly on the ground of the undue
advantage which the South would gain, politically,
that the admission of Missouri was distasteful to
the North.

It was not till after the Southern politicians had
firmly established their system of governing the
country by an alliance with the Democratic party
of the Free States, on the basis of a division of
offices, that they dreamed of making their " institution " the chief concern of the nation. As we
follow Mr. Greeley's narrative, we see them first
pleading for the existence of slavery, then for its
equality, and at last claiming for it an absolute dominion. Such had been the result of uniform concession on the part of the North for the sake of
Union, such the decline of public spirit, that within
sixty years of the time when slaveholders like

George Mason of Virginia could denounce slavery for its inconsistency with the principles on which our Revolution had triumphed, the leaders of a party at the North claiming a kind of patent in the rights of man as an expedient for catching votes were decrying the doctrines of the Declaration of Independence as visionary and impracticable. Was it the Slave or the Free States that had just cause to be alarmed for their peculiar institutions? And, meanwhile, it had been discovered that slavery was conservative! It would protect a country in which almost every voter was a landholder from any sudden frenzy of agrarianism! In the South it certainly conserved a privileged class, and prevented a general debauch of education; but in the North it preserved nothing but political corruption, subserviency, cant, and all those baser qualities which unenviably distinguish man from the brutes.

The nation had paid ten millions for Texas, an extension of the area of freedom, as it was shamelessly called, which was to raise the value of slaves in Virginia, according to Mr. Upshur, and did raise it, fifty per cent. It was next proposed to purchase Cuba for one hundred millions, or to take it by force if Spain refused to sell. And all this for fear of abolition. This was paying rather dearly for our conservative element, it should seem, especially when it stood in need of such continual and costly conservation. But it continued to be plain to a majority of voters that democratic institutions absolutely demanded a safeguard against demo-

cracy, and that the only insurance was something
that must be itself constantly insured at more and
more ruinous rates. It continued to be plain also
that slavery was purely a matter of local concern,
though it could help itself to the national money,
force the nation into an unjust war, and stain its
reputation in Europe with the buccaneering principles proclaimed in the Ostend Manifesto. All
these were plainly the results of the ever-increasing
and unprovoked aggressions of Northern fanaticism. To be the victims of such injustice seemed
not unpleasing to the South. Let us sum up the
items of their little bill against us. They demanded Missouri, — we yielded; they could not
get along without Texas, — we *re*-annexed it; they
must have a more stringent fugitive-slave law, —
we gulped it; they must no longer be insulted with
the Missouri Compromise, — we repealed it. Thus
far the North had surely been faithful to the terms
of the bond. We had paid our pound of flesh
whenever it was asked for, and with fewer wry
faces, inasmuch as Brother Ham underwent the in-
cision. Not at all. We had only surrendered the
principles of the Revolution; we must give up the
theory also, if we would be loyal to the Constitution.

We entirely agree with Mr. Greeley that the
quibble which would make the Constitution an
anti-slavery document, because the word *slave* is
not mentioned in it, cannot stand a moment if we
consider the speeches made in Convention, or the
ideas by which the action of its members was

guided. But the question of slavery in the Territories stands on wholly different ground. We know what the opinions of the men were who drafted the Constitution, by their own procedure in passing the Ordinance of 1787. That the North should yield all claim to the common lands was certainly a new interpretation of constitutional law. And yet this was practically insisted on by the South, and its denial was the more immediate occasion of rupture between the two sections. But, in our opinion, the real cause which brought the question to the decision of war was the habit of concession on the part of the North, and the inability of its representatives to say *No*, when policy as well as conscience made it imperative. Without that confidence in Northern pusillanimity into which the South had been educated by their long experience of this weakness, whatever might have been the secret wish of the leading plotters, they would never have dared to rush their fellow-citizens into a position where further compromise became impossible.

Inextricably confused with the question of Slavery, and essential to an understanding of the motives and character of the Southern people as distinguished from their politicians, is the doctrine of State Rights. On this topic also Mr. Greeley furnishes all the data requisite to a full understanding of the matter. The dispute resolves itself substantially into this: whether the adoption of the Constitution established a union or a confederacy, a government or a league, a nation or a committee.

This also is a question which can only be determined by a knowledge of what the Convention of 1787 intended and accomplished, and the States severally acceded to, — it being of course understood that no State had a right, or at the time pretended any right, to accept the Constitution with mental reservations. On this subject we have ample and unimpeachable testimony in the discussions which led to the calling of the Convention, and the debates which followed in the different conventions of the States called together to decide whether the new frame of government should be accepted or rejected. The conviction that it was absolutely necessary to remodel the Articles of Confederation was wrought wholly by an experience of the inadequacy of the existing plan (under which a single State could oppose its veto to a law of Congress), from the looseness of its cohesion and its want of power to compel obedience. The principle of coercive authority, which was represented as so oppressively unconstitutional by the friends of Secession in the North as well as the South four years ago, was precisely that which, as its absence had brought the old plan to a dead-lock, was deemed essential to the new. The formal proposal for a convention, originated by Hamilton, was seconded by one State after another. Here is a sample of Virginian public sentiment at that time, from the "instructions to their representatives," by several constituencies: "Government without coercion is a proposition at once so absurd and self-contradictory that the idea creates a confusion of the under-

standing; it is form without substance, at best a
body without a soul." Oliver Ellsworth, advocating the adoption of the Constitution in the Convention of Connecticut, says: " A more energetic
system is necessary. The present is merely advi-
sory. It has no coercive power. Without this,
government is ineffectual, or rather is no government at all." Earlier than this Madison had
claimed " an implied right of coercion " even for
the Confederate Congress, and Jefferson had gone
so far as to say that they possessed it " by the law
of nature." The leading objections to the new
Constitution were such as to show the general belief that the State sovereignties were to be absorbed into the general government in all matters
of national concern. But the unhappy ingenuity
of Mr. Jefferson afterwards devised that theory of
strict construction which would enable any State
to profit by the powers of the Constitution so long
as it was for her interest or convenience, and then,
by pleading its want of powers, to resolve the helpless organization once more into the incoherence of
confederacy. By this dexterous legerdemain, the
Union became a string of juggler's rings, which
seems a chain while it pleases the operator, but
which, by bringing the strain on the weak point
contrived for the purpose, is made to fall easily
asunder and become separate rings again. An
adroit use of this theory enabled the South to gain
one advantage after another by threatening disunion, and led naturally, on the first effective show
of resistance, to secession. But in order that the

threat might serve its purpose without the costly necessity of putting it in execution, the doctrine of State Rights was carefully inculcated at the South by the same political party which made belief in the value of the Union a fanaticism at the North. On one side of Mason and Dixon's line it was lawful, and even praiseworthy, to steal the horse; on the other, it was a hanging matter to look over the fence.

But in seeking for the cause of the rebellion, with any fairness toward the Southern people, and any wish to understand their motives and character, it would be unwise to leave out of view the fact that they have been carefully educated in the faith that secession is not only their right, but the only safeguard of their freedom. While it is perfectly true that the great struggle now going on is intrinsically between right and privilege, between law and license, and while on the part of its leaders the Southern revolt was a conspiracy against popular government, and an attempt to make a great Republic into a mere convenient drudge for Slavery, yet we should despair of our kind did we believe that the rank and file of the Confederate armies were consciously spending so much courage and endurance on behalf of barbarism. It is more consoling, as it is nearer the truth, to think that they are fighting for what they have been taught to believe their rights, and their inheritance as a free people. The high qualities they have undoubtedly shown in the course of the war, their tenacity, patience, and discipline, show that, under better influences, they may become worthy to take their part in advancing the true destinies of America.

It is yet too early to speculate with much confidence on the remote consequences of the war. One of its more immediate results has already been to disabuse the Southern mind of some of its most fatal misconceptions as to Northern character. They thought us a trading people, incapable of lofty sentiment, ready to sacrifice everything for commercial advantage,— a heterogeneous rabble, fit only to be ruled by a superior race. They are not likely to make that mistake again, and must have learned by this time that the best blood is that which has in it most of the iron of purpose and constancy. War, the sternest and dearest of teachers, has already made us a soberer and older people on both sides. It has brought questions of government and policy home to us as never before, and has made us feel that citizenship is a duty to whose level we must rise, and not a privilege to which we are born. The great principles of humanity and politics, which had faded into the distance of abstraction and history, have been for four years the theme of earnest thought and discussion at every fireside and wherever two men met together. They have again become living and operative in the heart and mind of the nation. What was before a mighty population is grown a great country, united in one hope, inspired by one thought, and welded into one power. But have not the same influences produced the same result in the South, and created there also a nation hope-

lessly alien and hostile? To a certain extent this
is true, but not in the unlimited way in which it
is stated by enemies in England, or politicians
at home, who would gladly put the people out of
heart, because they themselves are out of office.
With the destruction of slavery, the one object of
the war will have been lost by the Rebels, and its
one great advantage gained by the government.
Slavery is by no means dead as yet, whether
socially in its relation of man to man, or morally
in its hold on public opinion and its strength as
a political superstition. But there is no party at
the North, considerable in numbers or influence,
which could come into power on the platform of
making peace with the Rebels on their own terms.
No party can get possession of the government
which is not in sympathy with the temper of the
people, and the people, forced into war against
their will by the unprovoked attack of pro-slavery
bigotry, are resolved on pushing it to its legitimate conclusion. War means now, consciously
with many, unconsciously with most, but inevita-
bly, abolition. Nothing can save slavery but peace.
Let its doom be once accomplished, or its reconstruction (for reconstruction means nothing more)
clearly seen to be an impossibility, and the bond
between the men at the South who were willing to
destroy the Union, and those at the North who
only wish to save it, for the sake of slavery, will
be broken. The ambitious in both sections will
prefer their chances as members of a mighty
empire to what would always be secondary places

in two rival and hostile nations, powerless to command respect abroad or secure prosperity at home. The masses of the Southern people will not feel too keenly the loss of a kind of property in which they had no share, while it made them underlings, nor will they find it hard to reconcile themselves with a government from which they had no real cause of estrangement. If the war be waged manfully, as becomes a thoughtful people, without insult or childish triumph in success, if we meet opinion with wiser opinion, waste no time in badgering prejudice till it become hostility, and attack slavery as a crime against the nation, and not as individual sin, it will end, we believe, in making us the most powerful and prosperous community the world ever saw. Our example and our ideas will react more powerfully than ever on the Old World, and the consequence of a rebellion, aimed at the natural equality of all men, will be to hasten incalculably the progress of equalization over the whole earth. Above all, Freedom will become the one absorbing interest of the whole people, making us a nation alive from sea to sea with the consciousness of a great purpose and a noble destiny, and uniting us as slavery has hitherto combined and made powerful the most hateful aristocracy known to man.

McCLELLAN OR LINCOLN?

1864

THE spectacle of an opposition waiting patiently during several months for its principles to turn up would be amusing in times less critical than these. Nor was this the worst. If there might be persons malicious enough to think that the Democratic party could get along very well without principles, all would admit that a candidate was among the necessaries of life. Now, where not only immediate policy, but the very creed which that policy is to embody, is dependent on circumstances, and on circumstances so shifting and doubtful as those of a campaign, it is hard to find a representative man whose name may, in some possible contingency, mean enough, without, in some other equally possible contingency, meaning too much. The problem was to hunt up somebody who, without being anything in particular, might be anything in general, as occasion demanded. Of course, the professed object of the party was to save their country, but which *was* their country, and which it would be most profitable to save, whether America or Secessia, was a question that Grant or Sherman might answer one way or the other in a single battle. If only somebody or something would tell them whether they were for war or peace! The oracles were dumb, and all summer long they looked anxiously out, like Sister Anne from her tower, for the hero who should rescue unhappy Columbia from the Republican Bluebeard. Did they see a cloud of dust in the direction of Richmond or Atlanta? Perhaps Grant might be the man, after all, or even Sherman would answer at a pinch. When at last no great man would come along, it was debated whether it might not be better to nominate some one without a record, as it is called, since a nobody was clearly the best exponent of a party that was under the unhappy necessity of being still uncertain whether it had any recognizable soul or not. Meanwhile, the time was getting short and the public impatience peremptory.

"Under which king, bezonian? Speak, or die!"

The party found it alike inconvenient to do the one or the other, and ended by a compromise which might serve to keep them alive till after election, but which was as far from any distinct utterance as if their mouths were already full of that official pudding which they hope for as the reward of their amphibological patriotism. Since it was not safe to be either for peace or war, they resolved to satisfy every reasonable expectation by being at the same time both and neither. If you are warlike, there is General McClellan; if pacific, surely you must be suited with Mr. Pendleton; if neither, the combination of the two makes a *tertium quid* that is neither one thing nor another. As the politic Frenchman, kissing the foot of St. Peter's statue (recast out of a Jupiter), while he thus did homage to existing prejudices, hoped that the Thunderer would remember him if he ever came into power again, so the Chicago Convention compliments the prevailing warlike sentiment of the country with a soldier, but holds the civilian quietly in reserve for the future contingencies of submission. The nomination is a kind of political *What-is-it?* and voters are expected, without asking impertinent questions, to pay their money and make their own choice as to the natural history of the animal. Looked at from the Northern side, it is a raven, the bird of carnage, to be sure, but whitewashed and looking as decorously dove-like as it can; from the Southern, it is a dove, blackened over for the nonce, but letting the olive-branch peep from under its wing.

A more delicate matter for a convention, however, even than the selection of candidates, is the framing of a platform for them to stand upon. It was especially delicate for a gathering which represented so many heterogeneous and almost hostile elements. So incongruous an assemblage has not been seen since the host of Peter the Hermit, unanimous in nothing but the hope of plunder and of reconquering the Holy Land of office. There were War Democrats ready to unite in peace resolutions, and Peace Democrats eager to move the unanimous nomination of a war can-

didate. To make the confusion complete, Mr.
Franklin Pierce, the dragooner of Kansas, writes
a letter in favor of free elections, and the ma-
ligners of New England propose a Connecticut
Yankee as their favorite nominee. The Convention was a rag-bag of dissent, made up of bits so
various in hue and texture that the managers must
have been as much puzzled to arrange them in any
kind of harmonious pattern as the thrifty house-
wife in planning her coverlet out of the parings
of twenty years' dressmaking. All the odds and
ends of personal discontent, every shred of private
grudge, every resentful rag snipped off by official
shears, scraps of Rebel gray and leavings of Union
blue, — all had been gathered, as if for the tailor-
ing of Joseph's coat; and as a Chatham Street
broker first carefully removes all marks of previous
ownership from the handkerchiefs which find their
way to his counter, so the temporary chairman
advised his hearers, by way of a preliminary caution, to surrender their convictions. This, perhaps,
was superfluous, for it may be doubted whether
anybody present, except Mr. Fernando Wood, ever
legally had one, though Captain Rynders must
have brought many in his following who richly
deserved it. Mr. Belmont, being chosen to represent the Democracy of Mammon, did little more
than paraphrase in prose the speech of that fallen
financier in another rebellious conclave, as reported
by Milton : —

> " How in safety best we may
> Compose our present evils, with regard

Of what we are and were, dismissing quite
All thoughts of war."

But we turn from the momentary elevation of the banker, to follow the arduous labors of the Committee on Resolutions.[1] The single end to be served by the platform they were to construct was that of a bridge over which their candidate might make his way into the White House. But it must be so built as to satisfy the somewhat exacting theory of construction held by the Rebel emissaries at Niagara, while at the same time no apprehensions as to its soundness must be awakened in the loyal voters of the party. The war plank would offend the one, the State Rights plank excite the suspicion of the other. The poor fellow in Æsop, with his two wives, one pulling out the black hairs and the other the white, was not in a more desperate situation than the Committee, — MacHeath, between his two doxies, not more embarrassed. The result of their labors was, accordingly, as narrow as the pathway of the faithful into the Mahometan paradise, — so slender, indeed, that Blondin should have been selected as the only candidate who could hope to keep his balance on it, with the torrent of events rushing ever swifter and louder below. It might sustain the somewhat light Unionism of Mr. Pendleton, but would General McClellan dare to trust its fragile footing, with his Report and his West Point oration, with his record, in short, under his arm? Without these documents General Mc-

[1] The *Platform of the Chicago Convention* was published in the public journals 30th August.

Clellan is a nobody; with them, before he can step on a peace platform, he must eat an amount of leek that would have turned the stomach of Ancient Pistol himself. It remained to be seen whether he was more in favor of being President than of his own honor and that of the country.

The Resolutions of the Chicago Convention, though they denounce various wrongs and evils, some of them merely imaginary, and all the necessary results of civil war, propose only one thing, — surrender. Disguise it as you will, flavor it as you will, call it what you will, umble-pie is umble-pie, and nothing else. The people instinctively so understood it. They rejected with disgust a plan whose mere proposal took their pusillanimity for granted, and whose acceptance assured their self-contempt. At a moment when the Rebels would be checkmated in another move, we are advised to give them a knight and begin the game over again. If they are not desperate, what chance of their accepting offers which they rejected with scorn before the war began? If they are not desperate, why is their interest more intense in the result of our next Presidential election than even in the campaign at their very door? If they were not desperate, would two respectable men like Messrs. Clay and Holcomb endure the society of George Saunders? General McClellan himself admitted the righteousness of the war by volunteering in it, and, the war once begun, the only real question has been whether the principle of legitimate authority or that of wanton insurrection against it should prevail, —

whether we should have for the future a government of opinion or of brute force. When the rebellion began, its leaders had no intention to dissolve the Union, but to reconstruct it, to make the Montgomery Constitution and Jefferson Davis supreme over the whole country, and not over a feeble fragment of it. They knew, as we knew, the weakness of a divided country, and our experience of foreign governments during the last four years has not been such as to lessen the apprehension on that score, or to make the consciousness of it less pungent in either of the contending sections. Even now, Jefferson Davis is said to be in favor of a confederation between the Free and the Slave States. But what confederation could give us back the power and prestige of the old Union? The experience of Germany surely does not tempt to imitation. And in making overtures for peace, with whom are we to treat? Talking vaguely about "the South," "the Confederate States," or "the Southern people," does not help the matter; for the cat under all this meal is always the *government* at Richmond, men with everything to expect from independence, with much to hope from reconstruction, and sure of nothing but ruin from reunion. And these men, who were arrogant as equals and partners, are to be moderate in dictating terms as conquerors! If the people understood less clearly the vital principle which is at hazard in this contest, if they were not fully persuaded that Slavery and State Rights are merely the counters, and that free institutions are the real stake, they might be deluded with the hope of compromise. But there are things that are not subjects of compromise. The honor, the conscience, the very soul of a nation, cannot be compromised without ceasing to exist. When you propose to yield a part of them, there is already nothing left to yield.

And yet this is all that the party calling itself Democratic, after months of deliberation, after four years in which to study the popular mind, have to offer in the way of policy. It is neither more nor less than to confess that they have no real faith in popular self-government, for it is to assume that the people have neither common nor moral sense. General McClellan is to be put in command of the national citadel, on condition that he immediately offers to capitulate. To accept the nomination on these terms was to lose, not only his election, but his self-respect. Accordingly, no sooner was the damaging effect of the platform evident than it was rumored that he would consent to the candidacy, but reject the conditions on which alone it was offered. The singular uniform, half Union - blue and half Confederate - gray, in which it was proposed by the managers at Chicago to array the Democratic party, while it might be no novelty to some camp-followers of the New York delegation familiar with the rules of certain of our public institutions, could hardly be agreeable to one who had worn the livery of his country with distinction. It was the scene of Petruchio and the tailor over again : —

Gen. McC.	"Why, what, i' th' Devil's name, tailor, call'st thou this?"
Committee.	"You bid me make it orderly and well, According to the fashion and the time."
Gen. McC.	"Marry, I did; but, if you be remembered, *I did not bid you mar it to the time.*"

Between the nomination and acceptance came the taking of Atlanta, marring the coat to the time with a vengeance, and suggesting the necessity of turning it, — a sudden cure which should rank among the first in future testimonials to the efficacy of Sherman's lozenges. Had General McClellan thrust the resolutions away from him with an honest scorn, we should have nothing to say save in commendation. But to accept them with his own interpretation, to put upon them a meaning utterly averse from their plain intention, and from that understanding of them which the journals of his own faction clearly indicated by their exultation or their silence, according as they favored Confederacy or Union, is to prepare a deception for one of the parties to the bargain. In such cases, which is commonly cheated, the candidate, or the people who vote for him? If the solemn and deliberate language of resolutions is to be interpreted by contraries, what rule of hermeneutics shall we apply to the letter of a candidate? If the Convention meant precisely what they did not say, have we any assurance that the aspirant has not said precisely what he did not mean? Two negatives may constitute an affirmative, but surely the affirmation of two contradictory propositions by parties to the same bargain assures nothing but misunderstanding.

The resolutions were adopted with but four dissenting votes; their meaning was obvious, and the whole country understood it to be peace on any conditions that would be condescended to at Richmond. If a nation were only a contrivance to protect men in gathering gear, if territory meant only so many acres for the raising of crops, if power were of worth only as a police to prevent or punish crimes against person and property, then peace for the mere sake of peace were the one desirable thing for a people whose only history would be written in its cash-book. But if a nation be a living unity, leaning on the past by tradition, and reaching toward the future by continued aspiration and achievement, — if territory be of value for the raising of men formed to high aims and inspired to noble deeds by that common impulse which, springing from a national ideal, gradually takes authentic shape in a national character, — if power be but a gross and earthy bulk till it be ensouled with thought and purpose, and of worth only as the guardian and promoter of truth and justice among men, — then there are misfortunes worse than war and blessings greater than peace. At this moment, not the Democratic party only, but the whole country, longs for peace, and the difference is merely as to the price that shall be paid for it. Shall we pay in degradation, and sue for a cessation of hostilities which would make chaos the rule and order the exception, which would not be peace, but toleration, not the repose of manly security, but the helpless quiet of political death? Or shall we pay, in a little more present suffering, self-sacrifice, and earnestness of purpose, for a peace that shall be as lasting as honorable, won as it will be by the victory of right over wrong, and resting on the promise of God and the hope of man?   We believe the country has already made up its mind as to the answer, and will prove that a democracy may have as clear a conception of its interests and duties, as fixed a purpose in defending the one and fulfilling the other, a will as united and prompt, as have hitherto been supposed to characterize forms of government where the interests were more personal and the power less diffused.

Fortunately, though some of General McClellan's indiscreet friends would make the coming election to turn upon his personal quarrel with the administration, the question at issue between the two parties which seek to shape the policy of the country is one which manifestly transcends all lesser considerations, and must be discussed in the higher atmosphere of principle, by appeals to the reason, and not the passions, of the people.   However incongruous with each other in opinion the candidates of the Democratic party may be, in point of respectability they are unexceptionable.   It is true, as one of the candidates represents war and the other peace, and " when two men ride on one horse, one must ride behind," that it is of some consequence to know which is to be in the saddle and which on the croup ; but we will take it for granted that General McClellan will have no more delicacy about the opinions of Mr. Pendleton than he has

shown for those of the Convention. Still, we
should remember that the General may be impru-
dent enough to die, as General Harrison and General Taylor did before him, and that Providence
may again make " of our pleasant vices whips to
scourge us." We shall say nothing of the sectional
aspect of the nomination, for we do not believe
that what we deemed a pitiful electioneering clamor, when raised against our own candidates four
years ago, becomes reasonable argument in opposing those of our adversaries now. The point of
interest, then, is simply this : What can General
McClellan accomplish for the country which Mr.
Lincoln has failed to accomplish? In what respect would their policies differ? And, supposing
them to differ, which would be most consistent
with the honor and permanent well-being of the
nation?

General McClellan, in his letter of acceptance,[1]
assumes that, in nominating him, " the record of
his public life was kept in view " by the Convention. This will enable us to define with some certainty the points on which his policy would be
likely to differ from that of Mr. Lincoln. He
agrees with him that the war was a matter of necessity, not of choice. He agrees with him in assuming a right to emancipate slaves as a matter of
military expediency, differing only as to the method
and extent of its application, — a mere question of
judgment. He agrees with him as to the propriety
of drafting men for the public service, having, in-

---

[1] This letter was published in the public journals 9 September.

deed, been the first to recommend a draft of men
whom he was to command himself. He agrees
with him that it is not only lawful, but politic, to
make arrests without the ordinary forms of law
where the public safety requires it, and himself
both advised and accomplished the seizure of an
entire Legislature. So far there is no essential
difference, and beyond this we find very little, except that Mr. Lincoln was in a position where he
was called on to act with a view to the public welfare, and General McClellan in one where he could
express abstract opinions, without the responsibility
of trial, to be used hereafter for partisan purposes
as a part of his " record." For example, just after
his failure to coerce the State of Virginia, he took
occasion to instruct his superiors in their duty, and,
among other things, stated his opinion that the war
" should not be a war looking to the subjugation of
the people of any State," but " should be against
armed forces and political organizations." The
whole question of the right to " coerce a sovereign
State " appears to have arisen from a confusion of
the relations of a State to its own internal policy
and to the general government. But a State is
certainly a " political organization," and, if we understand General McClellan rightly, he would coerce a State, but not the people of it, — a distinction which we hope he appreciates better than its
victims would be likely to do. We find here also
no diversity in principle between the two men,
only that Mr. Lincoln has been compelled to do,
while General McClellan has had the easier task

of telling us what he would do. After the Peninsular campaign, we cannot but think that even the
latter would have been inclined to say, with the
wisest man that ever spoke in our tongue, " If to
do were as easy as to know what 't were good to
do, chapels had been churches, and poor men's cot-
tages princes' palaces."

The single question of policy on which General
McClellan differs from Mr. Lincoln, stripped of
the conventional phrases in which he drapes it, is
Slavery. He can mean nothing else when he talks
of " conciliation and compromise," of receiving
back any State that may choose to return " with a
full guaranty of all its constitutional rights." If
it be true that a rose by any other name will smell
as sweet, it is equally true that there is a certain
species of toadstool that would be none the less dis-
gusting under whatever *alias*. Compromise and
conciliation are both excellent things in their own
way, and in the fitting time and place, but right
cannot be compromised without surrendering it,
and to attempt conciliation by showing the white
feather ends, not in reconcilement, but subjection.
The combined ignorance of the Seven Sleepers of
Ephesus as to what had been going on while they
were in their cavern would hardly equal that of
General McClellan alone as to the political history
of the country. In the few months between Mr.
Lincoln's election and the attack on Fort Sumter
we tried conciliation in every form, carrying it
almost to the verge of ignominy. The Southern
leaders would have none of it. They saw in it

only a confession of weakness, and were but the more arrogant in their demand of all or nothing. Compromise we tried for three quarters of a century, and it brought us to where we are, for it was only a fine name for cowardice, and invited aggression. And now that the patient is dying of this drench of lukewarm water, Doctor Sangrado McClellan gravely prescribes another gallon. If that fail to finish him, why, give him a gallon more.

We wish it were as easy to restore General McClellan's army to what it was before the Peninsular campaign as he seems to think it is to put the country back where it was at the beginning of the war. The war, it is true, was undertaken to assert the sovereignty of the Constitution, but the true cause of quarrel was, not that the South denied the supremacy of that instrument, but that they claimed the sole right to interpret it, and to interpret it in a sense hostile to the true ideal of the country, and the clear interests of the people. But circumstances have changed, and what was at first a struggle to maintain the outward form of our government has become a contest to preserve the life and assert the supreme will of the nation. Even in April, 1861, underneath that desire for legal sanction common to our race, which expressed itself in loyalty to the Constitution, there was an instinctive feeling that the very germinating principle of our nationality was at stake, and that unity of territory was but another name for unity of idea ; nay, was impossible without it, and undesirable if it were possible. It was not against the

Constitution that the Rebels declared war, but against free institutions; and if they are beaten, they must submit to the triumph of those institutions. Their only chance of constitutional victory was at the polls. They rejected it, though it was in their grasp, and now it is for us, and not them, to dictate terms. After all the priceless blood they have shed, General McClellan would say to them, "Come back and rule us." Mr. Lincoln says, "Come back as equals, with every avenue of power open to you that is open to us; but the advantage which the slaveholding interest wrung from the weakness of the fathers your own madness has forfeited to the sons."

General McClellan tells us that if the war had been conducted "in accordance with those principles which he took occasion to declare when in active service, reconciliation would have been easy." We suppose he refers to his despatch of July 7th, 1862, when, having just demonstrated his incapacity in the profession for which he had been educated, he kindly offered to take the civil policy of the country under his direction, expecting, perhaps, to be more successful in a task for which he was fitted neither by training nor experience. It is true he had already been spoken of as a possible candidate for the Presidency, and that despatch was probably written to be referred to afterwards as part of the "record" to which he alludes in his recent letter. Indeed, he could have had no other conceivable object in so impertinent a proceeding, for, up to that time, the war had been conducted on the very principles he recommended; nay, was so conducted for six months longer, till it was demonstrated that reconciliation was not to be had on those terms, and that victory was incompatible with them.   Mr. Lincoln was forced into what General McClellan calls a radical policy by the necessity of the case.   The Rebels themselves insisted on convincing him that his choice was between that and failure.   They boasted that slavery was their bulwark and arsenal; that, while every Northern soldier withdrew so much from the productive industry of the Union, every fighting-man at the South could be brought into the field, so long as the negroes were left to do the work that was to feed and clothe him.   Were these negroes property?   The laws of war justified us in appropriating them to our own use.   Were they population?   The laws of war equally justified us in appealing to them for aid in a cause which was their own more than it was ours.   It was so much the worse for the South that its property was of a kind that could be converted from chattels into men, and from men into soldiers, by the scratch of a pen.   The dragon's teeth were not of our sowing, but, so far from our being under any obligation not to take into our service the army that sprang from them, it would have been the extreme of weakness and folly not to do it. If there be no provision in the Constitution for emancipating the negroes, neither is there any for taking Richmond; and we give General McClellan too much credit for intelligence and patriotism to suppose that if, when he asked for a hundred thousand more men at Harrison's Bar, he had been told that he could have black ones, he would have refused them.

But supposing the very improbable chance of General McClellan's election to the Presidency, how would he set about his policy of conciliation? Would he disarm the colored troops? In favor of prosecuting the war, as he declares himself to be, this would only necessitate the draft of just so many white ones in their stead. Would he recall the proclamation of freedom? This would only be to incite a servile insurrection. The people have already suffered too much by General McClellan's genius for retreat, to follow him in another even more disastrous. But it is idle to suppose that the Rebels are to be appeased by any exhibition of weakness. Like other men, they would take fresh courage from it. Force is the only argument to which they are in a condition to listen, and, like other men, they will yield to it at last, if it prove irresistible. We cannot think that General McClellan would wish to go down to posterity as the President who tried to restore the Union by the reënslaving of men who had fought in its defence, and had failed in the attempt. We doubt if he had any very clear conception of what he meant by conciliation and compromise, except as a gloss to make the unconditional surrender doctrine of the Chicago Convention a little less odious. If he meant more, if he hoped to gain political strength by an appeal to the old pro-slavery prejudices of the country, he merely shows the same unfortunate unconsciousness of the passage of time, and the changes it brings with it, that kept him in the trenches at Yorktown till his own defeat became inevitable. Perhaps he believes that the Rebels would accept from him what they rejected with contempt when offered by Mr. Lincoln, — that they would do in compliment to him what they refused to do from the interest of self-preservation. If they did, it would simply prove that they were in a condition to submit to terms, and not to dictate them. If they listened to his advances, their cause must be so hopeless that it would be a betrayal of his trust to make them. If they were obstinate, he would be left with the same war on his hands which has forced Mr. Lincoln into all his measures, and which would not be less exacting on himself. As a peace candidate he might solicit votes with some show of reason, but on a war platform we see no good reason for displacing Mr. Lincoln in his favor except on personal grounds; and we fear that our campaigns would hardly be conducted with vigor under a President whom the people should have invested with the office by way of poultice for his bruised sensibilities as a defeated commander. Once in the Presidential chair, with a country behind him insisting on a re-establishment of the Union, and a rebellion before him deaf to all offers from a government that faltered in its purposes, we do not see what form of conciliation he would hit upon by which to persuade a refractory " political organization," except that practised by Hood's butcher when he was advised to try it on a drove of sheep.

"He seized upon the foremost wether,
And hugged and lugged and tugged him neck and crop,
Just *nolens volens* through the open shop
(If tails came off he did not care a feather);
Then, walking to the door and smiling grim,
He rubbed his forehead and his sleeve together, —
'There! I 've *conciliated him!*'"

It is idle, however, to think of allaying angry feeling or appeasing resentment while the war lasts, and idler to hope for any permanent settlement, except in the complete subjugation of the rebellion. There are persons who profess to be so much shocked at the *word* subjugation as to be willing that we should have immediate experience of the *thing*, by receiving back the Rebels on their own conditions. Mr. Lincoln has already proclaimed an amnesty wide enough to satisfy the demands of the most exacting humanity, and they must reckon on a singular stupidity in their hearers who impute ferocious designs to a man who cannot nerve his mind to the shooting of a deserter or the hanging of a spy. Mr. Lincoln, in our judgment, has shown from the first the considerate wisdom of a practical statesman. If he has been sometimes slow in making up his mind, it has saved him the necessity of being hasty to change it when once made up, and he has waited till the gradual movement of the popular sentiment should help him to his conclusions and sustain him in them. To be moderate and unimpassioned in revolutionary times that kindle natures of more flimsy texture to a blaze may not be a romantic quality, but it is a rare one, and goes with those massive understandings on which a solid structure of achievement may be reared. Mr. Lincoln is a long-headed and long-purposed man, who knows when he is ready,— a secret General McClellan never learned. That he should be accused of playing Cromwell by the Opposition, and reproached with not being Cromwellian enough by the more ardent of his own supporters, is proof enough that his action has been of that firm but deliberate temper best suited to troublous times and to constitutional precedents. One of these accusations is the unworthy fetch of a party at a loss for argument, and the other springs from that exaggerated notion of the power of some exceptional characters upon events which Carlyle has made fashionable, but which was never even approximately true except in times when there was no such thing as public opinion, and of which there is no record personal enough to assure us what we are to believe. A more sincere man than Cromwell never lived, yet they know little of his history who do not know that his policy was forced to trim between Independents and Presbyterians, and that he so far healed the wounds of civil war as to make England dreaded without satisfying either. We have seen no reason to change our opinion of Mr. Lincoln since his wary scrupulousness won him the applause of one party, or his decided action, when he was at last convinced of its necessity, made him the momentary idol of the other. We will not call him a great man, for over-hasty praise is too apt to sour at last into satire, and greatness may be trusted safely to history and the future; but an honest one we believe him to be, and with no aim save to repair the glory and greatness of his country.

But fortunately it is no trial of the personal merits of opposing candidates on which the next election is to pronounce a verdict. The men set up by the two parties represent principles utterly antagonistic, and so far-reaching in their consequences that all personal considerations and contemporary squabbles become as contemptible in appearance as they always are in reality. However General McClellan may equivocate and strive to hide himself in a cloud of ink, the man who represents the party that deliberately and unanimously adopted the Chicago Platform is the practical embodiment of the principles contained in it. By ignoring the platform, he seems, it is true, to nominate himself; but this, though it may be good evidence of his own presumption, affords no tittle of proof that he could have been successful at Chicago without some distinct previous pledges of what his policy would be. If no such pledges were given, then the Convention nominated him with a clear persuasion that he was the sort of timber out of which tools are made. If they were not given, does not the acceptance of the nomination under false pretences imply a certain sacrifice of personal honor? And will the honor of the country be safe in the hands of a man who is careless of his own? General McClellan's election will be understood by the South and by the whole country as an acknowledgment of the right of secession, — an acknowledgment which will resolve the United States into an association for insurance against any risk of national strength and greatness by land or sea. Mr. Lincoln, on the other hand, is the exponent of principles vital to our peace, dignity, and renown, — of all that can save America from becoming Mexico, and insure popular freedom for centuries to come.

It is the merest electioneering trick to say that the war has been turned from its original intention, as if this implied that a cheat had thereby been put upon the country. The truth is, that the popular understanding has been gradually enlightened as to the real causes of the war, and, in consequence of that enlightenment, a purpose has grown up, defining itself slowly into clearer consciousness, to finish the war in the only way that will keep it finished, by rooting out the evil principle from which it sprang. The country has been convinced that a settlement which should stop short of this would be nothing more than a truce favorable only to the weaker party in the struggle, to the very criminals who forced it upon us. The single question is, Shall we have peace by submission or by victory? General McClellan's election insures the one, Mr. Lincoln's gives us our only chance of the other. It is Slavery, and not the Southern people, that is our enemy; we must conquer this to be at peace with them. With the relations of the several States of the Rebel Confederacy to the Richmond government we have nothing to do; but to say that, after being beaten as foreign enemies, they are to resume their previous relations to our own government as if nothing had happened, seems to us a manifest absurdity. From whom would General McClellan, if elected under his plan of conciliation, exact the penalties of rebellion? The States cannot be punished, and the only merciful way in which we can reach the real criminals is by that very policy of emancipation whose efficacy is proved by the bitter opposition of all the allies of the Rebellion in the North. This is a punishment which will not affect the independence of individual States, which will improve the condition of the mass of the Southern population, and which alone will remove the rock of offence from the pathway of democratic institutions. So long as slavery is left, there is antipathy between the two halves of the country, and the recurrence of actual war will be only a question of time. It is the nature of evil to be aggressive. Without moral force in itself, it is driven, by the necessity of things, to seek material props. It cannot make peace with truth, if it would. Good, on the other hand, is by its very nature peaceful. Strong in itself, strong in the will of God and the sympathy of man, its conquests are silent and beneficent as those of summer, warming into life, and bringing to blossom and fruitage, whatever is wholesome in men and the institutions of men.

ABRAHAM LINCOLN

1864–1865.

THERE have been many painful crises since the
impatient vanity of South Carolina hurried ten
prosperous Commonwealths into a crime whose
assured retribution was to leave them either at the
mercy of the nation they had wronged, or of the
anarchy they had summoned but could not control,
when no thoughtful American opened his morning
paper without dreading to find that he had no
longer a country to love and honor. Whatever the
result of the convulsion whose first shocks were
beginning to be felt, there would still be enough
square miles of earth for elbow-room; but that in-
effable sentiment made up of memory and hope, of
instinct and tradition, which swells every man's
heart and shapes his thought, though perhaps never
present to his consciousness, would be gone from
it, leaving it common earth and nothing more.
Men might gather rich crops from it, but that ideal
harvest of priceless associations would be reaped
no longer ; that fine virtue which sent up messages
of courage and security from every sod of it would
have evaporated beyond recall. We should be
irrevocably cut off from our past, and be forced to
splice the ragged ends of our lives upon whatever
new conditions chance might leave dangling for us.

We confess that we had our doubts at first whether the patriotism of our people were not too narrowly provincial to embrace the proportions of national peril. We felt an only too natural distrust of immense public meetings and enthusiastic cheers.

That a reaction should follow the holiday enthusiasm with which the war was entered on, that it should follow soon, and that the slackening of public spirit should be proportionate to the previous over-tension, might well be foreseen by all who had studied human nature or history. Men acting gregariously are always in extremes. As they are one moment capable of higher courage, so they are liable, the next, to baser depression, and it is often a matter of chance whether numbers shall multiply confidence or discouragement. Nor does deception lead more surely to distrust of men than self-deception to suspicion of principles. The only faith that wears well and holds its color in all weathers is that which is woven of conviction and set with the sharp mordant of experience. Enthusiasm is good material for the orator, but the statesman needs something more durable to work in, — must be able to rely on the deliberate reason and consequent firmness of the people, without which that presence of mind, no less essential in times of moral than of material peril, will be wanting at the critical moment. Would this fervor of the Free States hold out? Was it kindled by a just feeling of the value of constitutional liberty? Had it body enough to withstand the inevitable dampening of checks, reverses, delays? Had our population intelligence enough to comprehend that the choice was between order and anarchy, between the equilibrium of a government by law and the tussle of misrule by *pronunciamiento?* Could a war be maintained without the ordinary stimulus of hatred and plunder, and with the impersonal loyalty of principle? These were serious questions, and with no precedent to aid in answering them.

At the beginning of the war there was, indeed, occasion for the most anxious apprehension. A President known to be infected with the political heresies, and suspected of sympathy with the treason, of the Southern conspirators, had just surrendered the reins, we will not say of power, but of chaos, to a successor known only as the representative of a party whose leaders, with long training in opposition, had none in the conduct of affairs; an empty treasury was called on to supply resources beyond precedent in the history of finance; the trees were yet growing and the iron unmined with which a navy was to be built and armored; officers without discipline were to make a mob into an army; and, above all, the public opinion of Europe, echoed and reinforced with every vague hint and every specious argument of despondency by a powerful faction at home, was either contemptuously sceptical or actively hostile. It would be hard to over-estimate the force of this latter element of disintegration and discouragement among a people where every citizen at home, and every soldier in the field, is a reader of newspapers.

The pedlers of rumor in the North were the most
effective allies of the rebellion. A nation can be
liable to no more insidious treachery than that of
the telegraph, sending hourly its electric thrill of
panic along the remotest nerves of the community,
till the excited imagination makes every real danger loom heightened with its unreal double.

And even if we look only at more palpable difficulties, the problem to be solved by our civil war
was so vast, both in its immediate relations and
its future consequences; the conditions of its solution were so intricate and so greatly dependent on
incalculable and uncontrollable contingencies; so
many of the data, whether for hope or fear, were,
from their novelty, incapable of arrangement under any of the categories of historical precedent,
that there were moments of crisis when the firmest
believer in the strength and sufficiency of the democratic theory of government might well hold his
breath in vague apprehension of disaster. Our
teachers of political philosophy, solemnly arguing
from the precedent of some petty Grecian, Italian,
or Flemish city, whose long periods of aristocracy
were broken now and then by awkward paren-
theses of mob, had always taught us that democra-
cies were incapable of the sentiment of loyalty, of
concentrated and prolonged effort, of far-reaching
conceptions; were absorbed in material interests;
impatient of regular, and much more of exceptional
restraint; had no natural nucleus of gravitation,
nor any forces but centrifugal; were always on the
verge of civil war, and slunk at last into the nat-

ural almshouse of bankrupt popular government, a military despotism. Here was indeed a dreary outlook for persons who knew democracy, not by rubbing shoulders with it lifelong, but merely from books, and America only by the report of some fellow-Briton, who, having eaten a bad dinner or lost a carpet-bag here, had written to the "Times" demanding redress, and drawing a mournful inference of democratic instability. Nor were men wanting among ourselves who had so steeped their brains in London literature as to mistake Cockneyism for European culture, and contempt of their country for cosmopolitan breadth of view, and who, owing all they had and all they were to democracy, thought it had an air of high-breeding to join in the shallow epicedium that our bubble had burst.

But beside any disheartening influences which might affect the timid or the despondent, there were reasons enough of settled gravity against any overconfidence of hope. A war — which, whether we consider the expanse of the territory at stake, the hosts brought into the field, or the reach of the principles involved, may fairly be reckoned the most momentous of modern times — was to be waged by a people divided at home, unnerved by fifty years of peace, under a chief magistrate without experience and without reputation, whose every measure was sure to be cunningly hampered by a jealous and unscrupulous minority, and who, while dealing with unheard-of complications at home, must soothe a hostile neutrality abroad, waiting only a pretext to become war. All this was to be done without warning and without preparation, while at the same time a social revolution was to be accomplished in the political condition of four millions of people, by softening the prejudices, allaying the fears, and gradually obtaining the coöperation, of their unwilling liberators. Surely, if ever there were an occasion when the heightened imagination of the historian might see Destiny visibly intervening in human affairs, here was a knot worthy of her shears. Never, perhaps, was any system of government tried by so continuous and searching a strain as ours during the last three years; never has any shown itself stronger; and never could that strength be so directly traced to the virtue and intelligence of the people, — to that general enlightenment and prompt efficiency of public opinion possible only under the influence of a political framework like our own. We find it hard to understand how even a foreigner should be blind to the grandeur of the combat of ideas that has been going on here, — to the heroic energy, persistency, and self-reliance of a nation proving that it knows how much dearer greatness is than mere power; and we own that it is impossible for us to conceive the mental and moral condition of the American who does not feel his spirit braced and heightened by being even a spectator of such qualities and achievements. That a steady purpose and a definite aim have been given to the jarring forces which, at the beginning of the war, spent themselves in the discussion of schemes which could only become operative, if at all, after the war was

over; that a popular excitement has been slowly
intensified into an earnest national will; that a
somewhat impracticable moral sentiment has been
made the unconscious instrument of a practical
moral end; that the treason of covert enemies, the
jealousy of rivals, the unwise zeal of friends, have
been made not only useless for mischief, but even
useful for good; that the conscientious sensitive-
ness of England to the horrors of civil conflict has
been prevented from complicating a domestic with
a foreign war; — all these results, any one of which
might suffice to prove greatness in a ruler, have
been mainly due to the good sense, the good-humor,
the sagacity, the large-mindedness, and the unselfish honesty of the unknown man whom a blind
fortune, as it seemed, had lifted from the crowd to
the most dangerous and difficult eminence of modern times. It is by presence of mind in untried
emergencies that the native metal of a man is
tested; it is by the sagacity to see, and the fearless
honesty to admit, whatever of truth there may be
in an adverse opinion, in order more convincingly
to expose the fallacy that lurks behind it, that a
reasoner at length gains for his mere statement of
a fact the force of argument; it is by a wise forecast which allows hostile combinations to go so far
as by the inevitable reaction to become elements of
his own power, that a politician proves his genius
for state-craft; and especially it is by so gently
guiding public sentiment that he seems to follow it,
by so yielding doubtful points that he can be firm
without seeming obstinate in essential ones, and

thus gain the advantages of compromise without the weakness of concession ; by so instinctively comprehending the temper and prejudices of a people as to make them gradually conscious of the superior wisdom of his freedom from temper and prejudice, — it is by qualities such as these that a magistrate shows himself worthy to be chief in a commonwealth of freemen. And it is for qualities such as these that we firmly believe History will rank Mr. Lincoln among the most prudent of statesmen and the most successful of rulers. If we wish to appreciate him, we have only to conceive the inevitable chaos in which we should now be weltering, had a weak man or an unwise one been chosen in his stead.

" Bare is back," says the Norse proverb, " without brother behind it"; and this is, by analogy, true of an elective magistracy. The hereditary ruler in any critical emergency may reckon on the inexhaustible resources of *prestige*, of sentiment, of superstition, of dependent interest, while the new man must slowly and painfully create all these out of the unwilling material around him, by superiority of character, by patient singleness of purpose, by sagacious presentiment of popular tendencies and instinctive sympathy with the national character. Mr. Lincoln's task was one of peculiar and exceptional difficulty. Long habit had accustomed the American people to the notion of a party in power, and of a President as its creature and organ, while the more vital fact, that the executive for the time being represents the abstract idea of government as a permanent principle superior to all party and all private interest, had gradually become unfamiliar. They had so long seen the public policy more or less directed by views of party, and often even of personal advantage, as to be ready to suspect the motives of a chief magistrate compelled, for the first time in our history, to feel himself the head and hand of a great nation, and to act upon the fundamental maxim, laid down by all publicists, that the first duty of a government is to defend and maintain its own existence. Accordingly, a powerful weapon seemed to be put into the hands of the opposition by the necessity under which the administration found itself of applying this old truth to new relations. Nor were the opposition his only nor his most dangerous opponents.

The Republicans had carried the country upon an issue in which ethics were more directly and visibly mingled with politics than usual. Their leaders were trained to a method of oratory which relied for its effect rather on the moral sense than the understanding. Their arguments were drawn, not so much from experience as from general principles of right and wrong. When the war came, their system continued to be applicable and effective, for here again the reason of the people was to be reached and kindled through their sentiments. It was one of those periods of excitement, gathering, contagious, universal, which, while they last, exalt and clarify the minds of men, giving to the mere words *country*, *human rights*, *democracy*, a meaning and a force beyond that of sober and logical argument. They were convictions, maintained and defended by the supreme logic of passion. That penetrating fire ran in and roused those primary instincts that make their lair in the dens and caverns of the mind. What is called the great popular heart was awakened, that indefinable something which may be, according to circumstances, the highest reason or the most brutish unreason. But enthusiasm, once cold, can never be warmed over into anything better than cant, — and phrases, when once the inspiration that filled them with beneficent power has ebbed away, retain only that semblance of meaning which enables them to supplant reason in hasty minds. Among the lessons taught by the French Revolution there is none sadder or more striking than this, that you may make everything else out of the passions of men except a political system that will work, and that there is nothing so pitilessly and unconsciously cruel as sincerity formulated into dogma. It is always demoralizing to extend the domain of sentiment over questions where it has no legitimate jurisdiction; and perhaps the severest strain upon Mr. Lincoln was in resisting a tendency of his own supporters which chimed with his own private desires, while wholly opposed to his convictions of what would be wise policy.

The change which three years have brought about is too remarkable to be passed over without comment, too weighty in its lesson not to be laid to heart. Never did a President enter upon office

with less means at his command, outside his own
strength of heart and steadiness of understanding,
for inspiring confidence in the people, and so winning it for himself, than Mr. Lincoln. All that
was known of him was that he was a good stump-
speaker, nominated for his *availability*, — that is,
because he had no history, — and chosen by a party
with whose more extreme opinions he was not in
sympathy. It might well be feared that a man past
fifty, against whom the ingenuity of hostile partisans could rake up no accusation, must be lacking
in manliness of character, in decision of principle,
in strength of will; that a man who was at best
only the representative of a party, and who yet did
not fairly represent even that, would fail of political, much more of popular, support. And certainly no one ever entered upon office with so few
resources of power in the past, and so many materials of weakness in the present, as Mr. Lincoln.
Even in that half of the Union which acknowledged him as President, there was a large and at
that time dangerous minority, that hardly admitted
his claim to the office, and even in the party that
elected him there was also a large minority that
suspected him of being secretly a communicant
with the church of Laodicea. All that he did was
sure to be virulently attacked as ultra by one side;
all that he left undone, to be stigmatized as proof
of lukewarmness and backsliding by the other.
Meanwhile, he was to carry on a truly colossal
war by means of both; he was to disengage the
country from diplomatic entanglements of unpre-

cedented peril undisturbed by the help or the hindrance of either, and to win from the crowning dangers of his administration, in the confidence of the people, the means of his safety and their own. He has contrived to do it, and perhaps none of our Presidents since Washington has stood so firm in the confidence of the people as he does after three years of stormy administration.

Mr. Lincoln's policy was a tentative one, and rightly so. He laid down no programme which must compel him to be either inconsistent or unwise, no cast-iron theorem to which circumstances must be fitted as they rose, or else be useless to his ends. He seemed to have chosen Mazarin's motto, *Le temps et moi*. The *moi*, to be sure, was not very prominent at first; but it has grown more and more so, till the world is beginning to be persuaded that it stands for a character of marked individuality and capacity for affairs. Time was his prime-minister, and, we began to think, at one period, his general-in-chief also. At first he was so slow that he tired out all those who see no evidence of progress but in blowing up the engine; then he was so fast, that he took the breath away from those who think there is no getting on safely while there is a spark of fire under the boilers. God is the only being who has time enough; but a prudent man, who knows how to seize occasion, can commonly make a shift to find as much as he needs. Mr. Lincoln, as it seems to us in reviewing his career, though we have sometimes in our impatience thought otherwise, has always waited, as a wise man should, till the right moment brought up all his reserves. *Semper nocuit differre paratis* is a sound axiom, but the really efficacious man will also be sure to know when he is *not* ready, and be firm against all persuasion and reproach till he is.

One would be apt to think, from some of the criticisms made on Mr. Lincoln's course by those who mainly agree with him in principle, that the chief object of a statesman should be rather to proclaim his adhesion to certain doctrines, than to achieve their triumph by quietly accomplishing his ends. In our opinion, there is no more unsafe politician than a conscientiously rigid *doctrinaire*, nothing more sure to end in disaster than a theoretic scheme of policy that admits of no pliability for contingencies. True, there is a popular image of an impossible He, in whose plastic hands the submissive destinies of mankind become as wax, and to whose commanding necessity the toughest facts yield with the graceful pliancy of fiction; but in real life we commonly find that the men who control circumstances, as it is called, are those who have learned to allow for the influence of their eddies, and have the nerve to turn them to account at the happy instant. Mr. Lincoln's perilous task has been to carry a rather shaky raft through the rapids, making fast the unrulier logs as he could snatch opportunity, and the country is to be congratulated that he did not think it his duty to run straight at all hazards, but cautiously to assure himself with his setting-pole where the main current was, and keep steadily to that. He is still in wild water, but we have faith that his skill and sureness of eye will bring him out right at last.

A curious, and, as we think, not inapt parallel might be drawn between Mr. Lincoln and one of the most striking figures in modern history, — Henry IV. of France. The career of the latter may be more picturesque, as that of a daring captain always is; but in all its vicissitudes there is nothing more romantic than that sudden change, as by a rub of Aladdin's lamp, from the attorney's office in a country town of Illinois to the helm of a great nation in times like these. The analogy between the characters and circumstances of the two men is in many respects singularly close. Succeeding to a rebellion rather than a crown, Henry's chief material dependence was the Huguenot party, whose doctrines sat upon him with a looseness distasteful certainly, if not suspicious, to the more fanatical among them. King only in name over the greater part of France, and with his capital barred against him, it yet gradually became clear to the more far-seeing even of the Catholic party that he was the only centre of order and legitimate authority round which France could reorganize itself. While preachers who held the divine right of kings made the churches of Paris ring with declamations in favor of democracy rather than submit to the heretic dog of a Béarnois, — much as our *soi-disant* Democrats have lately been preaching the divine right of slavery, and denouncing the heresies of the Declaration of Independence, — Henry bore both parties in hand till he was convinced that only one

course of action could possibly combine his own interests and those of France. Meanwhile the Protestants believed somewhat doubtfully that he was
theirs, the Catholics hoped somewhat doubtfully
that he would be theirs, and Henry himself turned
aside remonstrance, advice, and curiosity alike with
a jest or a proverb (if a little *high*, he liked them
none the worse), joking continually as his manner
was. We have seen Mr. Lincoln contemptuously
compared to Sancho Panza by persons incapable
of appreciating one of the deepest pieces of wisdom
in the profoundest romance ever written; namely,
that, while Don Quixote was incomparable in theoretic and ideal statesmanship, Sancho, with his
stock of proverbs, the ready money of human experience, made the best possible practical governor.
Henry IV. was as full of wise saws and modern instances as Mr. Lincoln, but beneath all this was
the thoughtful, practical, humane, and thoroughly
earnest man, around whom the fragments of France
were to gather themselves till she took her place
again as a planet of the first magnitude in the European system. In one respect Mr. Lincoln was
more fortunate than Henry. However some may
think him wanting in zeal, the most fanatical can
find no taint of apostasy in any measure of his, nor
can the most bitter charge him with being influenced by motives of personal interest. The leading distinction between the policies of the two is
one of circumstances. Henry went over to the
nation; Mr. Lincoln has steadily drawn the nation
over to him. One left a united France; the other,

we hope and believe, will leave a reunited America. We leave our readers to trace the further points of difference and resemblance for themselves, merely suggesting a general similarity which has often occurred to us. One only point of melancholy interest we will allow ourselves to touch upon. That Mr. Lincoln is not handsome nor elegant, we learn from certain English tourists who would consider similar revelations in regard to Queen Victoria as thoroughly American in their want of *bienséance.* It is no concern of ours, nor does it affect his fitness for the high place he so worthily occupies; but he is certainly as fortunate as Henry in the matter of good looks, if we may trust contemporary evidence. Mr. Lincoln has also been reproached with Americanism by some not unfriendly British critics; but, with all deference, we cannot say that we like him any the worse for it, or see in it any reason why he should govern Americans the less wisely.

People of more sensitive organizations may be shocked, but we are glad that in this our true war of independence, which is to free us forever from the Old World, we have had at the head of our affairs a man whom America made, as God made Adam, out of the very earth, unancestried, unprivileged, unknown, to show us how much truth, how much magnanimity, and how much state-craft await the call of opportunity in simple manhood when it believes in the justice of God and the worth of man. Conventionalities are all very well in their proper place, but they shrivel at the touch of nature like stubble in the fire. The genius that sways a nation by its arbitrary will seems less august to us than that which multiplies and reinforces itself in the instincts and convictions of an entire people. Autocracy may have something in it more melodramatic than this, but falls far short of it in human value and interest.

Experience would have bred in us a rooted distrust of improvised statesmanship, even if we did not believe politics to be a science, which, if it cannot always command men of special aptitude and great powers, at least demands the long and steady application of the best powers of such men as it can command to master even its first principles. It is curious, that, in a country which boasts of its intelligence, the theory should be so generally held that the most complicated of human contrivances, and one which every day becomes more complicated, can be worked at sight by any man able to talk for an hour or two without stopping to think.

Mr. Lincoln is sometimes claimed as an example of a ready-made ruler. But no case could well be less in point; for, besides that he was a man of such fair-mindedness as is always the raw material of wisdom, he had in his profession a training precisely the opposite of that to which a partisan is subjected. His experience as a lawyer compelled him not only to see that there is a principle underlying every phenomenon in human affairs, but that there are always two sides to every question, both of which must be fully understood in order to understand either, and that it is of greater advantage to an advocate to appreciate the strength than the weakness of his antagonist's position. Nothing is more remarkable than the unerring tact with which, in his debate with Mr. Douglas, he went straight to the reason of the question; nor have we ever had a more striking lesson in political tactics than the fact, that, opposed to a man exceptionally adroit in using popular prejudice and bigotry to his purpose, exceptionally unscrupulous in appealing to those baser motives that turn a meeting of citizens into a mob of barbarians, he should yet have won his case before a jury of the people. Mr. Lincoln was as far as possible from an impromptu politician. His wisdom was made up of a knowledge of things as well as of men; his sagacity resulted from a clear perception and honest acknowledgment of difficulties, which enabled him to see that the only durable triumph of political opinion is based, not on any abstract right, but upon so much of justice, the highest attainable at any given moment in human affairs, as may be had in the balance of mutual concession. Doubtless he had an ideal, but it was the ideal of a practical statesman, — to aim at the best, and to take the next best, if he is lucky enough to get even that. His slow, but singularly masculine, intelligence taught him that precedent is only another name for embodied experience, and that it counts for even more in the guidance of communities of men than in that of the individual life. He was not a man who held it good public economy to pull down on the mere chance of rebuilding better. Mr. Lincoln's faith in

God was qualified by a very well-founded distrust of the wisdom of man. Perhaps it was his want of self-confidence that more than anything else won him the unlimited confidence of the people, for they felt that there would be no need of retreat from any position he had deliberately taken. The cautious, but steady, advance of his policy during the war was like that of a Roman army. He left behind him a firm road on which public confidence could follow; he took America with him where he went; what he gained he occupied, and his advanced posts became colonies. The very homeliness of his genius was its distinction. His kingship was conspicuous by its workday homespun. Never was ruler so absolute as he, nor so little conscious of it; for he was the incarnate common-sense of the people. With all that tenderness of nature whose sweet sadness touched whoever saw him with something of its own pathos, there was no trace of sentimentalism in his speech or action. He seems to have had but one rule of conduct, always that of practical and successful politics, to let himself be guided by events, when they were sure to bring him out where he wished to go, though by what seemed to unpractical minds, which let go the possible to grasp at the desirable, a longer road.

Undoubtedly the highest function of statesmanship is by degrees to accommodate the conduct of communities to ethical laws, and to subordinate the conflicting self-interests of the day to higher and more permanent concerns. But it is on the understanding, and not on the sentiment, of a nation that all safe legislation must be based. Voltaire's saying, that "a consideration of petty circumstances is the tomb of great things," may be true of individual men, but it certainly is not true of governments. It is by a multitude of such considerations, each in itself trifling, but all together weighty, that the framers of policy can alone divine what is practicable and therefore wise. The imputation of inconsistency is one to which every sound politician and every honest thinker must sooner or later subject himself. The foolish and the dead alone never change their opinion. The course of a great statesman resembles that of navigable rivers, avoiding immovable obstacles with noble bends of concession, seeking the broad levels of opinion on which men soonest settle and longest dwell, following and marking the almost imperceptible slopes of national tendency, yet always aiming at direct advances, always recruited from sources nearer heaven, and sometimes bursting open paths of progress and fruitful human commerce through what seem the eternal barriers of both. It is loyalty to great ends, even though forced to combine the small and opposing motives of selfish men to accomplish them; it is the anchored cling to solid principles of duty and action, which knows how to swing with the tide, but is never carried away by it, — that we demand in public men, and not obstinacy in prejudice, sameness of policy, or a conscientious persistency in what is impracticable. For the impracticable, however theoretically enticing, is always politically unwise, sound statesmanship being the application of that prudence to the public business which is the safest guide in that of private men.

No doubt slavery was the most delicate and embarrassing question with which Mr. Lincoln was called on to deal, and it was one which no man in his position, whatever his opinions, could evade; for, though he might withstand the clamor of partisans, he must sooner or later yield to the persistent importunacy of circumstances, which thrust the problem upon him at every turn and in every shape.

It has been brought against us as an accusation abroad, and repeated here by people who measure their country rather by what is thought of it than by what it is, that our war has not been distinctly and avowedly for the extinction of slavery, but a war rather for the preservation of our national power and greatness, in which the emancipation of the negro has been forced upon us by circumstances and accepted as a necessity. We are very far from denying this; nay, we admit that it is so far true that we were slow to renounce our constitutional obligations even toward those who had absolved us by their own act from the letter of our duty. We are speaking of the government which, legally installed for the whole country, was bound, so long as it was possible, not to overstep the limits of orderly prescription, and could not, without abnegating its own very nature, take the lead in making rebellion an excuse for revolution. There were, no doubt, many ardent and sincere persons who seemed to think this as simple a thing to do as to

lead off a Virginia reel. They forgot what should
be forgotten least of all in a system like ours, that
the administration for the time being represents
not only the majority which elects it, but the minority as well, — a minority in this case powerful,
and so little ready for emancipation that it was opposed even to war. Mr. Lincoln had not been
chosen as general agent of an antislavery society,
but President of the United States, to perform certain functions exactly defined by law. Whatever
were his wishes, it was no less duty than policy to
mark out for himself a line of action that would
not further distract the country, by raising before
their time questions which plainly would soon
enough compel attention, and for which every day
was making the answer more easy.

Meanwhile he must solve the riddle of this new
Sphinx, or be devoured. Though Mr. Lincoln's
policy in this critical affair has not been such as to
satisfy those who demand an heroic treatment for
even the most trifling occasion, and who will not
cut their coat according to their cloth, unless they
can borrow the scissors of Atropos, it has been at
least not unworthy of the long-headed king of
Ithaca. Mr. Lincoln had the choice of Bassanio
offered him. Which of the three caskets held the
prize that was to redeem the fortunes of the country? There was the golden one whose showy spe-
ciousness might have tempted a vain man; the sil-
ver of compromise, which might have decided the
choice of a merely acute one; and the leaden, —
dull and homely looking, as prudence always is, —

yet with something about it sure to attract the eye
of practical wisdom. Mr. Lincoln dallied with his
decision perhaps longer than seemed needful to
those on whom its awful responsibility was not to
rest, but when he made it, it was worthy of his
cautious but sure-footed understanding. The moral
of the Sphinx-riddle, and it is a deep one, lies in
the childish simplicity of the solution. Those who
fail in guessing it, fail because they are over-
ingenious, and cast about for an answer that shall
suit their own notion of the gravity of the occasion
and of their own dignity, rather than the occasion
itself.

In a matter which must be finally settled by public opinion, and in regard to which the ferment of
prejudice and passion on both sides has not yet
subsided to that equilibrium of compromise from
which alone a sound public opinion can result, it
is proper enough for the private citizen to press
his own convictions with all possible force of argument and persuasion; but the popular magistrate,
whose judgment must become action, and whose
action involves the whole country, is bound to wait
till the sentiment of the people is so far advanced
toward his own point of view, that what he does
shall find support in it, instead of merely confusing
it with new elements of division. It was not un-
natural that men earnestly devoted to the saving
of their country, and profoundly convinced that
slavery was its only real enemy, should demand
a decided policy round which all patriots might
rally,— and this might have been the wisest course

for an absolute ruler. But in the then unsettled state of the public mind, with a large party decrying even resistance to the slaveholders' rebellion as not only unwise, but even unlawful; with a majority, perhaps, even of the would-be loyal so long accustomed to regard the Constitution as a deed of gift conveying to the South their own judgment as to policy and instinct as to right, that they were in doubt at first whether their loyalty were due to the country or to slavery; and with a respectable body of honest and influential men who still believed in the possibility of conciliation, — Mr. Lincoln judged wisely, that, in laying down a policy in deference to one party, he should be giving to the other the very fulcrum for which their disloyalty had been waiting.

It behooved a clear-headed man in his position not to yield so far to an honest indignation against the brokers of treason in the North as to lose sight of the materials for misleading which were their stock in trade, and to forget that it is not the falsehood of sophistry which is to be feared, but the grain of truth mingled with it to make it specious, — that it is not the knavery of the leaders so much as the honesty of the followers they may seduce, that gives them power for evil. It was especially his duty to do nothing which might help the people to forget the true cause of the war in fruitless disputes about its inevitable consequences.

The doctrine of state rights can be so handled by an adroit demagogue as easily to confound the distinction between liberty and lawlessness in the

minds of ignorant persons, accustomed always to
be influenced by the sound of certain words, rather
than to reflect upon the principles which give them
meaning. For, though Secession involves the manifest absurdity of denying to a State the right of
making war against any foreign power while per-
mitting it against the United States; though it sup-
poses a compact of mutual concessions and guaranties among States without any arbiter in case of
dissension; though it contradicts common-sense in
assuming that the men who framed our government
did not know what they meant when they substi-
tuted Union for Confederation; though it falsifies
history, which shows that the main opposition to
the adoption of the Constitution was based on the
argument that it did not allow that independence
in the several States which alone would justify
them in seceding; — yet, as slavery was universally
admitted to be a reserved right, an inference could
be drawn from any direct attack upon it (though
only in self-defence) to a natural right of resistance, logical enough to satisfy minds untrained to
detect fallacy, as the majority of men always are,
and now too much disturbed by the disorder of
the times to consider that the order of events had
any legitimate bearing on the argument. Though
Mr. Lincoln was too sagacious to give the Northern allies of the Rebels the occasion they desired
and even strove to provoke, yet from the beginning
of the war the most persistent efforts have been
made to confuse the public mind as to its origin
and motives, and to drag the people of the loyal

States down from the national position they had instinctively taken to the old level of party squabbles and antipathies. The wholly unprovoked rebellion of an oligarchy proclaiming negro slavery the corner-stone of free institutions, and in the first flush of over-hasty confidence venturing to parade the logical sequence of their leading dogma, " that slavery is right in principle, and has nothing to do with difference of complexion," has been represented as a legitimate and gallant attempt to maintain the true principles of democracy. The rightful endeavor of an established government, the least onerous that ever existed, to defend itself against a treacherous attack on its very existence, has been cunningly made to seem the wicked effort of a fanatical clique to force its doctrines on an oppressed population.

Even so long ago as when Mr. Lincoln, not yet convinced of the danger and magnitude of the crisis, was endeavoring to persuade himself of Union majorities at the South, and to carry on a war that was half peace in the hope of a peace that would have been all war, — while he was still enforcing the Fugitive Slave Law, under some theory that Secession, however it might absolve States from their obligations, could not escheat them of their claims under the Constitution, and that slaveholders in rebellion had alone among mortals the privilege of having their cake and eating it at the same time, — the enemies of free government were striving to persuade the people that the war was an Abolition crusade. To rebel without reason was proclaimed as one of the rights of man, while it was carefully kept out of sight that to suppress rebellion is the first duty of government. All the evils that have come upon the country have been attributed to the Abolitionists, though it is hard to see how any party can become permanently powerful except in one of two ways, — either by the greater truth of its principles, or the extravagance of the party opposed to it. To fancy the ship of state, riding safe at her constitutional moorings, suddenly engulfed by a huge kraken of Abolitionism, rising from unknown depths and grasping it with slimy tentacles, is to look at the natural history of the matter with the eyes of Pontoppidan. To believe that the leaders in the Southern treason feared any danger from Abolitionism would be to deny them ordinary intelligence, though there can be little doubt that they made use of it to stir the passions and excite the fears of their deluded accomplices. They rebelled, not because they thought slavery weak, but because they believed it strong enough, not to overthrow the government, but to get possession of it; for it becomes daily clearer that they used rebellion only as a means of revolution, and if they got revolution, though not in the shape they looked for, is the American people to save them from its consequences at the cost of its own existence? The election of Mr. Lincoln, which it was clearly in their power to prevent had they wished, was the occasion merely, and not the cause, of their revolt. Abolitionism, till within a year or two, was the despised heresy of a few earnest persons, without political weight enough to carry the election of a parish constable; and their cardinal principle was disunion, because they were convinced that within the Union the position of slavery was impregnable. In spite of the proverb, great effects do not follow from small causes, — that is, disproportionately small, — but from adequate causes acting under certain required conditions. To contrast the size of the oak with that of the parent acorn, as if the poor seed had paid all costs from its slender strong-box, may serve for a child's wonder; but the real miracle lies in that divine league which bound all the forces of nature to the service of the tiny germ in fulfilling its destiny. Everything has been at work for the past ten years in the cause of anti-slavery, but Garrison and Phillips have been far less successful propagandists than the slaveholders themselves, with the constantly growing arrogance of their pretensions and encroachments. They have forced the question upon the attention of every voter in the Free States, by defiantly putting freedom and democracy on the defensive. But, even after the Kansas outrages, there was no wide-spread desire on the part of the North to commit aggressions, though there was a growing determination to resist them. The popular unanimity in favor of the war three years ago was but in small measure the result of anti-slavery sentiment, far less of any zeal for abolition. But every month of the war, every movement of the allies of slavery in the Free States, has been making Abolitionists by the thousand. The masses of any people, however intelligent, are very little moved by abstract principles of humanity and justice, until those principles are interpreted for them by the stinging commentary of some infringement upon their own rights, and then their instincts and passions, once aroused, do indeed derive an incalculable reinforcement of impulse and intensity from those higher ideas, those sublime traditions, which have no motive political force till they are allied with a sense of immediate personal wrong or imminent peril. Then at last the stars in their courses begin to fight against Sisera. Had any one doubted before that the rights of human nature are unitary, that oppression is of one hue the world over, no matter what the color of the oppressed, — had any one failed to see what the real essence of the contest was, — the efforts of the advocates of slavery among ourselves to throw discredit upon the fundamental axioms of the Declaration of Independence and the radical doctrines of Christianity could not fail to sharpen his eyes.

While every day was bringing the people nearer to the conclusion which all thinking men saw to be inevitable from the beginning, it was wise in Mr. Lincoln to leave the shaping of his policy to events. In this country, where the rough and ready understanding of the people is sure at last to be the controlling power, a profound common-sense is the best genius for statesmanship. Hitherto the wisdom of the President's measures has been justified by the fact that they have always resulted in more firmly uniting public opinion. One of the things particu-

larly admirable in the public utterances of President
Lincoln is a certain tone of familiar dignity, which,
while it is perhaps the most difficult attainment of
mere style, is also no doubtful indication of personal character. There must be something essen-
tially noble in an elective ruler who can descend to
the level of confidential ease without forfeiting respect, something very manly in one who can break
through the etiquette of his conventional rank and
trust himself to the reason and intelligence of those
who have elected him. No higher compliment was
ever paid to a nation than the simple confidence,
the fireside plainness, with which Mr. Lincoln always addresses himself to the reason of the American people. This was, indeed, a true democrat,
who grounded himself on the assumption that a
democracy can think. "Come, let us reason together about this matter," has been the tone of all
his addresses to the people; and accordingly we
have never had a chief magistrate who so won to
himself the love and at the same time the judgment
of his countrymen. To us, that simple confidence
of his in the right-mindedness of his fellow-men is
very touching, and its success is as strong an argument as we have ever seen in favor of the theory
that men can govern themselves. He never appeals to any vulgar sentiment, he never alludes to
the humbleness of his origin; it probably never
occurred to him, indeed, that there was anything
higher to start from than manhood; and he put
himself on a level with those he addressed, not by
going down to them, but only by taking it for

granted that they had brains and would come up to a common ground of reason. In an article lately printed in "The Nation," Mr. Bayard Taylor mentions the striking fact, that in the foulest dens of the Five Points he found the portrait of Lincoln. The wretched population that makes its hive there threw all its votes and more against him, and yet paid this instinctive tribute to the sweet humanity of his nature. Their ignorance sold its vote and took its money, but all that was left of manhood in them recognized its saint and martyr.

Mr. Lincoln is not in the habit of saying, "This is *my* opinion, or *my* theory," but, "This is the conclusion to which, in my judgment, the time has come, and to which, accordingly, the sooner we come the better for us." His policy has been the policy of public opinion based on adequate discussion and on a timely recognition of the influence of passing events in shaping the features of events to come.

One secret of Mr. Lincoln's remarkable success in captivating the popular mind is undoubtedly an unconsciousness of self which enables him, though under the necessity of constantly using the capital *I*, to do it without any suggestion of egotism. There is no single vowel which men's mouths can pronounce with such difference of effect. That which one shall hide away, as it were, behind the substance of his discourse, or, if he bring it to the front, shall use merely to give an agreeable accent of individuality to what he says, another shall make an offensive challenge to the self-satisfaction of all

his hearers, and an unwarranted intrusion upon
each man's sense of personal importance, irritating
every pore of his vanity, like a dry northeast wind,
to a goose-flesh of opposition and hostility.   Mr.
Lincoln has never studied Quinctilian ; but he has,
in the earnest simplicity and unaffected Americanism of his own character, one art of oratory worth
all the rest.   He forgets himself so entirely in his
object as to give his *I* the sympathetic and persuasive effect of *We* with the great body of his countrymen.   Homely, dispassionate, showing all the
rough-edged process of his thought as it goes along,
yet arriving at his conclusions with an honest kind
of every-day logic, he is so eminently our representative man, that, when he speaks, it seems as if the
people were listening to their own thinking aloud.
The dignity of his thought owes nothing to any
ceremonial garb of words, but to the manly movement that comes of settled purpose and an energy
of reason that knows not what rhetoric means.
There has been nothing of Cleon, still less of Strep-
siades striving to underbid him in demagogism, to
be found in the public utterances of Mr. Lincoln.
He has always addressed the intelligence of men,
never their prejudice, their passion, or their ignorance.

On the day of his death, this simple Western attorney, who according to one party was a vulgar
joker, and whom the *doctrinaires* among his own
supporters accused of wanting every element of
statesmanship, was the most absolute ruler in Chris-

tendom, and this solely by the hold his good-humored sagacity had laid on the hearts and understandings of his countrymen. Nor was this all, for it appeared that he had drawn the great majority, not only of his fellow-citizens, but of mankind also, to his side. So strong and so persuasive is honest manliness without a single quality of romance or unreal sentiment to help it! A civilian during times of the most captivating military achievement, awkward, with no skill in the lower technicalities of manners, he left behind him a fame beyond that of any conqueror, the memory of a grace higher than that of outward person, and of a gentlemanliness deeper than mere breeding. Never before that startled April morning did such multitudes of men shed tears for the death of one they had never seen, as if with him a friendly presence had been taken away from their lives, leaving them colder and darker. Never was funeral panegyric so eloquent as the silent look of sympathy which strangers exchanged when they met on that day. Their common manhood had lost a kinsman.

tional existence has never been in such peril as to force upon us the conviction that it was both the title-deed of our greatness and its only safeguard. But what splendid possibilities has not our trial revealed even to ourselves! What costly stuff whereof to make a nation! Here at last is a state whose life is not narrowly concentred in a despot or a class, but feels itself in every limb; a government which is not a mere application of force from without, but dwells as a vital principle in the will of every citizen. Our enemies — and wherever a man is to be found bribed by an abuse, or who profits by a political superstition, we have a natural enemy — have striven to laugh and sneer and lie this apparition of royal manhood out of existence. They conspired our murder; but in this vision is the prophecy of a dominion which is to push them from their stools, and whose crown doth scar their eyeballs. America lay asleep, like the princess of the fairy tale, enchanted by prosperity; but at the first fiery kiss of war the spell is broken, the blood tingles along her veins again, and she awakes conscious of her beauty and her sovereignty.

It is true that, by the side of the self-devotion and public spirit, the vices and meannesses of troubled times have shown themselves, as they will and must. We have had shoddy, we have had contracts, we have had substitute-brokerage, we have had speculators in patriotism, and, still worse, in military notoriety. Men have striven to make the blood of our martyrs the seed of wealth or office. But in times of public and universal extremity, when habitual standards of action no longer serve, and ordinary currents of thought are swamped in the flood of enthusiasm or excitement, it always happens that the evil passions of some men are stimulated by what serves only to exalt the nobler qualities of others. In such epochs, evil as well as good is exaggerated. A great social convulsion shakes up the lees which underlie society, forgotten because quiescent, and the stimulus of calamity brings out the extremes of human nature, whether for good or evil.

What is especially instructive in the events we have been witnessing for the past four years is the fact that the people have been the chief actors in the drama. They have not been the led, but the leaders. They have not been involved in war by the passions or interests of their rulers, but deliberately accepted the ordeal of battle in defence of institutions which were the work of their own hands, and of whose beneficence experience had satisfied them. Loyalty has hitherto been a sentiment rather than a virtue; it has been more often a superstition or a prejudice than a conviction of the conscience or of the understanding. Now for the first time it is identical with patriotism, and has its seat in the brain, and not the blood. It has before been picturesque, devoted, beautiful, as forgetfulness of self always is, but now it is something more than all these, — it is logical. Here we have testimony that cannot be gainsaid to the universal vitality and intelligence which our system diffuses with healthy pulse through all its members. Every

man feels himself a part, and not a subject, of the government, and can say in a truer and higher sense than Louis XIV., "I am the state." But we have produced no Cromwell, no Napoleon. Let us be thankful that we have passed beyond that period of political development when such productions are necessary, or even possible. It is but another evidence of the excellence of the democratic principle. Where power is the privilege of a class or of a single person, it may be usurped; but where it is the expression of the common will, it can no more be monopolized than air or light. The ignorant and unreasoning force of a populace, sure of losing nothing and with a chance of gaining something by any change, that restless material out of which violent revolutions are made, if it exist here at all, is to be found only in our great cities, among a class who have learned in other countries to look upon all law as their natural enemy. Nor is it by any fault of American training, but by the want of it, that these people are what they are. When Lord Derby says that the government of this country is at the mercy of an excited mob, he proves either that the demagogue is no exclusive product of a democracy, or that England would be in less danger of war if her governing class knew something less of ancient Greece and a little more of modern America.

Whether or no there be any truth in the assertion that democracy tends to bring men down to a common level (as it surely brings them up to one), we shall not stop to inquire, for the world has not yet had a long enough experience of it to warrant any safe conclusion. During our revolutionary struggle, it seems to us that both our civil and military leaders compare very well in point of ability with the British product of the same period, and the same thing may very well be true at the present time. But while it may be the glory, it can hardly be called the duty of a country to produce great men; and if forms of polity have anything to do in the matter, we should incline to prefer that which could make a great nation felt to be such and loved as such by every human fibre in it, to one which stunted the many that a few favored specimens might grow the taller and fairer.

While the attitude of the government was by the necessity of the case expectant so far as slavery was concerned, it is also true that the people ran before it, and were moved by a deeper impulse than the mere instinct of self-preservation. The public conscience gave energy and intention to the public will, and the bounty which drew our best soldiers to the ranks was an idea. The game was the ordinary game of war, and they but the unreasoning pieces on the board; but they felt that a higher reason was moving them in a game where the stake was the life not merely of their country, but of a principle whose rescue was to make America in very deed a New World, the cradle of a fairer manhood. Weakness was to be no longer the tyrant's opportunity, but the victim's claim; labor should never henceforth be degraded as a curse, but honored as that salt of the earth which keeps life sweet, and gives its savor to duty. To be of good family should mean being a child of the one Father of us all; and good birth, the being born into God's world, and not into a fool's paradise of man's invention. But even had this moral leaven been wanting, had the popular impulse been merely one of patriotism, we should have been well content to claim as the result of democracy that for the first time in the history of the world it had mustered an army that knew for what it was fighting. Nationality is no dead abstraction, no unreal sentiment, but a living and operative virtue in the heart and moral nature of men. It enlivens the dullest soul with an ideal out of and beyond itself, lifting every faculty to a higher level of vision and action. It enlarges the narrowest intellect with a fealty to something better than self. It emancipates men from petty and personal interests, to make them conscious of sympathies whose society ennobles. Life has a deeper meaning when its throb beats time to a common impulse and catches its motion from the general heart.

But while the experience of the last four years has been such, with all its sorrows, as to make us proud of our strength and grateful for the sources of it, we cannot but feel that peace will put to the test those higher qualities which war leaves in reserve. What are we to do with the country our arms have regained? It is by our conduct in this stewardship, and not by our rights under the original compact of the States, that our policy is to be justified. The glory of conquest is trifling and barren, unless victory clear the way to a higher civilization, a more solid prosperity, and a Union based upon reciprocal benefits. In what precise manner the seceding States shall return, whether by inherent right, or with some preliminary penance and ceremony of readoption, is of less consequence than what they shall be after their return. Dependent provinces, sullenly submitting to a destiny which they loathe, would be a burden to us, rather than an increase of strength or an element of prosperity. War would have won us a peace stripped of all the advantages that make peace a blessing. We should have so much more territory, and so much less substantial greatness. We did not enter upon war to open a new market, or fresh fields for speculators, or an outlet for redundant population, but to save the experiment of democracy from destruction, and put it in a fairer way of success by removing the single disturbing element. Our business now is not to allow ourselves to be turned aside from a purpose which our experience thus far has demonstrated to have been as wise as it was necessary, and to see to it that, whatever be the other conditions of reconstruction, democracy, which is our real strength, receive no detriment.

We would not be understood to mean that Congress should lay down in advance a fixed rule not to be departed from to suit the circumstances of special cases as they arise. What may do very well for Tennessee may not be as good for South Carolina. Wise statesmanship does not so much consist in the agreement of its forms with any abstract ideal, however perfect, as in its adaptation to the wants of the governed and its capacity of shaping itself to the demands of the time. It is not to be judged by its intention, but by its results, and those will be proportioned to its practical, and not its theoretic, excellence. The Anglo-Saxon soundness of understanding has shown itself in nothing more clearly than in allowing institutions to be formulated gradually by custom, convenience, or necessity, and in preferring the practical comfort of a system that works, to the French method of a scientific machinery of perpetual motion, demonstrably perfect in all its parts, and yet refusing to go. We do not wish to see scientific treatment, however admirable, applied to the details of reconstruction, if that is to be, as now seems probable, the next problem that is to try our intelligence and firmness. But there are certain points, it seems to us, on which it is important that public opinion should come to some sort of understanding in advance.

The peace negotiations have been of service in demonstrating that it is not any ill blood engendered by war, any diversity of interests properly national, any supposed antagonism of race, but simply the slaveholding class, that now stands between us and peace, as four years ago it forced us into war. Precisely as the principle of Divine right could make no lasting truce with the French Revolution, the Satanic right of the stronger to enslave the weaker can come to no understanding

with democracy. The conflict is in the things, not
in the men, and one or the other must abdicate.
Of course the leaders, to whom submission would
be ruin, and a few sincere believers in the doctrine of State rights, are willing to sacrifice even
slavery for independence, a word which has a
double meaning for some of them; but there can
be no doubt that an offer to receive the seceding
States back to their old position under the Constitution would have put the war party in a hopeless
minority at the South. We think there are manifest symptoms that the chinks made by the four
years' struggle have let in new light to the Southern people, however it may be with their ruling
faction, and that they begin to suspect a diversity
of interest between themselves, who chiefly suffer
by the war, and the small class who bullied them
into it for selfish purposes of their own. However
that may be, the late proposal of Davis and Lee
for the arming of slaves, though they certainly did
not so intend it, has removed a very serious obstacle from our path. It is true that the emancipating clause was struck out of the act as finally
passed by the shadowy Congress at Richmond.
But this was only for the sake of appearances.
Once arm and drill the negroes, and they can
never be slaves again. This is admitted on all
hands, and accordingly, whatever the words of the
act may be, it practically at once promotes the
negro to manhood by brevet, as it were, but at any
rate to manhood. For the offer of emancipation
as a bounty implies reason in him to whom it is

offered ; nay, more, implies a capacity for progress and a wish for it, which are in themselves valid titles to freedom. This at a step puts the South back to the position held by her greatest men in regard to slavery. All the Scriptural arguments, all the fitness of things, all the physiological demonstrations, all Mr. Stephens's corner-stones, Ham, Onesimus, heels, hair, and facial angle, — all are swept out, by one flirt of the besom of Fate, into the inexorable limbo of things that were and never should have been. How is Truth wounded to death in the house of her friends ! The highest authority of the South has deliberately renounced its vested interest in the curse of Noah, and its right to make beasts of black men because St. Paul sent back a white one to his master. Never was there a more exact verification of the Spanish proverb, that he who went out for wool may come back shorn. Alas for Nott and Gliddon ! Thrice alas for Bishop Hopkins ! With slavery they lose their hold on the last clue by which human reason could find its way to a direct proof of the benevolence of God and the plenary inspiration of Scripture.

All that we have learned of the blacks during the war makes the plan of arming a part of them to help maintain the master's tyranny over the rest seem so futile, and the arguments urged against it by Mr. Gholson and Mr. Hunter are so convincing, that we can hardly persuade ourselves that the authors of it did not intend it to make the way easier, not to independence, but to reunion. It is said to argue desperation on the part of the chief conspirators at Richmond, and it undoubtedly does; but we see in what we believe to be the causes of their despair something more hopeful than the mere exhaustion it indicates. It is simply incredible that the losses of a four years' war should have drained the fighting men of a population of five millions, or anything like it; and the impossibility of any longer filling the Rebel armies even by the most elaborate system of press-gangs proves to our mind that the poorer class of whites have for some reason or other deserted the cause of the wealthy planters. The men are certainly there, but they have lost all stomach for fighting. Here again we see something which is likely to make a final settlement more easy than it would have been even a year ago. Though the fact that so large a proportion of the Southern people cannot read makes it harder to reach them, yet our soldiers have circulated among them like so many Northern newspapers, and it is impossible that this intercourse, which has been constant, should not have suggested to them many ideas of a kind which their treacherous guides would gladly keep from them. The frantic rage of Southern members of Congress against such books as Helper's can be explained only by their fear lest their poorer constituents should be set a-thinking, for the notion of corrupting a field-hand by an Abolition document is too absurd even for a Wigfall or a Charleston editor.

Here, then, are two elements of a favorable horoscope for our future; an acknowledgment of the

human nature of the negro by the very Sanhedrim
of the South, thus removing his case from the court
of ethics to that of political economy; and a suspicion on the part of the Southern majority that
something has been wrong, which makes them
readier to see and accept what is right. We do not
mean to say that there is any very large amount of
even latent Unionism at the South, but we believe
there is plenty of material in solution there which
waits only to be precipitated into whatever form of
crystal we desire. We must not forget that the
main elements of Southern regeneration are to be
sought in the South itself, and that such elements
are abundant. A people that has shown so much
courage and constancy in a bad cause, because they
believed it a good one, is worth winning even by
the sacrifice of our natural feeling of resentment.
If we forgive the negro for his degradation and
his ignorance, in consideration of the system of
which he has been the sacrifice, we ought also to
make every allowance for the evil influence of
that system upon the poor whites. It is the fatal
necessity of all wrong to revenge itself upon those
who are guilty of it, or even accessory to it. The
oppressor is dragged down by the victim of his
tyranny. The eternal justice makes the balance
even; and as the sufferer by unjust laws is lifted
above his physical abasement by spiritual compensations and that nearness to God which only suffering is capable of, in like measure are the material
advantages of the wrong-doer counterpoised by a
moral impoverishment. Our duty is not to punish,

but to repair ; and the cure must work both ways, emancipating the master from the slave, as well as the slave from the master. Once rid of slavery, which was the real criminal, let us have no more reproaches, justifiable only while the Southern sin made us its forced accomplices ; and while we bind up the wounds of our black brother who had fallen among thieves that robbed him of his rights as a man, let us not harden our hearts against our white brethren, from whom interest and custom, those slyer knaves, whose fingers we have felt about our own pockets, had stolen away their conscience and their sense of human brotherhood.

The first question that arises in the mind of everybody in thinking of reconstruction is, What is to be done about the negro? After the war is over, there will be our Old Man of the Sea, as ready to ride us as ever. If we only emancipate him, he will not let us go free. We must do something more than merely this. While the suffering from them is still sharp, we should fix it in our minds as a principle, that the evils which have come upon us are the direct and logical consequence of our forefathers having dealt with a question of man as they would with one of trade or territory, — as if the rights of others were something susceptible of compromise, — as if the laws that govern the moral, and, through it, the material world, would stay their operation for our convenience. It is well to keep this present in the mind, because in the general joy and hurry of peace we shall be likely to forget it again, and to make concessions, or to leave things at loose ends for time to settle, — as time has settled the blunders of our ancestors. Let us concede everything except what does not belong to us, but is only a trust-property, namely, the principle of democracy and the prosperity of the future involved in the normal development of that principle.

We take it for granted at the outset, that the mind of the country is made up as to making no terms with slavery in any way, large or limited, open or covert. Not a single good quality traceable to this system has been brought to light in the white race at the South by the searching test of war. In the black it may have engendered that touching piety of which we have had so many proofs, and it has certainly given them the unity of interest and the sympathy of intelligence which make them everywhere our friends, and which have saved them from compromising their advantage, and still further complicating the difficulties of civil war by insurrection. But what have been its effects upon the ruling class, which is, after all, the supreme test of institutions? It has made them boastful, selfish, cruel, and false, to a degree unparalleled in history. So far from having given them any special fitness for rule, it has made them incapable of any but violent methods of government, and unable to deal with the simplest problems of political economy. An utter ignorance of their own countrymen at the North led them to begin the war, and an equal misconception of Europe encouraged them to continue it. That they have shown courage is true, but that is no exclusive property of theirs, and the military advantage they seemed to possess is due less to any superiority of their own than to the extent of their territory and the roadless wildernesses which are at once the reproach and the fortification of their wasteful system of agriculture. Their advantages in war have been in proportion to their disadvantages in peace, and it is peace which most convincingly tries both the vigor of a nation and the wisdom of its polity. It is with this class that we shall have to deal in arranging the conditions of settlement; and we must do it with a broad view of the interests of the whole country and of the great mass of the Southern people, whose ignorance and the prejudices consequent from it made it so easy to use them as the instruments of their own ruin. No immediate advantage must blind us to the real objects of the war, — the securing our external power and our internal tranquillity, and the making them inherent and indestructible by founding them upon the common welfare.

The first condition of permanent peace is to render those who were the great slaveholders when the war began, and who will be the great landholders after it is over, powerless for mischief. What punishment should be inflicted on the chief criminals is a matter of little moment. The South has received a lesson of suffering which satisfies all the legitimate ends of punishment, and as for vengeance, it is contrary to our national temper and the spirit of our government. Our great object should be, not to weaken, but to strengthen the South, — to make it richer, and not poorer. We must not repeat the stupid and fatal blunder of slaveholding publicists, that the wealth and power of one portion of the country are a drain upon the resources of the rest, instead of being their natural feeders and invigorators. Any general confiscation of Rebel property, therefore, seems to us unthrifty housekeeping, for it is really a levying on our own estate, and a lessening of our own resources. The people of the Southern States will be called upon to bear their part of the grievous burden of taxation which the war will leave upon our shoulders, and that is the fairest as well as the most prudent way of making them contribute to our national solvency. All irregular modes of levying contributions, however just, — and exactly just they can seldom be, — leave discontent behind them, while a uniform system, where every man knows what he is to pay and why he is to pay it, tends to restore stability by the very evenness of its operation, by its making national interests familiar to all, and by removing any sense of injustice. Any sweeping confiscation, such as has sometimes been proposed in Congress with more heat than judgment, would render the South less available for revenue, would retard the return of industry to its legitimate channels, by lessening its means, and would not destroy the influence of the misgoverning aristocracy. On the contrary, it would give them that prestige of misfortune whose power over the sentiments of mankind is the moral of the story of Stuarts and

Bourbons and Bonapartes. Retribution they should have, but let them have it in the only way worthy of a great people to inflict. Let it come in a sense of their own folly and sin, brought about by the magnanimity of their conquerors, by the return of a more substantial prosperity born of the new order of things, so as to convince, instead of alienating. We should remember that it is our country which we have regained, and not merely a rebellious faction which we have subdued.

Whether it would not be good policy for the general government to assume all the wild lands in the rebellious States, and to devote the proceeds of their sale to actual settlers to the payment of the national debt, is worth consideration. Texas alone, on whose public lands our assumption of her indebtedness gives us an equitable claim, would suffice to secure our liabilities and to lighten our taxation, and in all cases of land granted to freedmen no title should vest till a fair price had been paid, — a principle no less essential to their true interests than our own. That these people, who are to be the peasantry of the future Southern States, should be made landholders, is the main condition of a healthy regeneration of that part of the country, and the one warranty of our rightful repossession of it. The wealth that makes a nation really strong, and not merely rich, is the opportunity for industry, intelligence, and well-being of its laboring population. This is the real country of poor men, as the great majority must always be. No glories of war or art, no luxurious refinement of the few, can give them a sense of nationality where this is wanting. If we free the slave without giving him a right in the soil, and the inducement to industry which this offers, we reproduce only a more specious form of all the old abuses. We leave all political power in the hands of the wealthy landholders, where it was before. We leave the poorer whites unemancipated, for we leave labor still at the mercy of capital, and with its old stigma of degradation. Blind to the lessons of all experience, we deliberately make the South what Ireland was when Arthur Young travelled there, the country richest in the world by nature, reduced to irredeemable poverty and hopeless weakness by an upper class who would not, and a lower class who could not, improve. We have no right to purchase dominion, no right to purchase even abolition, at such a price as that. No *uti possidetis* conveys any legitimate title, except on the condition of wise administration and mutual benefit.

But will it be enough to make the freedmen landholders merely? Must we not make them voters also, that they may have that power of self-protection which no interference of government can so safely, cheaply, and surely exercise in their behalf? We answer this question in the affirmative, for reasons both of expediency and justice. At best, the difficulty, if not settled now, will come up again for settlement hereafter, when it may not be so easy of solution. As a matter of expediency, it is always wisest to shape a system of policy with a view to permanence, much more than to immediate convenience. When things are put upon a right footing at first, — and the only right footing is one which will meet the inevitable demands of the future as well as the more noisy ones of the present, — all subsidiary relations will of necessity arrange themselves by mutual adaptation, without constantly calling for the clumsy interference of authority. We must leave behind us no expectation and no fear of change, to unsettle men's minds and dishearten their industry. Both the late master and the late slave should begin on the new order of things with a sense of its permanence on the one hand and its rightfulness on the other. They will soon learn that neither intelligence can do without labor, nor labor without intelligence, and that wealth will result only from a clearly understood and reciprocally beneficial dependence of each upon the other. Unless we make the black a citizen, we take away from the white the strongest inducement to educate and enlighten him. As a mere proletary, his ignorance is a temptation to the stronger race ; as a voter, it is a danger to them which it becomes their interest to remove. It is easy to manage the mob of New York for the time with grape-shot, but it is the power for evil which their suffrage gives them that will at last interest all classes, by reform and education, to make it a power for good.

Under the head of expediency comes also this other consideration, — that, unless made citizens, the emancipated blacks, reckoned as they must be in the basis of representation, and yet without power to modify the character of the representatives chosen, will throw so much more power into the hands of men certain to turn it to their disadvantage, and only too probably to our own. This mass, if we leave it inert, may, in any near balance of parties, be enough to crush us; while, if we endow it with life and volition, if we put it in the way of rising in intelligence and profiting by self-exertion, it will be the best garrison for maintaining the supremacy of our ideas, till they have had time to justify themselves by experience. Have we endured and prosecuted this war for the sake of bringing back our old enemies to legislate for us, stronger than ever, with all the resentment and none of the instruction of defeat?

But as a measure of justice also, which is always the highest expediency, we are in favor of giving the ballot to the freedmen. Our answer to the question, What are we to do with the negro? is short and simple. Give him a fair chance. We must get rid of the delusion that right is in any way dependent on the skin, and not on an inward virtue. Our war has been carried on for the principles of democracy, and a cardinal point of those principles is, that the only way in which to fit men for freedom is to make them free, the only way to teach them how to use political power is to give it them. Both South and North have at last conceded the manhood of the negro, and the question now is how we shall make that manhood available and profitable to him and to us. Democracy does not mean, to any intelligent person, an attempt at the impossibility of making one man as good as another. But it certainly does mean the making of one man's manhood as good as another's and the giving to every human being the right of unlimited free trade in all his faculties and acquirements. We believe the white race, by their intellectual and traditional superiority, will retain sufficient ascendency to prevent any serious mischief from the new order of things. We admit that the whole subject bristles with difficulties, and we would by no means discuss or decide it on sentimental grounds. But our choice would seem to be between unqualified citizenship, to depend on the ability to read and write, if you will, and setting the blacks apart in some territory by themselves. There are, we think, insuperable objections to this last plan. It would put them beyond the reach of all good influence from the higher civilization of the whites, without which they might relapse into barbarism like the Maroons of Surinam, and it would deprive the whole Southern country of the very labor it needs. As to any prejudices which should prevent the two races from living together, it would soon yield to interest and necessity. The mere antipathy of color is not so strong there as here, and the blacks would form so very large a majority of the laboring class as not to excite the jealousy of rivalry. We can remember when the prejudice against the Celt was as strong in many of the Free States as that against the African could ever be at the South. It is not very long since this prejudice nearly gave a new direction to the politics of the country. Yet, like all prejudices, it had not coherence enough to keep any considerable party long together.

The objections to the plan are, of course, the same which lie against any theory of universal suffrage. These are many and strong, if considered abstractly; but we assume that theory to be admitted now as the rule of our political practice, and its evils as a working system have not been found so great, taking the country at large, as nearly to outweigh its advantages. Moreover, as we have said before, it compels the redress of its own abuses, and the remedy is one which is a benefit to the whole community, for it is simply to raise the general standard of intelligence. It is superior, certainly, to the English system, in which the body of the nation is alienated from its highest intellect and culture. We think the objections are quite as strong to any elective plan of government, for a select majority is as liable to be governed by its interests and passions as any popular one. Witness the elections at Oxford. Is the average wisdom or unselfishness of mankind so high that there should be no narrow minds and no selfish hearts in any body of electors, however carefully selected? The only infallible sovereign on earth is chosen by the majority of a body in which passion and intrigue and the influence (sometimes none of the purest) of conflicting courts are certainly not inoperative. Man is perhaps not the wisest of animals, but he has at least as keen a sense of his own advantage in a hovel as in a palace, and what is for the interest of the masses of the people is not very far from being for that of the country. It is said, to be sure, that we are inadequately represented in Congress; but a representative is apt to be a tolerably exact exponent of the merits of his constituency, and we must look for relief to the general improvement of our people in morals, manners, and culture. We doubt if the freedmen would send worse members to Congress than some in whose election merchants and bankers and even doctors of divinity have been accomplices.

With the end of the war the real trial of our statesmanship, our patriotism, and our patience will begin. The passions excited by it will, no doubt, subside in due time, but meanwhile it behooves the party in possession of the government to conciliate patriotic men of all shades of opinion by a liberal, manly and unpartisan policy. Republicans must learn to acknowledge that all criticisms of their measures have not been dictated by passion or disloyalty, that many moderate and honest men, many enlightened ones, have really found reason for apprehension in certain arbitrary stretches of authority, nay, may even have been opposed to the war itself, without being in love with slavery, and without deserving to be called Copperheads. Many have doubted the wisdom of our financial policy, without being unpatriotic. It is precisely this class, dispassionate and moderate in their opinions, whose help we shall need in healing the wounds of war and giving equanimity to our counsels. We hope to see a course of action entered upon which shall draw them to its support. In peace, governments cannot, as in war, find strength in the enthusiasm and even the passions of the people, but must seek it in the approval of their judgment and convictions. During war, all the measures of the dominant party have a certain tincture of patriotism; declamation serves very well the purposes of eloquence, and fervor of persuasion passes muster as reason; but in peaceful times everything must come back to a specific standard, and stand or fall on its own merits. Our faith is not unmixed with apprehension when we think of the immediate future, yet it is an abiding faith nevertheless; and with the experience of the last four years to sustain us, we are willing to believe almost anything good of the American people, and to say with the saint, *Credimus quia impossibile est.* We see no good reason why, if we use our victory with the moderation becoming men who profess themselves capable of self-government, conceding all that can be conceded without danger to the great principle which has been at stake, the North and the South should not live more harmoniously together in the future than in the past, now that the one rock of offence has been blasted out of the way. We do not believe that the war has tended to lessen their respect for each other, or that it has left scars which will take to aching again with every change of the political weather. We must bind the recovered communities to us with hooks of interest, by convincing them that we desire their prosperity as an integral part of our own. For a long while yet there will be a latent disaffection, even when the outward show may be fair, as in spring the ground often stiffens when the thermometer is above the freezing point. But we believe, in spite of this, that all this untowardness will yield to the gradual wooing of circumstances, and that it is to May, and not December, that we are to look forward. Even in our finances, which are confessedly our weakest point, we doubt if the experience of any other nation will enable us to form a true conception of our future. We shall have, beyond question, the ordinary collapse of speculation that follows a sudden expansion of paper currency. We shall have that shivering and expectant period when the sails flap and the ship trembles ere it takes the wind on the new tack. But it is no idle boast to say that there never was a country with such resources as ours. In Europe the question about a man always is, What *is* he? Here it is as invariably, What does he *do?* And in that little difference lies the security of our national debt for whoever has eyes. In America there is no idle class supported at the expense of the nation, there is no splendid poor-house of rank or office, but every man is at work adding his share to the wealth, and to that extent insuring the solvency, of the country. Our farm, indeed, is mortgaged, but it is a mortgage which the yearly profits will pay off.

Those who look upon the war as a wicked crusade of the North against the divinely sanctioned institutions of the South, and those who hope even yet to reknit the monstrous league between slavery and a party calling itself Democratic, will of course be willing to take back the seceding States without conditions. Neither of these classes is any longer formidable, either by its numbers or the character of its leaders. But there is yet a third class, who seem to have confused their minds with some fancied distinction between civil and foreign war. Holding the States to be indestructible, they seem to think that, by the mere cessation of hostilities, they are to resume their places as if nothing had happened, or rather as if this had been a mere political contest which we had carried. But it is with the people of the States, and not with any abstract sovereignty, that we have been at war, and it is of them that we are to exact conditions, and not of some convenient quasi-entity, which is not there when the battle is raging, and is there when the terms of capitulation are to be settled. No, it is slavery which made this war, and slavery which must pay the damages. While we should not by any unseemly exultation remind the Southern people that they have been conquered, we should also not be weak enough to forget that we have won the right of the victor. And what is that right, if it be not to exact indemnity for the past and security for the future? And what more nobly and satisfactorily fulfils both those conditions, than utterly to extinguish the cause of quarrel? What we fear is the foolish and weak good-nature inherent in popular government, but against which monarchies and aristocracies are insured by self-interest, which the prospect of peace is sure to arouse, and which may make our settlement a stage-reconciliation, where everybody rushes into the arms of everybody else with a fervor which has nothing to do with the living relations of the actors. We believe that the public mind should be made up as to what are the essential conditions of real and lasting peace, before it is subjected to the sentimental delusions of the inevitable era of good feeling, in which the stronger brother is so apt to play the part of Esau. If we are to try the experiment of democracy fairly, it must be tried in its fullest extent, and not half-way. The theory which grants political power to the ignorant white foreigner need not be squeamish about granting it to the ignorant black native, for the gist of the matter is in the dark mind, and not the more or less dusky skin. Of course we shall be met by the usual fallacy, — Would you confer equality on the blacks? But the answer is a very simple one. Equality cannot be conferred on any man, be he white or black. If he be capable of it, his title is from God, and not from us. The opinion of the North is made up on the subject of emancipation, and Mr. Lincoln has announced it as the one essential preliminary to the readmission of the insurgent States. To our mind, citizenship is the necessary consequence, as it is the only effectual warranty, of freedom; and accordingly we are in favor of distinctly settling beforehand some conditional right of admission to it. We have purposely avoided any discussion on gradualism as an element in emancipation, because we consider its evil results to have been demonstrated in the British West Indies. True conservative policy is not an anodyne hiding away our evil from us in a brief forgetfulness. It looks to the long future of a nation, and dares the heroic remedy where it is scientifically sure of the nature of the disease. The only desperate case for a people is where its moral sense is paralyzed, and the first symptom is a readiness to accept an easy expedient at the sacrifice of a difficult justice. The relation which is to be final and permanent cannot be too soon decided on and put in working order, whether for the true interest of master or slave; and the only safe relation is one that shall be fearlessly true to the principles in virtue of which we asserted our own claim to autonomy, and our right to compel obedience to the government so established. Anything short of that has the weakness of an expedient which will erelong compel us to reconstruct our reconstruction, and the worse weakness of hypocrisy, which will sooner or later again lay us open to the retribution of that eternal sincerity which brings all things at last to the test of its own unswerving standard.

SCOTCH THE SNAKE, OR KILL IT?

1865

IT has been said that the American people are less apt than others to profit by experience, because the bustle of their lives keeps breaking the thread of that attention which is the material of memory, till no one has patience or leisure to spin from it a continuous thread of thought. We suspect that this is not more true of us than of other nations, — than it is of all people who read newspapers. Great events are perhaps not more common than they used to be, but a vastly greater number of trivial incidents are now recorded, and this dust of time gets in our eyes. The telegraph strips history of everything down to the bare fact, but it does not observe the true proportions of things, and we must make an effort to recover them. In brevity and cynicism it is a mechanical Tacitus, giving no less space to the movements of Sala than of Sherman, as impartial a leveller as death. It announces with equal *sangfroid* the surrender of Kirby Smith and the capture of a fresh rebel governor, reducing us to the stature at which posterity shall reckon us. Eminent contemporaneousness may see here how much space will be allotted to it in the historical compends and biographical dictionaries of the next generation. In artless irony the telegraph is unequalled among the satirists of this generation. But this short-hand diarist confounds all distinctions of great and little, and roils the memory with minute particles of what is oddly enough called intelligence. We read in successive paragraphs the appointment of a Provisional Governor of North Carolina, whose fitness or want of it may be the turning-point of our future history, and the nomination of a minister, who will at most only bewilder some foreign court with a more desperately helpless French than his predecessor. The conspiracy trial at Washington, whose result will have absolutely no effect on the real affairs of the nation, occupies for the moment more of the public mind and thought than the question of reconstruction, which involves the life or death of the very principle we have been fighting for these four years.

Undoubtedly the event of the day, whatever it may be, is apt to become unduly prominent, and to thrust itself obscuringly between us and the perhaps more important event of yesterday, where the public appetite demands fresh gossip rather than real news, and the press accordingly keeps its spies everywhere on the lookout for trifles that become important by being later than the last. And yet this minuteness of triviality has its value also. Our sensitive sheet gives us every morning the photograph of yesterday, and enables us to detect and to study at leisure that fleeting expression of the time which betrays its character, and which might altogether escape us in the idealized historical portrait. We cannot estimate the value of the *items* in our daily newspaper, because the world to which they relate is too familiar and prosaic; but a hundred years hence some Thackeray will find them full of picturesque life and spirit. The "Chronicle" of the Annual Register makes the England of the last century more vividly real to us than any history. The jests which Pompeian idlers scribbled on the walls, while Vesuvius was brooding its fiery conspiracy under their feet, bring the scene nearer home to us than the letter of Pliny, and deepen the tragedy by their trifling contrast, like the grave-diggers' unseemly gabble in Hamlet. Perhaps our judgment of history is made sounder, and our view of it more lifelike, when we are so constantly reminded how the little things of life assert their place alongside the great ones, and how healthy the constitution of the race is, how sound its digestion, how gay its humor, that can take the world so easily while our continent is racked with fever and struggling for life against the doctors.

> " Let Hercules himself do what he may,
>   The cat will mew, the dog must have his day."

It is always pleasant to meet Dame Clio over the tea-table, as it were, where she is often more entertaining, if not more instructive, than when she puts on the loftier port and more ceremonious habit of a Muse. These inadvertences of history are pleasing. We are no longer foreigners, in any age of the world, but feel that in a few days we could have accommodated ourselves there, and that, wherever men are, we are not far from home. The more we can individualize and personify, the more lively our sympathy. Man interests us scientifically, but men claim us through all that we have made a part of our nature by education and custom. We would give more to know what Xenophon's soldiers gossiped about round their camp-fires, than for all the particulars of their retreat. Sparta becomes human to us when we think of Agesilaus on his hobby-horse. Finding that those heroic figures romped with their children, we begin for the first time to suspect that they ever really existed as much as Robinson Crusoe. Without these personal traits, antiquity seems as unreal to us as Sir Thomas More's Utopia. It is, indeed, surprising how little of real life what is reckoned solid literature has preserved to us, voluminous as it is. Where does chivalry at last become something more than a mere procession of plumes and armor, to be lamented by Burke, except in some of the less ambitious verses of the Trouvères, where we hear the canakin clink too emphatically, perhaps, but which at least paint living men and possible manners? Tennyson's knights are cloudy, gigantic, of no age or country, like the heroes of Ossian. They are creatures without stomachs. Homer is more condescending, and though we might not be able to draw the bow of Ulysses, we feel quite at home with him and Eumœus over their roast pork.

We cannot deny that the poetical view of any

period is higher, and in the deepest sense truer, than all others; but we are thankful also for the penny-a-liner, whether ancient or modern, who reflects the whims and humors, the enthusiasms and weaknesses, of the public in unguarded moments. Is it so certain, after all, that we should not be interesting ourselves in other quite as nugatory matters if these were denied us? In one respect, and no unimportant one, the instantaneous dispersion of news and the universal interest in it have affected the national thought and character. The whole people have acquired a certain metropolitan temper; they feel everything at once and in common; a single pulse sends anger, grief, or triumph through the whole country; one man sitting at the keyboard of the telegraph in Washington sets the chords vibrating to the same tune from sea to sea; and this simultaneousness, this unanimity, deepens national consciousness and intensifies popular emotion. Every man feels himself a part, sensitive and sympathetic, of this vast organism, a partner in its life or death. The sentiment of patriotism is etherealized and ennobled by it, is kindled by the more or less conscious presence of an ideal element; and the instinctive love of a few familiar hills and fields widens, till Country is no longer an abstraction, but a living presence, felt in the heart and operative in the conscience, like that of an absent mother. It is no trifling matter that thirty millions of men should be thinking the same thought and feeling the same pang at a single moment of time, and that these vast parallels of latitude should become a neighborhood more intimate than many a country village. The dream of Human Brotherhood seems to be coming true at last. The peasant who dipped his net in the Danube, or trapped the beaver on its banks, perhaps never heard of Cæsar or of Cæsar's murder; but the shot that shattered the forecasting brain, and curdled the warm, sweet heart of the most American of Americans, echoed along the wires through the length and breadth of a continent, swelling all eyes at once with tears of indignant sorrow. Here was a tragedy fulfilling the demands of Aristotle, and purifying with an instantaneous throb of pity and terror a theatre of such proportions as the world never saw. We doubt if history ever recorded an event so touching and awful as this sympathy, so wholly emancipated from the toils of space and time that it might seem as if earth were really sentient, as some have dreamed, or the great god Pan alive again to make the hearts of nations stand still with his shout. What is Beethoven's " Funeral March for the Death of a Hero " to the symphony of love, pity, and wrathful resolve which the telegraph of that April morning played on the pulses of a nation?

It has been said that our system of town meetings made our Revolution possible, by educating the people in self-government. But this was at most of partial efficacy, while the newspaper and telegraph gather the whole nation into a vast town-meeting, where every one hears the affairs of the country discussed, and where the better judgment is pretty sure to make itself valid at last. No memorable thing is said or done, no invention or discovery is made, that some mention of it does not sooner or later reach the ears of a majority of Americans. It is this constant mental and moral stimulus which gives them the alertness and viva-city, the wide-awakeness of temperament, charac-teristic of dwellers in great cities, and which has been remarked on by English tourists as if it were a kind of physiological transformation. They seem to think we have lost something of that solidity of character which (with all other good qualities) they consider the peculiar inheritance of the British race, though inherited in an elder brother's pro-portion by the favored dwellers in the British Isles. We doubt if any substantial excellence is lost by this suppling of the intellectual faculties, and bringing the nervous system nearer the surface by the absorption of superfluous fat. What is lost in bulk may be gained in spring. It is true that the clown, with his parochial horizon, his diet inconveniently thin, and his head conveni-ently thick, whose notion of greatness is a prize pig, and whose patriotism rises or falls with the strength of his beer, is a creature as little likely to be met with here as the dodo, his only rival in the qualities that make up a good citizen; but this is no result of climatic influences. Such crea-tures are the contemporaries of an earlier period of civilization than ours. Nor is it so clear that solidity is always a virtue, and lightness a vice in character, any more than in bread, or that the leaven of our institutions works anything else than a wholesome ferment and aeration. The experience of the last four years is enough to prove that sensibility may consist with tenacity of purpose, and that enthusiasm may become a permanent motive where the conviction of the worth of its object is profound and logical. There are things in this universe deeper and higher, more solid even, than the English Constitution. If that is the perfection of human wisdom and a sufficing object of faith and worship for our cousins over the water, on the other hand God's dealing with this chosen people is preparing them to conceive of a perfection of divine wisdom, of a constitution in the framing of which man's wit had no share, and which shall yet be supreme, as it is continually more or less plainly influential in the government of the world. We may need even sterner teaching than any we have yet had, but we have faith that the lesson will be learned at last.

If the assertion which we alluded to at the outset were true, if we, more than others, are apt to forget the past in the present, the work of Mr. Moore [1] would do much in helping us to recover what we have lost. Had its execution been as complete as its plan was excellent, it would have left nothing to be desired. Its want of order may be charged upon the necessity of monthly publication; but there are other defects which this will hardly excuse. The editor seems to have become gradually helpless before the mass of material that

[1] *The Rebellion Record.* Edited by Frank Moore. Six vols.

heaped itself about him, and to have shovelled
from sheer despair of selection. In the documen-
tary part he is sufficiently, sometimes even depres-
singly full, and he has preserved a great deal of
fugitive poetry from both sides, much of it spirited,
and some of it vigorously original;[1] but he has
frequently neglected to give his authorities. His
extracts from the newspapers of the day, especially
from Southern and foreign ones, are provokingly
few, and his department of "incidents and rumors,"
the true mirror of the time, inadequate both in
quantity and quality. In spite of these defects,
however, there is enough to recall vividly the features of the time at any marked period during the
war, to renew the phases of feeling, to trace the
slowly gathering current of opinion, and to see
a definite purpose gradually orbing itself out of
the chaos of plans and motives, hopes, fears, enthusiasms, and despondencies. We do not propose
to review the book, — we might, indeed, almost as
well undertake to review the works of Father Time
himself, — but, relying chiefly on its help in piecing
out our materials, shall try to freshen the memory
of certain facts and experiences worth bearing in
mind either for example or warning.

It is of importance, especially considering the
part which what are called the "leading minds" of
the South are expected to play in reconstruction, to
keep clearly before our eyes the motives and the
manner of the Rebellion. Perhaps we should say

[1] See especially *The Old Sergeant*, a remarkable poem by For-
ceythe Willson, in the sixth volume.

inducements rather than motives, for of these there was but a single one put forward by the seceding States, namely, the obtaining security, permanence, and extension for the system of slavery. We do not use the qualifying epithet "African," because the franker propagandists of Southern principles affirmed the divine institution of slavery pure and simple, without regard to color or the curse of Canaan. This being the single motive of the Rebellion, what was its real object? Primarily, to possess itself of the government by a sudden *coup d'état;* or that failing, then, secondarily, by a peaceful secession, which should paralyze the commerce and manufactures of the Free States, to bring them to terms of submission. Whatever may have been the opinion of some of the more far-sighted, it is clear that a vast majority of the Southern people, including their public men, believed that their revolution would be peaceful. Their inducements to moving precisely when they did were several. At home the treasury was empty; faithless ministers had supplied the Southern arsenals with arms, and so disposed the army and navy as to render them useless for any sudden need; but above all, they could reckon on several months of an administration which, if not friendly, was so feeble as to be more dangerous to the country than to its betrayers, and there was a great party at the North hitherto their subservient allies, and now sharing with them in the bitterness of a common political defeat.[1]

[1] Mr. A. H. Stephens, Vice-President of the late Confederacy, attributed the Secession movement to disappointed ambition.

Abroad there was peace, with the prospect of its continuance; the two great maritime powers were also the great consumers of cotton, were both deadly enemies, like themselves, to the democratic principle, and, if not actively interfering, would at least throw all the moral weight of their sympathy and encouragement on the Southern side. They were not altogether mistaken in their reckoning. The imbecility of Mr. Buchanan bedded the ship of state in an ooze of helpless inaction, where none of her guns could be brought to bear, and whence nothing but the tide of indignation which followed the attack on Sumter could have set her afloat again, while prominent men and journals of the Democratic party hastened to assure the Rebels, not only of approval, but of active physical assistance. England, with indecent eagerness, proclaimed a neutrality which secured belligerent rights to a conspiracy that was never to become a nation, and thus enabled members of Parliament to fit out privateers to prey with impunity on the commerce of a friendly power. The wily Napoleon followed, after an interval long enough to throw all responsibility for the measure, and to direct all the natural irritation it excited in this country, upon his neighbor over the way. England is now endeavoring to evade the consequences of her hasty proclamation and her jaunty indifference to the enforcement of it upon her own subjects. The principle of international law involved is a most important one; but it was not so much the act itself, or the pecuniary damage resulting from it, as the *animus* that so plainly prompted it, which Americans find it hard to forgive.

It would be unwise in us to forget that independence was a merely secondary and incidental consideration with the Southern conspirators at the beginning of the Rebellion, however they may have thought it wise to put it in the front, both for the sake of their foreign abettors who were squeamish about seeming, though quite indifferent about being, false to their own professions and the higher interests of their country, and also for the sake of its traditionary influence among the Southern people. Some, it is true, were bold enough or logical enough to advocate barbarism as a good in itself; and in estimating the influences which have rendered some minds, if not friendly to the Rebellion, at least indifferent to the success of the Union, we should not forget that reaction against the softening and humanizing effect of modern civilization, led by such men as Carlyle, and joined in by a multitude whose intellectual and moral fibre is too much unstrung to be excited by anything less pungent than paradox. Protestants against the religion which sacrifices to the polished idol of Decorum and translates Jehovah by *Comme-il-faut*, they find even the divine manhood of Christ too tame for them, and transfer their allegiance to the shaggy Thor with his mallet of brute force. This is hardly to be wondered at when we hear England called prosperous for the strange reason that she no longer dares to act from a noble impulse, and when, at whatever page of her recent history one opens, he

finds her statesmanship to consist of one Noble
Lord or Honorable Member asking a question, and
another Noble Lord or Honorable Member endeavoring to dodge it, amid cries of *Hear! Hear!*
enthusiastic in proportion to the fruitlessness of
listening. After all, we are inclined to think there
is more real prosperity, more that posterity will
find to have a deep meaning and reality, in a democracy spending itself for a principle, and, in spite
of the remonstrances, protests, and sneers of a
world busy in the eternal seesaw of the balance of
Europe, persisting in a belief that life and property
are mere counters, of no value except as representatives of a higher idea. May it be long ere government become in the New World, as in the Old,
an armed police and fire - department, to protect
property as it grows more worthless by being sel-
fishly clutched in fewer hands, and keep God's fire
of manhood from reaching that gunpowder of the
dangerous classes which underlies all institutions
based only on the wisdom of our ancestors.

As we look back to the beginnings of the Rebellion, we are struck with the thoughtlessness with
which both parties entered upon a war of whose
vast proportions and results neither was even dimly
conscious. But a manifest difference is to be remarked. In the South this thoughtlessness was the
result of an ignorant self-confidence, in the North
of inexperience and good humor. It was long before either side could believe that the other was in
earnest: the one in attacking a government which
they knew only by their lion's share in its offices

and influence, the other in resisting the unprovoked assault of a race born in the saddle, incapable of subjugation, and unable to die comfortably except in the last ditch of jubilant oratory. When at last each was convinced of the other's sincerity, the moods of both might have been predicted by any observer of human nature. The side which felt that it was not only in the wrong, but that it had made a blunder, lost all control of its temper, all regard for truth and honor. It betook itself forthwith to lies, bluster, and cowardly abuse of its antagonist. But beneath every other expression of Southern sentiment, and seeming to be the base of it, was a ferocity not to be accounted for by thwarted calculations or by any resentment at injuries received, but only by the influence of slavery on the character and manners. "Scratch a Russian," said Napoleon, "and you come to the Tartar beneath." Scratch a slaveholder, and beneath the varnish of conventionalism you come upon something akin to the man-hunter of Dahomey. Nay, the selfishness engendered by any system which rests on the right of the strongest is more irritable and resentful in the civilized than the savage man, as it is enhanced by a consciousness of guilt. In the first flush of over-confidence, when the Rebels reckoned on taking Washington, the air was to be darkened with the gibbeted carcasses of dogs and caitiffs. Pollard, in the first volume of his *Southern History of the War*, prints without comment the letter of a ruffian who helped butcher our wounded in Sudley Church after the first battle of

Manassas, in which he says that he had resolved to give no quarter. In Missouri the Rebels took scalps as trophies, and that they made personal ornaments of the bones of our unburied dead, and that women wore them, though seeming incredible, has been proved beyond question. Later in the war, they literally starved our prisoners in a country where Sherman's army of a hundred thousand men found supplies so abundant that they could dispense with their provision train. Yet these were the "gentry" of the country, in whose struggle to escape from the contamination of mob-government the better classes of England so keenly sympathized. Our experience is thrown away unless it teach us that every form of conventionalized injustice is instinctively in league with every other, the world over, and that all institutions safe only in law, but forever in danger from reason and conscience, beget first selfishness, next fear, and then cruelty, by an incurable degeneration. Having been thus taught that a rebellion against justice and mercy has certain natural confederates, we must be blind indeed not to see whose alliance at the South is to give meaning and permanence to our victory over it.

In the North, on the other hand, nothing is more striking than the persistence in good nature, the tenacity with which the theories of the erring brother and the prodigal son were clung to, despite all evidence of facts to the contrary. There was a kind of boyishness in the rumors which the newspapers circulated (not seldom with intent to dis-

pirit), and the people believed on the authority of
reliable gentlemen from Richmond, or Union refu-
gees whose information could be trusted. At one
time the Rebels had mined eleven acres in the
neighborhood of Bull Run ; at another, there were
regiments of giants on their way from Texas, who,
first paralyzing our batteries by a yell, would rush
unscathed upon the guns, and rip up the unresist-
ing artillerymen with bowie-knives three feet long,
made for that precise service, and the only weapon
to which these Berserkers would condescend ; again,
for the fiftieth time, France and England had de-
finitely agreed upon a forcible intervention ; finally,
in order to sap the growing confidence of the people in President Lincoln, one of his family was
accused of communicating our plans to the Rebels,
and this at a time when the favorite charge against
his administration was the having no plan at all.
The public mind, as the public folly is generally
called, was kept in a fidget by these marvels and
others like them. But the point to which we would
especially call attention is this : that while the
war slowly educated the North, it has had comparatively little effect in shaking the old nonsense out
of the South. Nothing is more striking, as we
trace Northern opinion through those four years
that seemed so long and seem so short, than to see
how the minds of men were sobered, braced, and
matured as the greatness of the principles at stake
became more and more manifest; how their purpose, instead of relaxing, was strained tighter by
disappointment, and by the growing sense of a

guidance wiser than their own. Nor should we
forget how slow the great body of the people were
in being persuaded of the expediency of directly
attacking slavery, and after that of enlisting colored
troops ; of the fact, in short, that it must always be
legal to preserve the source of the law's authority,
and constitutional to save the country. The prudence of those measures is now acknowledged by
all, and justified by the result; but we must not
be blind to the deeper moral, that justice is always
and only politic, that it needs no precedent, and
that we were prosperous in proportion as we were
willing to be true to our nobler judgment. In one
respect only the popular understanding seems always to have been, and still to remain, confused.
Our notion of treason is a purely traditional one,
derived from countries where the question at issue
has not been the life of the nation, but the conflicting titles of this or that family to govern it.
Many people appear to consider civil war as merely
a more earnest kind of political contest, which
leaves the relative position of the parties as they
would be after a Presidential election. But no
treason was ever so wicked as that of Davis and his
fellow-conspirators, for it had no apology of injury
or even of disputed right, and it was aimed against
the fairest hope and promise of the world. They
did not attempt to put one king in place of another,
but to dethrone human nature and discrown the
very manhood of the race. And in what respect
does a civil war differ from any other in the discretion which it leaves to the victor of exacting

indemnity for the past and security for the future?
A contest begun for such ends and maintained by
such expedients as this has been, is not to be concluded by merely crying *quits* and shaking hands.
The slaveholding States chose to make themselves
a foreign people to us, and they must take the consequences. We surely cannot be expected to take
them back as if nothing had happened, as if victory
rendered us helpless to promote good or prevent
evil, and took from us all title to insist on the admission of the very principle for which we have
sacrificed so much. The war has established the
unity of the government, but no peace will be anything more than a pretence unless it rest upon the
unity of the nation, and that can only be secured
by making everywhere supreme the national idea
that freedom is a right inherent in man himself,
and not a creature of the law, to be granted to
one class of men or withheld from it at the option
of another.

What have we conquered? The Southern
States? The Southern people? A cessation of
present war? Surely not these or any one of
these merely. The fruit of our victory, as it was
always the object of our warfare, is the everlasting
validity of the theory of the Declaration of Independence in these United States, and the obligation
before God and man to make it the rule of our
practice. It was in that only that we were stronger
than our enemies, stronger than the public opinion
of the world; and it is from that alone that we
derive our right of the strongest, for it is wisdom,

justice, and the manifest will of Him who made of one blood all the nations of the earth. It were a childish view of the matter to think this is a mere trial of strength or struggle for supremacy between the North and South. The war sprang from the inherent antipathy between two forms of political organization radically hostile to each other. Is the war over, will it ever be over, if we allow the incompatibility to remain, childishly satisfied with a mere change of shape? This has been the grapple of two brothers that already struggled with each other even in the womb. One of them has fallen under the other; but let simple, good-natured Esau beware how he slacken his grip till he has got back his inheritance, for Jacob is cunninger with the tongue than he.

We have said that the war has given the North a higher conception of its manhood and its duties, and of the vital force of ideas. But do we find any parallel change in the South? We confess we look for it in vain. There is the same arrogance, the same materialistic mode of thought, which reckons the strength and value of a country by the amount of its crops rather than by the depth of political principle which inspires its people, the same boyish conceit on which even defeat wastes its lesson. Here is a clear case for the interference of authority. The people have done their part by settling the fact that we have a government; and it is for the government now to do its duty toward the people by seeing to it that their blood and treasure shall not have been squandered in a meaningless conflict. We must not let ourselves be misled by the terms North and South, as if those names implied any essential diversity of interest, or the claim to any separate share in the future destiny of the country. Let us concede every right to the several States except that of mischief, and never again be deceived by the fallacy that a moral wrong can be local in its evil influence, or that a principle alien to the instincts of the nation can be consistent either with its prosperity or its peace. We must not be confused into a belief that it is with States that we are dealing in this matter. The very problem is how to reconstitute safely a certain territory or population as States. It is not we that take anything from them. The war has left them nothing that they can fairly call their own politically but helplessness and confusion. We propose only to admit them for the first time into a real union with us, and to give them an equal share in privileges, our belief in whose value we have proved by our sacrifices in asserting them. There is always a time for doing what is fit to be done ; and if it be done wisely, temperately, and firmly, it need appeal for its legality to no higher test than success. It is the nation, and not a section, which is victorious, and it is only on principles of purely national advantage that any permanent settlement can be based.

The South will come back to the Union intent on saving whatever fragments it can from the wreck of the evil element in its social structure, which it clings to with that servile constancy which

men often show for the vice that is making them
its victims. If they must lose slavery, they will
make a shift to be comfortable on the best substi-
tute they can find in a system of caste. The question for a wise government in such a case seems to
us not to be, Have we the right to interfere? but
much rather, Have we the right to let them alone?
If we are entitled, as conquerors, — and it is only
as such that we are so entitled, — to stipulate for
the abolition of slavery, what is there to prevent
our exacting further conditions no less essential to
our safety and the prosperity of the South? The
national unity we have paid so dearly for will turn
out a pinchbeck counterfeit, without that sympathy
of interests and ideas, that unity of the people,
which can spring only from homogeneousness of
institutions. The successive advances toward justice which we made during the war, and which
looked so difficult and doubtful before they were
made, the proclamation of freedom and the arming
of the blacks, seem now to have been measures of
the simplest expediency, as the highest always
turns out to be the simplest when we have the wit
to try it. The heavens were to have come crash-
ing down after both those measures; yet the pil-
lars of the universe not only stood firm on their
divinely laid foundations, but held us up also, and,
to the amazement of many, God did not frown on
an experiment of righteousness. People are not
yet agreed whether these things were constitutional;
we believe, indeed, that the weight of legal opinion
is against them, but nevertheless events are toler-

ably unanimous that without them we should have had a fine Constitution left on our hands with no body politic for it to animate.

Laws of the wisest human device are, after all, but the sheath of the sword of Power, which must not be allowed to rust in them till it cannot be drawn swiftly in time of need. President Lincoln had many scruples to overcome ere he could overstep the limits of precedent into the divine air of moral greatness. Like most men, he was reluctant to be the bearer of that message of God with which his name will be linked in the grateful memory of mankind. If he won an immortality of fame by consenting to ally himself with the eternal justice, and to reinforce his armies by the inspiration of their own nobler instincts, an equal choice of renown is offered to his successor in applying the same loyalty to conscience in the establishment of peace. We could not live together half slave and half free; shall we succeed better in trying a second left-handed marriage between democracy and another form of aristocracy, less gross, but not less uncongenial? They who before misled the country into a policy false and deadly to the very truth which was its life and strength, by the fear of abolitionism, are making ready to misrule it again by the meaner prejudice of color. We can have no permanent peace with the South but by Americanizing it, by compelling it, if need be, to accept the idea, and with it the safety of democracy. At present we seem on the brink of contracting to protect from insurrection States in which a majority of the population, many of them now trained to arms, and all of them conscious of a claim upon us to make their freedom strong enough to protect them, are to be left at the mercy of laws which they have had no share in enacting.

The gravity of this consideration alone should make us pause. The more thought we bestow upon the matter, the more thoroughly are we persuaded that the only way to get rid of the negro is to do him justice. Democracy is safe because it is just, and safe only when it is just to all. Here is no question of white or black, but simply of man. We have hitherto been strong in proportion as we dared be true to the sublime thought of our own Declaration of Independence, which for the first time proposed to embody Christianity in human laws, and announced the discovery that the security of the state is based on the moral instincts and the manhood of its members. In the very midnight of the war, when we were compassed round with despondency and the fear of man, that peerless utterance of human policy rang like a trumpet announcing heavenly succor, and lifted us out of the darkness of our doubts into that courage which comes of the fear of God. Now, if ever, may a statesman depend upon the people sustaining him in doing what is simply right, for they have found out the infinite worth of freedom, and how much they love it, by being called on to defend it. We have seen how our contest has been watched by a breathless world; how every humane and generous heart, every intellect bold enough to believe that men may be safely trusted with government as well as with any other of their concerns, has wished us God-speed. And we have felt as never before the meaning of those awful words, "Hell beneath is stirred for thee," as we saw all that was mean and timid and selfish and wicked, by a horrible impulsion of nature, gathering to the help of our enemies. Why should we shrink from embodying our own idea as if it would turn out a Frankenstein? Why should we let the vanquished dictate terms of peace? A choice is offered that may never come again, unless after another war. We should sin against our own light, if we allowed mongrel republics to grow up again at the South, and deliberately organized anarchy, as if it were better than war. Let the law be made equal for all men. If the power does not exist in the Constitution, find it somewhere else, or confess that democracy, strongest of all governments for war, is the weakest of all in the statesmanship that shall save us from it. There is no doubt what the wishes of the administration are. Let them act up to their own convictions and the emergency of the hour, sure of the support of the people; for it is one of the chief merits of our form of polity that the public reason, which gives our Constitution all its force, is always a reserve of power to the magistrate, open to the appeal of justice, and ready to ratify the decisions of conscience. There is no need of hurry in readmitting the States that locked themselves out of the old homestead. It is not enough to conquer unless we convert them, and time, the best means of quiet persuasion, is in our own hands. Shall we hasten to cover with the thin ashes of another compromise that smouldering war which we called peace for seventy years, only to have it flame up again when the wind of Southern doctrine has set long enough in the old quarter? It is not the absence of war, but of its causes, that is in our grasp. That is what we fought for, and there must be a right somewhere to enforce what all see to be essential. To quibble away such an opportunity would be as cowardly as unwise.

THE PRESIDENT ON THE STUMP

1866

MR. JOHNSON is the first of our Presidents who has descended to the stump, and spoken to the people as if they were a mob. We do not care to waste words in criticising the taste of this proceeding, but deem it our duty to comment on some of its graver aspects. We shall leave entirely aside whatever was personal in the extraordinary diatribe of the 22d of February, merely remarking that we believe the majority of Americans have too much good sense to be flattered by an allusion to the humbleness of their chief magistrate's origin; the matter of interest for them being rather to ascertain what he has arrived at than where he started from, — we do not mean in station, but in character, intelligence, and fitness for the place he occupies. We have reason to suspect, indeed, that pride of origin, whether high or low, springs from the same principle in human nature, and that one is but the positive, the other the negative, pole of a single weakness. The people do not take it as a compliment to be told that they have chosen a plebeian to the highest office, for they are not fond of a plebeian tone of mind or manners. What they do like, we believe, is to be represented by their foremost man, their highest type of courage, sense, and patriotism, no matter what his origin. For, after all, no one in this country incurs any natal disadvantage unless he be born to an ease which robs him of the necessity of exerting, and so of increasing and maturing, his natural powers. It is of very little consequence to know what our President was ; of the very highest, to ascertain what he is, and to make the best of him. We may say, in passing, that the bearing of Congress, under the temptations of the last few weeks, has been most encouraging, though we must except from our commendation the recent speech of Mr. Stevens of Pennsylvania. There is a pride of patriotism that should make all personal pique seem trifling ; and Mr. Stevens ought to have remembered that it was not so much the nakedness of an antagonist that he was uncovering as that of his country.

The dangers of popular oratory are always great, and unhappily ours is nearly all of this kind. Even a speaker in Congress · addresses his real hearers through the reporters and the post-office. The merits of the question at issue concern him less than what *he* shall say about it so as not to ruin his own chance of reëlection, or that of some fourth cousin to a tidewaitership. Few men have any great amount of gathered wisdom, still fewer of extempory, while there are unhappily many who have a large stock of accumulated phrases, and hold their parts of speech subject to immediate draft. In a country where the party newspapers and speakers have done their best to make us be-

lieve that consistency is of so much more importance than statesmanship, and where every public
man is more or less in the habit of considering
what he calls his " record " as the one thing to be
saved in the general deluge, a hasty speech, if the
speaker be in a position to make his words things,
may, by this binding force which is superstitiously
attributed to the word once uttered, prove to be of
public detriment. It would be well for us if we
could shake off this baleful system of requiring
that a man who has once made a fool of himself
shall always thereafter persevere in being one.
Unhappily it is something more easy of accomplishment than the final perseverance of the saints.
Let us learn to be more careful in distinguishing
between betrayal of principle, and breaking loose
from a stupid consistency that compels its victims
to break their heads against the wall instead of
going a few steps round to the door. To eat our
own words would seem to bear some analogy to
that diet of east-wind which is sometimes attributed to the wild ass, and might therefore be wholesome for the tame variety of that noble and necessary animal, which, like the poor, we are sure to
have always with us. If the words have been
foolish, we can conceive of no food likely to be
more nutritious, and could almost wish that we
might have public establishments at the common
charge, like those at which the Spartans ate black
broth, where we might all sit down together to a
meal of this cheaply beneficial kind. Among other
amendments of the Constitution, since every Sena-

tor seems to carry half a dozen in his pocket nowadays, a sort of legislative six-shooter, might we
not have one to the effect that a public character
might change his mind as circumstances changed
theirs, say once in five years, without forfeiting the
confidence of his fellow-citizens?

We trust that Mr. Johnson may not be so often
reminded of his late harangue as to be provoked
into maintaining it as part of his settled policy,
and that every opportunity will be given him for
forgetting it, as we are sure his better sense will
make him wish to do. For the more we reflect
upon it, the more it seems to us to contain, either
directly or by implication, principles of very dangerous consequence to the well-being of the Republic. We are by no means disposed to forget Mr.
Johnson's loyalty when it was hard to be loyal, nor
the many evidences he has given of a sincere desire to accomplish what seemed to him best for the
future of the whole country ; but, at the same time,
we cannot help thinking that some of his over-
frank confidences of late have shown alarming misconceptions, both of the position he holds either in
the public sentiment or by virtue of his office, and
of the duty thereby devolved upon him. We do
not mean to indulge ourselves in any nonsensical
rhetoric about usurpations like those which cost
an English king his head, for we consider the matter in too serious a light, and no crowded galleries
invite us to thrill them with Bulwerian common-
place; but we have a conviction that the exceptional
circumstances of the last five years, which gave a

necessary predominance to the executive part of our government, have left behind them a false impression of the prerogative of a President in ordinary times. The balance-wheel of our system has insensibly come to think itself the motive power, whereas that, to be properly effective, should always be generated by the deliberate public opinion of the country. Already the Democratic party, anxious to profit by any chance at resuscitation, — for it is extremely inconvenient to be dead so long, — is more than hinting that the right of veto was given to the President that he might bother and baffle a refractory Congress into concession, not to his reasons, but to his whim. There seemed to be a plan at one time of forming a President's party, with no principle but that of general opposition to the policy of that great majority which carried him into power. Such a scheme might have had some chance of success in the good old times when it seemed to the people as if there was nothing more important at stake than who should be in and who out; but it would be sure of failure now that the public mind is intelligently made up as to the vital meaning of whatever policy we adopt, and the necessity of establishing our institutions, once for all, on a basis as permanent as human prudence can make it.

Congress is sometimes complained of for wasting time in discussion, and for not having, after a four months' session, arrived at any definite plan of settlement. There has been, perhaps, a little eagerness on the part of honorable members to associate their names with the particular nostrum that is to build up our national system again. In a country where, unhappily, any man may be President, it is natural that a means of advertising so efficacious as this should not be neglected. But really, we do not see how Congress can be blamed for not being ready with a plan definite and precise upon every point of possible application, when it is not yet in possession of the facts according to whose varying complexion the plan must be good or bad. The question with us is much more whether another branch of the government, — to which, from its position and its opportunity for a wider view, the country naturally looks for initiative suggestion, and in which a few months ago even decisive action would have been pardoned, — whether this did not let the lucky moment go by without using it. That moment was immediately after Mr. Lincoln's murder, when the victorious nation was ready to apply, and the conquered faction would have submitted without a murmur to that bold and comprehensive policy which is the only wise as it is the only safe one for great occasions. To let that moment slip was to descend irrecoverably from the vantage ground where statesmanship is an exact science to the experimental level of tentative politics. We cannot often venture to set our own house on fire with civil war, in order to heat our iron up to that point of easy forging at which it glowed, longing for the hammer of the master-smith, less than a year ago. That Occasion is swift we learned long ago from the adage; but this volatility is meant only of moments where force of personal character is decisive, where the fame or fortune of a single man is at stake. The life of nations can afford to take less strict account of time, and in their affairs there may always be a hope that the slow old tortoise, Prudence, may over-take again the opportunity that seemed flown by so irrecoverably. Our people have shown so much of this hard-shelled virtue during the last five years, that we look with more confidence than ap-prehension to the result of our present difficulties. Never was the common-sense of a nation more often and directly appealed to, never was it readier in coming to its conclusion and making it operative in public affairs, than during the war whose wounds we are now endeavoring to stanch. It is the duty of patriotic men to keep this great popular faculty always in view, to satisfy its natural demand for clearness and practicality in the measures proposed, and not to distract it and render it nugatory by the insubstantial metaphysics of abstract policy. From the splitting of heads to the splitting of hairs would seem to be a long journey, and yet some are already well on their way to the end of it, who should be the leaders of public opinion and not the skirmishing harassers of its march. It would be well if some of our public men would consider that Providence has saved their modesty the trial of an experiment in cosmogony, and that their task is the difficult, no doubt, but much sim-pler and less ambitious one, of bringing back the confused material which lies ready to their hand,

always with a divinely implanted instinct of order
in it, to as near an agreement with the providential
intention as their best wisdom can discern.   The
aggregate opinion of a nation moves slowly.   Like
those old migrations of entire tribes, it is encumbered with much household stuff; a thousand un-
foreseen things may divert or impede it; a hostile
check or the temptation of present convenience
may lead it to settle far short of its original aim;
the want of some guiding intellect and central will
may disperse it; but experience shows one constant
element of its progress, which those who aspire to
be its leaders should keep in mind, namely, that
the place of a wise general should be oftener in the
rear or the centre than the extreme front.   The
secret of permanent leadership is to know how to
be moderate.   The rashness of conception that
makes opportunity, the gallantry that heads the
advance, may win admiration, may possibly achieve
a desultory and indecisive exploit; but it is the
slow steadiness of temper, bent always on the main
design and the general movement, that gains by
degrees a confidence as unshakable as its own, the
only basis for permanent power over the minds of
men.   It was the surest proof of Mr. Lincoln's
sagacity and the deliberate reach of his understanding, that he never thought time wasted while
he waited for the wagon that brought his supplies.
The very immovability of his purpose, fixed always
on what was attainable, laid him open to the shallow criticism of having none, — for a shooting star
draws more eyes, and seems for the moment to have

a more definite aim, than a planet, — but it gained him at last such a following as made him irresistible. It lays a much lighter tax on the intellect, and proves its resources less, to suggest a number of plans, than to devise and carry through a single one.

Mr. Johnson has an undoubted constitutional right to choose any, or to reject all, of the schemes of settlement proposed by Congress, though the wisdom of his action in any case is a perfectly proper subject of discussion among those who put him where he is, who are therefore responsible for his power of good or evil, and to whom the consequences of his decision must come home at last. He has an undoubted personal right to propose any scheme of settlement himself, and to advocate it with whatever energy of reason or argument he possesses, but is liable, in our judgment, to very grave reprehension if he appeal to the body of the people against those who are more immediately its representatives than himself in any case of doubtful expediency, before discussion is exhausted, and where the difference may well seem one of personal pique rather than of considerate judgment. This is to degrade us from a republic, in whose foreordered periodicity of submission to popular judgment democracy has guarded itself against its own passions, to a mass meeting, where momentary interest, panic, or persuasive sophistry — all of them gregarious influences, and all of them contagious — may decide by a shout what years of afterthought may find it hard, or even impossible, to undo. There have been some things in the deportment of the President of late that have suggested to thoughtful men rather the pettish foible of wilfulness than the strength of well-trained and conscientious will. It is by the objects for whose sake the force of volition is called into play that we decide whether it is childish or manly, whether we are to call it obstinacy or firmness. Our own judgment can draw no favorable augury from meetings gathered "to sustain the President," as it is called, especially if we consider the previous character of those who are prominent in them, nor from the ill-considered gossip about a "President's party;" and they would excite our apprehension of evil to come, did we not believe that the experience of the last five years had settled into convictions in the mind of the people. The practical result to which all benevolent men finally come is that it is idle to try to sustain any man who has not force of character enough to sustain himself without their help, and the only party which has any chance now before the people is that of resolute good sense. What is now demanded of Congress is unanimity in the best course that is feasible. They should recollect that Wisdom is more likely to be wounded in the division of those who should be her friends, than either of the parties to the quarrel. Our difficulties are by no means so great as timid or interested people would represent them to be. We are to decide, it is true, for posterity; but the question presented to us is precisely that which every man has to decide in making his will, — neither greater nor less than that, nor demanding a wisdom above what that demands. The power is in our own hands, so long as it is prudent for us to keep it there; and we are justified, not in doing simply what we will with our own, but what is best to be done. The great danger in the present posture of affairs seems to be lest the influence which in Mr. Lincoln's case was inherent in the occasion and the man should have held over in the popular mind as if it were entailed upon the office. To our minds more is to be apprehended in such a conjuncture from the weakness than from the strength of the President's character.

There is another topic which we feel obliged to comment on, regretting deeply, as we do, that the President has given us occasion for it, and believing, as we would fain do, that his own better judgment will lead him to abstain from it in the future. He has most unfortunately permitted himself to assume a sectional ground. Geography is learned to little purpose in Tennessee, if it does not teach that the Northeast as well as the Southwest is an integral and necessary part of the United States. By the very necessity of his high office, a President becomes an American, whose concern is with the outward boundaries of his country, and not its internal subdivisions. One great object of the war, we had supposed, was to abolish all fallacies of sectional distinction in a patriotism that could embrace something wider than a township, a county, or even a State. But Mr. Johnson has chosen to revive the paltry party-cries from before that deluge which we hoped had washed everything clean, and to talk of treason at both ends of the Union, as if there were no difference between men who attempted the life of their country, and those who differ from him in their judgment of what is best for her future safety and greatness. We have heard enough of New England radicalism, as if that part of the country where there is the most education and the greatest accumulation of property in the hands of the most holders were the most likely to be carried away by what are called agrarian theories. All that New England and the West demand is that America should be American; that every relic of a barbarism more archaic than any institution of the Old World should be absolutely and irrecoverably destroyed; that there should be no longer two peoples here, but one, homogeneous and powerful by a sympathy in idea. Does Mr. Johnson desire anything more? Does he, alas! desire anything less? If so, it may be the worse for his future fame, but it will not and cannot hinder the irresistible march of that national instinct which forced us into war, brought us out of it victorious, and will not now be cheated of its fruits. If we may trust those who have studied the matter, it is moderate to say that more than half the entire population of the Free States is of New England descent, much more than half the native population. It is by the votes of these men that Mr. Johnson holds his office; it was as the exponent of their convictions of duty and policy that he was chosen to it. Not a vote

did he or could he get in a single one of the States
in rebellion. If they were the American people
when they elected him to execute their will, are they
less the American people now? It seems to us the
idlest of all possible abstractions now to discuss the
question whether the rebellious States were ever
out of the Union or not, as if that settled the right
of secession. The victory of superior strength
settled it, and nothing else. For four years they
were practically as much out of the Union as
Japan; had they been strong enough, they would
have continued out of it; and what matters it
where they were theoretically? Why, until Queen
Victoria, every English sovereign assumed the
style of King of France. The King of Sardinia
was, and the King of Italy, we suppose, is still tit-
ular King of Jerusalem. Did either monarch ever
exercise sovereignty or levy taxes in those imaginary dominions? What the war accomplished for
us was the reduction of an insurgent population;
and what it settled was, not the right of secession,
for that must always depend on will and strength,
but that every inhabitant of every State was a subject as well as a citizen of the United States, — in
short, that the theory of freedom was limited by
the equally necessary theory of authority. We
hoped to hear less in future of the possible inter-
pretations by which the Constitution may be made
to mean this or that, and more of what will help
the present need and conduce to the future strength
and greatness of the whole country. It was by
precisely such constitutional quibbles, educating

men to believe they had a right to claim whatever they could sophistically demonstrate to their own satisfaction, — and self-interest is the most cunning of sophists, — that we were interpreted, in spite of ourselves, into civil war. It was by just such a misunderstanding of one part of the country by another as that to which Mr. Johnson has lent the weight of his name and the authority of his place, that rendered a hearty national sympathy, and may render a lasting reorganization, impossible.

If history were still written as it was till within two centuries, and the author put into the mouth of his speakers such words as his conception of the character and the situation made probable and fitting, we could conceive an historian writing a hundred years hence to imagine some such speech as this for Mr. Johnson in an interview with a Southern delegation.

" Gentlemen, I am glad to meet you once more as friends, I wish I might say as fellow-citizens. How soon we may again stand in that relation to each other depends wholly upon yourselves. You have been pleased to say that my birth and life-long associations gave you confidence that I would be friendly to the South. In so saying, you do no more than justice to my heart and my intentions; but you must allow me to tell you frankly, that, if you use the word South in any other than a purely geographical sense, the sooner you convince yourselves of its impropriety as addressed to an American President, the better. The South as a political entity was Slavery, and went out of existence with it. And let me also, as naturally connected with this topic, entreat you to disabuse your minds of the fatally mistaken theory that you have been conquered by the North. It is the American people who are victors in this conflict, and who intend to inflict no worse penalty on you than that of admitting you to an entire equality with themselves. They are resolved, by God's grace, to Americanize you, and America means education, equality before the law, and every upward avenue of life made as free to one man as another. You urge upon me, with great force and variety of argument, the manifold evils of the present unsettled state of things, the propriety and advantage of your being represented in both houses of Congress, the injustice of taxation without representation. I admit the importance of every one of these considerations, but I think you are laboring under some misapprehension of the actual state of affairs. I know not if any of you have been in America since the spring of 1861, or whether (as I rather suspect) you have all been busy in Europe endeavoring to — but I beg pardon, I did not intend to say anything that should recall old animosities. But intelligence is slow to arrive in any part of the world, and intelligence from America painfully so in reaching Europe. You do not seem to be aware that *something has happened here during the last four years*, something that has made a very painful and lasting impression on the memory of the American people, whose voice on this occasion I have the honor to be. They feel constrained to demand that you shall enter into bonds to keep the peace. They do not, I regret to say, agree with you in looking upon what has happened here of late as only a more emphatic way of settling a Presidential election, the result of which leaves both parties entirely free to try again. They seem to take the matter much more seriously. Nor do they, so far as I can see, agree with you in your estimate of the importance of conserving your several state sovereignties, as you continue to call them, insisting much rather on the conservation of America and of American ideas. They say that the only thing which can individualize or perpetuate a commonwealth is to have a history; and they ask which of the States lately in rebellion, except Virginia and South Carolina, had anything of the kind? In spite of my natural sympathies, gentlemen, my reason compels me to agree with them. Your strength, such as it was, was due less to the fertility of your brains than to that of your soil and to the invention of the Yankee Whitney which you used and never paid for. You tell me it is hard to put you on a level with your negroes. As a believer in the superiority of the white race, I cannot admit the necessity of enforcing that superiority by law. A Roman emperor once said that gold never retained the unpleasant odor of its source, and I must say to you that loyalty is sweet to me, whether it throb under a black skin or a white. The American people has learned of late to set a greater value on the color of ideas than on shades of complexion. As to the injustice of taxation without representation, that is an idea derived from our English ancestors, and is liable, like all rules, to the exceptions of necessity. I see no reason why a State may not as well be disfranchised as a borough for an illegal abuse of its privileges; nor do I quite feel the parity of the reason which should enable you to do that with a loyal black which we may not do with a disloyal white. Remember that this government is bound by every obligation, ethical and political, to protect these people because they are weak, and to reward them (if the common privilege of manhood may be called a reward) because they are faithful. We are not fanatics, but a nation that has neither faith in itself nor faith toward others must soon crumble to pieces by moral dry-rot. If we may conquer you, gentlemen, (and you forced the necessity upon us,) we may surely impose terms upon you; for it is an old principle of law that *cui liceat majus, ei licet etiam minus.*

"In your part of the country, gentlemen, that which we should naturally appeal to as the friend of order and stability — property — is blindly against us; prejudice is also against us; and we have nothing left to which we can appeal but human nature and the common privilege of manhood. You seem to have entertained some hope that I would gather about myself a 'President's party,' which should be more friendly to you and those animosities which you mistake for interests. But you grossly deceive yourselves; I have no sympathy but with my whole country, and there is nothing out of which such a party as you dream of could be constructed, except the broken remnant of those who deserted you when for the first time you needed their help and not their subserviency, and those feathery characters who are drawn hither and thither by the chances of office. I need not say to you that I am and can be nothing in this matter but the voice of the nation's deliberate resolve. The recent past is too painful, the immediate future too momentous, to tolerate any personal considerations. You throw yourselves upon our magnanimity, and I must be frank with you. My predecessor, Mr. Buchanan, taught us the impolicy of weakness and concession. The people are magnanimous, but they understand by magnanimity a courageous steadiness in principle. They do not think it possible that a large heart should consist with a narrow brain; and they would consider it pusillanimous in them to consent to the weakness of their country by admitting you to a share in its government before you have given evidence of sincere loyalty to its principles, or, at least, of wholesome fear of its power. They believe, and I heartily agree with them, that a strong nation begets strong citizens, and a weak one weak, — that the powers of the private man are invigorated and enlarged by his confidence in the power of the body politic; and they see no possible means of attaining or securing this needed strength but in that homogeneousness of laws and institutions which breeds unanimity of ideas and sentiments, no way of arriving at that homogeneousness but the straightforward path of perfect confidence in freedom. All nations have a right to

security, ours to greatness ; and must have the one
as an essential preliminary to the other. If your
prejudices stand in the way, and you are too weak
to rid yourselves of them, it will be for the American people to consider whether the plain duty of
conquering them for you will be, after all, so difficult a conquest as some they have already achieved.
By yourselves or us they must be conquered.
Gentlemen, in bidding you farewell, I ask you to
consider whether you have not forgotten that, in
order to men's living peacefully together in communities, the idea of government must precede
that of liberty, and that the one is as much the
child of necessity as the other is a slow concession
to civilization, which itself mainly consists in the
habit of obedience to something more refined than
force."

THE SEWARD–JOHNSON REACTION

1866

THE late Philadelphia experiment at making a party out of nullities reminds us of nothing so much as of the Irishman's undertaking to produce a very palatable soup out of no more costly material than a pebble. Of course he was to be furnished with a kettle as his field of operations, and after that he asked only for just the least bit of beef in the world to give his culinary miracle a flavor, and a pinch of salt by way of relish. As nothing could be more hollow and empty than the pretence on which the new movement was founded, nothing more coppery than the material out of which it was mainly composed, we need look no further for the likeness of a kettle wherewith to justify our comparison; as for the stone, nothing could be more like that than the Northern disunion faction, which was to be the chief ingredient in the newfangled pottage, and whose leading characteristic for the last five years has been a uniform alacrity in going under; the offices in the gift of the President might very well be reckoned on to supply the beef which should lead by their noses the weary expectants whose hunger might be too strong for their nicety of stomach; and the pinch of salt, —

why could not that be found in the handful of Republicans who might be drawn over by love of
notoriety, private disgusts, or that mixture of motives which has none of the substance of opinion,
much less of the tenacity of principle, but which
is largely operative in the action of illogical minds?
But the people? Would they be likely to have
their appetite aroused by the fumes of this thin
decoction? Where a Chinaman is cook, one is apt
to be a little suspicious; and if the Address in
which the Convention advertised their ingenious
mess had not a little in its verbiage to remind one
of the flowery kingdom, there was something in
that part of the assemblage which could claim any
bygone merit of Republicanism calculated to stim-
ulate rather than to allay any dreadful surmise of
the sagacious rodent which our antipodes are said
to find savory. And as for the people, it is a curious fact, that the party which has always been
loudest to profess its faith in their capacity of self-
government has been the last to conceive it possible that they should apprehend a principle, arrive
at a logical conclusion, or be influenced by any
other than a mean motive. The *cordons bleus* of
the political cooks at Philadelphia were men admirably adapted for the petty intrigues of a local
caucus, but by defect of nature profoundly unconscious of that simple process of generalization from
a few plain premises by which the popular mind
is guided in times like these, and upon questions
which appeal to the moral instincts of men.

The Convention was well managed, we freely

admit, — and why not, when all those who were allowed to have any leading part in it belonged exclusively to that class of men who are known as party managers, and who, like the director of a theatre or a circus, look upon the mass of mankind as creatures to be influenced by a taking title, by amplitude of posters, and by a thrilling sensation or two, no matter how coarse? As for the title, nothing could be better than that of the " Devoted Unionists," — and were not the actors, no less than the scenery and decorations, for the most part entirely new, — at least in that particular play? Advertisement they did not lack, with the whole Democratic press and the Department of State at their service, not to speak of the real clown being allowed to exhibit himself at short intervals upon the highest platform in this or any other country. And if we ask for sensation, never were so many performers exhibited together in their grand act of riding two horses at once, or leaping through a hoop with nothing more substantial to resist them than the tissue-paper of former professions, nay, of recent pledges. And yet the skill of the managers had something greater still behind, in Massachusetts linked arm in arm with South Carolina. To be sure, a thoughtful mind might find something like a false syllogism in pairing off a Commonwealth whose greatest sin it has been to lead the van in freedom of opinion, and in those public methods of enlightenment which make it a safeguard of popular government, with an Oligarchy whose leadership has been in precisely the opposite direction, as if both had equally sinned against American ideas. But such incongruities are trifles no greater than those of costume so common on every stage; and perhaps the only person to be pitied in the exhibition was Governor Orr, who had once uttered a hope that his own State might one day walk abreast with the daughter of Puritan forethought in the nobler procession of prosperous industry, and who must have felt a slight shock of surprise, if nothing more, at the form in which Massachusetts had chosen to incarnate herself on that particular occasion. We cannot congratulate the Convention on the name of its chairman, for there is something ominously suggestive in it. But, on the other hand it is to be remembered that Mr. Doolittle has a remarkably powerful voice, which is certainly one element in the manufacture of sound opinions. A little too much latitude was allowed to Mr. Raymond in the Address, though on the whole perhaps it was prudent to make that document so long as to insure it against being read. In their treatment of Mr. Vallandigham the managers were prudent. He was allowed to appear just enough not quite to alienate his party, on whom the new movement counts largely for support, and just not enough to compromise the Convention with the new recruits it had made among those who would follow the name Conservative into anything short of downright anarchy. The Convention, it must be confessed, had a rather hard problem to solve,—nothing less than to make their patent reconciliation cement out of fire and gunpowder, both useful things in themselves, but liable in concert to bring about some odd results in the way of harmonious action. It is generally thought wiser to keep them apart, and accordingly Mr. Vallandigham was excluded from the Convention altogether, and the Southern delegates were not allowed any share in the Address or Resolutions. Indeed, as the Northern members were there to see what they could make, and the Southern to find out how much they could save, and whatever could be made or saved was to come out of the North, it was more prudent to leave all matters of policy in the hands of those who were supposed to understand best the weak side of the intended victim. The South was really playing the game, and is to have the lion's share of the winnings; but it is only as a disinterested bystander, who looks over the cards of one of the parties, and guides his confederate by hints so adroitly managed as not to alarm the pigeon. The Convention avoided the reef where the wreck of the Chicago lies bleaching; but we are not so sure that they did not ground themselves fast upon the equally dangerous mud-bank that lies on the opposite side of the honest channel. At Chicago they were so precisely frank as to arouse indignation; at Philadelphia they are so careful of generalities that they make us doubtful, if not suspicious. Does the expectation or even the mere hope of pudding make the utterance as thick as if the mouth were already full of it? As to the greater part of the Resolutions, they were political truisms in which everybody would agree as so harmless that the Convention might almost as well have resolved the multiplication table article by article. The Address was far less explicit; and where there is so very much meal, it is perhaps not altogether uncharitable to suspect that there may be something under it. There is surely a suspicious bulge here and there, that has the look of the old Democratic cat. But, after all, of what consequence are the principles of the party, when President Johnson covers them all when he puts on his hat, and may change them between dinner and tea, as he has done several times already? The real principle of the party, its seminal and vital principle alike, is the power of the President, and its policy is every moment at the mercy of his discretion. That power has too often been the plaything of whim, and that discretion the victim of ill-temper or vanity, for us to have any other feeling left than regret for the one and distrust of the other.

The new party does not seem to have drawn to itself any great accession of strength from the Republican side, or indeed to have made many converts that were not already theirs in fact, though not in name. It was joined, of course, at once by the little platoon of gentlemen calling themselves, for some mystical reason, Conservatives, who have for some time been acting with the Democratic faction, carefully keeping their handkerchiefs to their noses all the while. But these involuntary Catos are sure, as if by instinct, to choose that side which is doomed not to please the gods, and their adhesion is as good as a warranty of defeat.

During the President's progress they must often have been driven to their handkerchiefs again. It was a great blunder of Mr. Seward to allow him to assume the apostolate of the new creed in person, for every word he has uttered must have convinced many, even of those unwilling to make the admission, that a doctrine could hardly be sound which had its origin and derives its power from a source so impure. For so much of Mr. Johnson's harangues as is not positively shocking, we know of no parallel so close as in his Imperial Majesty Kobes I. : —

> "Er rühmte dass er nie studirt
>   Auf Universitäten
>   Und Reden sprach aus sich selbst heraus,
>   Ganz ohne Facultäten."

And when we consider his power of tears; when we remember Mr. Reverdy Johnson and Mr. Andrew Johnson confronting each other like two augurs, the one trying not to laugh while he saw the other trying to cry; when we recall the touching scene at Canandaigua, where the President was overpowered by hearing the pathetic announcement that Stephen A. Douglas had for two years attended the academy in what will doubtless henceforward be dubbed that "classic locality," we cannot help thinking of

> "In seinem schönen Auge glänzt
>   Die Thräne, die Stereotype."

Indeed, if the exhibition of himself were not so profoundly sad, when we think of the high place he occupies and the great man he succeeded in it, nothing could well be so comic as some of the incidents of Mr. Johnson's tour. No satirist could have conceived anything so bewitchingly absurd as the cheers which greeted the name of Simeon at the dinner in New York, whether we suppose the audience to have thought him some eminent member of their party of whom they had never heard, or whom they had forgotten as thoroughly as they had Mr. Douglas, or if we consider that they were involuntarily giving vent to their delight at the pleasing prospect opened by their "illustrious guest's" allusion to his speedy departure. Nor could anything have been imagined beforehand so ludicrously ominous as Mr. Seward's fears lest the platform should break down under them at Niagara. They were groundless fears, it is true, for the Johnson platform gave way irreparably on the 22d of February; but they at least luckily prevented Nicholas Bottom Cromwell from uttering his after-dinner threat against the people's immediate representatives, against the very body whose vote supplies the funds of his party, and whose money, it seems, is constitutional, even if its own existence as a Congress be not. We pity Mr. Seward in his new office of bear-leader. How he must hate his Bruin when it turns out that his tricks do not even please the crowd!

But the ostensible object of this indecent orgy seems to us almost as discreditable as the purpose it veiled so thinly. Who was Stephen A. Douglas, that the President, with his Cabinet and the two highest officers of the army and navy, should add their official dignity to the raising of his monument, and make the whole country an accomplice in consecrating his memory? His name is not associated with a single measure of national importance, unless upon the wrong side. So far was he from being a statesman that, even on the lower ground of politics, both his principles and his expression of them were tainted with the reek of vulgar associations. A man of naturally great abilities he certainly was, but wholly without that instinct for the higher atmosphere of thought or ethics which alone makes them of value to any but their possessor, and without which they are more often dangerous than serviceable to the commonwealth. He habitually courted those weaknesses in the people which tend to degrade them into a populace, instead of appealing to the virtues that grow by use, and whose mere acknowledgment in a man in some sort ennobles him. And by doing this he proved that he despised the very masses whose sweet breaths he wooed, and had no faith in the system under which alone such a one as he could have been able to climb so high. He never deserted the South to take side with the country till the South had both betrayed and deserted him. If such a man were the fairest outcome of Democracy, then is it indeed a wretched failure. But for the factitious importance given to his name by the necessity of furnishing the President with a pretext for stumping the West in the interest of Congress, Mr. Douglas would be wellnigh as utterly forgotten as Cass or Tyler, or Buchanan or Fillmore; nor

should we have alluded to him now but that the
recent pilgrimage has made his name once more
public property, and because we think it a common
misfortune when such men are made into saints,
though for any one's advantage but their own.
We certainly have no wish to play the part of
advocatus diaboli on such an occasion, even were
it necessary at a canonization where the office of
Pontifex Maximus is so appropriately filled by Mr.
Johnson.

In speaking of the late unhappy exposure of
the unseemly side of democratic institutions, we
have been far from desirous of insisting on Mr.
Seward's share in it.   We endeavored to account
for it at first by supposing that the Secretary of
State, seeing into the hands of how vain and weak
a man the reins of administration had fallen, was
willing, by flattering his vanity, to control his
weakness for the public good.   But we are forced
against our will to give up any such theory, and to
confess that Mr. Seward's nature has been "subdued to what it works in."   We see it with sincere
sorrow, and are far from adding our voice to the
popular outcry against a man the long and honorable services of whose prime we are not willing to
forget in the decline of his abilities and that dry-
rot of the mind's nobler temper which so often results from the possession of power.   Long contact
with the meaner qualities of men, to whose infec-
tion place and patronage are so unhappily exposed,
could not fail of forcing to a disproportionate
growth any germs of that cynicism always latent

in temperaments so exclusively intellectual and unmitigated by any kindly lenitive of humor. Timid by nature, the war which he had prophesied, but had not foreseen, and which invigorated bolder men, unbraced him; and while the spendthrift verbosity of his despatches was the nightmare of foreign ministries, his uncertain and temporizing counsels were the perpetual discouragement of his party at home. More than any minister with whose official correspondence we are acquainted, he carried the principle of paper money into diplomacy, and bewildered Earl Russell and M. Drouyn de Lhuys with a horrible doubt as to the real value of the verbal currency they were obliged to receive. But, unfortunately, his own countrymen were also unprovided with a price-current of the latest quotation in phrases, and the same gift of groping and inconclusive generalities which perhaps was useful as a bewilderment to would-be hostile governments abroad was often equally effective in disheartening the defenders of nationality at home. We cannot join with those who accuse Mr. Seward of betraying his party, for we think ourselves justified by recent events in believing that he has always looked upon parties as the mere ladders of ambitious men; and when his own broke under him at Chicago in 1860, he forthwith began to cast about for another, the rounds of which might be firmer under his feet. He is not the first, and we fear will not be the last, of our public men who have thought to climb into the White House by a back window, and have come ignominiously to the ground in attempting it. Mr. Seward's view of the matter probably is that the Republican party deserted him six years ago, and that he was thus absolved of all obligations to it. But might there not have been such a thing as fidelity to its principles? Or was Mr. Seward drawn insensibly into the acceptance of them by the drift of political necessity, and did he take them up as if they were but the hand that had been dealt him in the game, not from any conviction of their moral permanence and power, perhaps with no perception of it, but from a mere intellectual persuasion of the use that might be made of them politically and for the nonce by a skilful gamester? We should be very unwilling to admit such a theory of his character; but surely what we have just seen would seem to justify it, for we can hardly conceive that any one should suddenly descend from real statesmanship to the use of such catch-rabble devices as those with which he has lately disgusted the country. A small politician cannot be made out of a great statesman, for there is an oppugnancy of nature between the two things, and we may fairly suspect the former winnings of a man who has been once caught with loaded dice in his pocket. However firm may be Mr. Seward's faith in the new doctrine of Johnsonian infallibility, surely he need not have made himself a partner in its vulgarity. And yet he has attempted to vie with the Jack-pudding tricks of the unrivalled performer whose man-of-business he is, in attempting a *populacity* (we must coin a new word for a new thing) for which he was

exquisitely unfitted. What more stiffly awkward
than his essays at easy familiarity? What more
painfully remote from drollery than his efforts to
be droll? In the case of a man who descends so
far as Mr. Seward, such feats can be characterized by no other word so aptly as by tumbling.
The thing would be sad enough in any prominent
man, but in him it becomes a public shame, for
in the eyes of the world it is the nation that
tumbles in its Prime Minister. The Secretary of
State's place may be dependent on the President,
but the dignity of it belongs to the country, and
neither of them has any right to trifle with it. Mr.
Seward might stand on his head in front of what
Jenkins calls his "park gate," at Auburn, and we
should be the last to question his perfect right as
a private citizen to amuse himself in his own way,
but in a great officer of the government such
pranks are no longer harmless. They are a national scandal, and not merely so, but a national
detriment, inasmuch as they serve to foster in
foreign statesmen a profound misapprehension of
the American people and of the motives which influence them in questions of public policy. Never
was so great a wrong done to democracy, nor so
great an insult offered to it, as in this professional
circuit of the presidential Punch and his ministerial
showman.

Fortunately, the exhibitions of this unlucky pair,
and their passing round the hat without catching
even the greasy pence they courted, have very
little to do with the great question to be decided

at the next elections, except in so far as we may
be justified in suspecting their purity of motive
who could consent to such impurity of means, and
the soundness of their judgment in great things
who in small ones show such want of sagacity.
The crowds they have drawn are no index of popular approval. We remember seeing the prodigious
nose of Mr. Tyler (for the person behind it had
been added by nature merely as the handle to so
fine a hatchet) drawn by six white horses through
the streets, and followed by an eager multitude,
nine tenths of whom thought the man belonging
to it a traitor to the party which had chosen him.
But then the effigy at least of a grandiose, if not
a great man, sat beside him, and the display was
saved from contempt by the massive shape of
Webster, beneath which he showed like a swallow
against a thunder-cloud. Even Mr. Fillmore, to
whom the Fugitive Slave Law denies the complete
boon of an otherwise justly earned oblivion, had
some dignity given to his administration by the
presence of Everett. But in this late advertising-
tour of a policy in want of a party, Cleon and
Agoracritus seem to have joined partnership, and
the manners of the man match those of the master.
Mr. Johnson cannot so much as hope for the success in escaping memory achieved by the last of
those small Virginians whom the traditionary fame
of a State once fertile in statesmen lifted to four
years of imperial pillory, where his own littleness
seemed to heighten rather than lower the grandeur
of his station; his name will not be associated

with the accomplishment of a great wrong against humanity, let us hope not with the futile attempt at one; but he will be indignantly remembered as the first, and we trust the last, of our chief magistrates who believed in the brutality of the people, and gave to the White House the ill-savor of a corner-grocery. *He* a tribune of the people? A lord of misrule, an abbot of unreason, much rather!

No one can object more strongly than we to the mixing of politics with personal character; but they are here inextricably entangled together, and we hold it to be the duty of every journal in the country to join in condemning a spectacle which silence might seem to justify as a common event in our politics. We turn gladly from the vulgarity of the President and his minister to consider the force of their arguments. Mr. Johnson seems to claim that he has not betrayed the trust to which he was elected, mainly because the Union party have always affirmed that the rebellious States could not secede, and therefore *ex vi termini* are still in the Union. The corollary drawn from this is, that they have therefore a manifest right to immediate representation in Congress. What we have always understood the Union party as meaning to affirm was, that a State had no right to secede; and it was upon that question, which is a very different thing from the other, that the whole controversy hinged. To assert that a State or States could not secede, if they were strong enough, would be an absurdity. In point of fact, all but three of the Slave States did secede, and for four years it would have been treason throughout their whole territory, and death on the nearest tree, to assert the contrary. The law forbids a man to steal, but he may steal, nevertheless; and then, if he had Mr. Johnson's power as a logician, he might claim to escape all penalty by pleading that when the law said *should not* it meant *could not*, and therefore he *had not*. If a four years' war, if a half million lives, and if a debt which is counted by the thousand million are not satisfactory proofs that somebody did contrive to secede practically, whatever the theoretic right may have been, then nothing that ought not to be done ever has been done. We do not, however, consider the question as to whether the Rebel States were constitutionally, or in the opinion of any political organization, out of the Union or not as of the least practical importance; for we have never known an instance in which any party has retreated into the thickets and swamps of constitutional interpretation, where it had the least chance of maintaining its ground in the open field of common sense or against the pressure of popular will. The practical fact is, that the will of the majority, or the national necessity for the time being, has always been constitutional; which is only as much as to say that the Convention of 1787 was not wholly made up of inspired prophets, who could provide beforehand for every possible contingency. The doctrine of a strict and even pettifogging interpretation of the Constitution had its rise among men who looked upon that instrument as a treaty, and at a time when the conception of a national power which should receive that of the States into its stream as tributary was something which had entered the head of only here and there a dreamer. The theorists of the Virginia school would have dammed up and diverted the force of each State into a narrow channel of its own, with its little saw-mill and its little grist-mill for local needs, instead of letting it follow the slopes of the continental water-shed to swell the volume of one great current ample for the larger uses and needful for the higher civilization of all. That there should always be a school who interpret the Constitution by its letter is a good thing, as interposing a check to hasty or partial action, and gaining time for ample discussion ; but that in the end we should be governed by its spirit, living and operative in the energies of an advancing people, is a still better thing ; since the levels and shore-lines of politics are no more stationary than those of continents, and the ship of state would in time be left aground far inland, to long in vain for that open sea which is the only pathway to fortune and to glory.

Equally idle with the claim that the Union party is foreclosed from now dealing with the Rebel States as seceded, because four years ago it declared that they had no right to secede, is the assertion that the object of the war was proclaimed to be for the restoration of the Union and the Constitution as they were. Even were we to admit that 1861 is the same thing as 1866, the question comes back again to precisely the point that is at issue between the President and Congress, namely, What is the wisest way of restoring the Union? for which both profess themselves equally anxious. As for the Constitution, we cannot have that as it was, but only as its framers hoped it would be, with its one weak and wicked element excluded. But as to Union, are we in favor of a Union in form or in fact? of a Union on the map and in our national style merely, or one of ideas, interests, and aspirations? If we cannot have the latter, the former is a delusion and a snare; and the strength of the nation would be continually called away from prosperous toil to be wasted in holding a wolf by the ears, which would still be a wolf, and known by all our enemies for such, though we called heaven and earth to witness, in no matter how many messages or resolves, that the innocent creature was a lamb. That somebody has a right to dictate some kind of terms is admitted by Mr. Johnson's own repeated action in the matter; but who that somebody should be, whether a single man, of whose discretion even his own partisans are daily becoming more doubtful, or the immediate representatives of that large majority of the States and of the people who for the last five years have been forced against their will to represent and to be the United States, is certainly too grave an affair to be settled by that single man himself.

We have seen to what extremes the party calling itself Conservative has hinted its willingness to go, under the plea of restored Union, but with the object of regained power. At Philadelphia, they went as far as they publicly dared in insinuating that the South would be justified in another rebellion, and their journals have more than once prompted the President to violent measures, which would as certainly be his ruin as they would lead to incalculable public disaster. The President himself has openly announced something like a design of forcibly suppressing a Congress elected by the same votes and secured by the same guaranties that elected him to his place and secure him in it, — a Congress whose validity he has acknowledged by sending in his messages to it, by signing its bills, and by drawing his pay under its vote ; and yet thinking men are not to be allowed to doubt the propriety of leaving the gravest measure that ever yet came up for settlement by the country to a party and a man so reckless as these have shown themselves to be. Mr. Johnson talks of the danger of centralization, and repeats the old despotic fallacy of many tyrants being worse than one, — a fallacy originally invented, and ever since repeated, as a slur upon democracy, but which is a palpable absurdity when the people who are to be tyrannized over have the right of displacing their tyrants every two years. The true many-headed tyrant is the Mob, that part of the deliberative body of a nation which Mr. Johnson, with his Southern notions of popular government, has been vainly seeking, that he might pay court to it, from the seaboard to St. Louis, but which hardly exists, we are thankful to say, as a constituent body, in any part of the Northern States outside the city of New York.

Mr. Seward, with that playfulness which sits upon him so gracefully, and which draws its resources from a reading so extensive that not even *John Gilpin* has escaped its research, puts his argument to the people in a form where the Socratic and arithmetic methods are neatly combined, and asks, " How many States are there in the Union? " He himself answers his own question for an audience among whom it might have been difficult to find any political adherent capable of so arduous a solution, by asking another, " Thirty-six? " Then he goes on to say that there is a certain party which insists that the number shall be less by ten, and ends by the clincher, " Now how many stars do you wish to see in your flag? " The result of some of Mr. Johnson's harangues was so often a personal collision, in which the more ardent on both sides had an opportunity to see any number of new constellations, that this astronomical view of the case must have struck the audience rather by its pertinence than its novelty. But in the argument of the Secretary, as in that of the President, there is a manifest confusion of logic, and something very like a *petitio principii*. We might answer Mr. Seward's question with, " As many fixed stars as you please, but no more shooting stars with any consent of ours." But really this matter is of more interest to heralds of arms than to practical men. The difference between Congress and the President is not, as Mr. Seward would insinuate, that Congress or anybody else wishes to keep the ten States out, but that the Radical party (we cheerfully accept our share in the opprobrium of the name) insists that they shall come in on a footing of perfect equality with the rest; while the President would reward them for rebellion by giving them an additional weight of nearly one half in the national councils. The cry of "Taxation without representation" is foolish enough as raised by the Philadelphia Convention, for do we not tax every foreigner that comes to us while he is in process of becoming a citizen and a voter? But under the Johnsonian theory of reconstruction, we shall leave a population which is now four millions not only taxed without representation, but doomed to be so forever without any reasonable hope of relief. The true point is not as to the abstract merits of universal suffrage (though we believe it the only way toward an enlightened democracy and the only safeguard of popular government), but as to whether we shall leave the freedmen without the only adequate means of self-defence. And however it may be now, the twenty-six States certainly *were* the Union when they accepted the aid of these people and pledged the faith of the government to their protection. Jamaica, at the end of nearly thirty years since emancipation, shows us how competent former masters are to accomplish the elevation of their liberated slaves, even though their own interests would prompt them to it. Surely it is a strange plea to be effective in a democratic country, that we owe these people nothing because they cannot help themselves; as if governments were instituted for the care of the strong only. The argument against their voting which is based upon their ignorance strikes us oddly in the mouths of those whose own hope of votes lies in the ignorance, or, what is often worse, the prejudice, of the voters. Besides, we do not demand that the seceding States should at once confer the right of suffrage on the blacks, but only that they should give them the same chance to attain it, and the same inducement to make themselves worthy of it, as to every one else. The answer that they have not the right in some of the Northern States may be a reproach to the intelligence of those States, but has no relevancy if made to the general government. It is not with these States that we are making terms or claim any right to make them, nor is the number of their non-voting population so large as to make them dangerous, or the prejudice against them so great that it may not safely be left to time and common sense. It was not till all men were made equal before the law, and the fact recognized that government is something that does not merely preside over, but reside in, the rights of all, that even white peasants were enabled to rise out of their degradation, and to become the strength instead of the danger of France. Nothing short of such a reform could have conquered the contempt and aversion with which the higher classes looked upon the emancipated serf. Norman-French literature reeks with the outbreak of this feeling toward the ances-

tors, whether Jews or villeins, of the very men who
are now the aristocracy of South Carolina, — a feeling as intense, as nauseous in its expression, and as
utterly groundless, as that against the negro now.
We are apt, it would seem, a little to confound the
meaning of the two terms *government* and *self-government*, and the principles on which they respec-
tively rest. If the latter has its rights, the former
has quite as plainly its duties; and one of them
certainly is to see that no freedom should be allowed to the parts which would endanger the safety
of the whole. An occasion calling for the exercise
of this duty is forced upon us now, and we must be
equal to it. Self-government, in any rightful defi-
nition of it, can hardly be stretched so far that it
will cover, as the late Rebels and their Northern
advocates contend, the right to dispose absolutely
of the destinies of four millions of people, the allies
and hearty friends of the United States, without
allowing them any voice in the matter.

It is alleged by reckless party orators that those
who ask for guaranties before readmitting the seceded States wish to treat them with harshness, if
not with cruelty. Mr. Thaddeus Stevens is triumphantly quoted, as if his foolish violence fairly
represented the political opinions of the Union
party. They might as well be made responsible
for his notions of finance. We are quite willing to
let Mr. Stevens be paired off with Mr. Vallandigham, and to believe that neither is a fair exponent of the average sentiment of his party. Calling names should be left to children, with whom,

as with too large a class of our political speakers, it seems to pass for argument. We believe it never does so with the people; certainly not with the intelligent, who make a majority among them, unless (as in the case of "Copperhead") there be one of those hardly-to-be-defined realities behind the name which they are so quick to detect. We cannot say that we have any great sympathy for the particular form of mildness which discovers either a "martyr," or a "pure-hearted patriot," or even a "lofty statesman," in Mr. Jefferson Davis, the latter qualification of him having been among the discoveries of the London *Times* when it thought his side was going to win; but we can say that nothing has surprised us more, or seemed to us a more striking evidence of the humanizing influence of democracy, than the entire absence of any temper that could be called revengeful in the people of the North toward their late enemies. If it be a part of that inconsistent mixture of purely personal motives and more than legitimate executive action which Mr. Johnson is pleased to call his "policy," — if it be a part of that to treat the South with all the leniency that is short of folly and all the conciliation that is short of meanness, — then we were advocates of it before Mr. Johnson. While he was yet only ruminating in his vindictive mind, sore with such rancor as none but a "plebeian," as he used to call himself, can feel against his social superiors, the only really agrarian proclamation ever put forth by any legitimate ruler, and which was countersigned by the now suddenly "conservative" Secretary of State, we were in favor of measures that should look to governing the South by such means as the South itself afforded, or could be made to afford. It is true that, as a part of the South, we reckoned the colored people bound to us by every tie of honor, justice, and principle, but we never wished to wink out of sight the natural feelings of men suddenly deprived of what they conceived to be their property, — of men, too, whom we respected for their courage and endurance even in a bad cause. But we believed then, as we believe now, and as events have justified us in believing, that there could be no graver error than to flatter our own feebleness and uncertainty by calling it magnanimity, — a virtue which does not scorn the society of patience and prudence, but which cannot subsist apart from courage and fidelity to principle. A people so boyish and conceited as the Southerners have always shown themselves to be, unwilling ever to deal with facts, but only with their own imagination of them, would be sure to interpret indecision as cowardice, if not as an unwilling tribute to that superiority of which men who really possess it are the last to boast. They have learned nothing from the war but to hate the men who subdued them, and to misinterpret and misrepresent the causes of their subduing ; and even now, when a feeling has been steadily growing in the rest of the country for the last nine months deeper and more intense than any during the war, because mixed with an angry sense of unexpected and treacherous disappointment, instead of setting their strength to the rebuilding of their shattered social fabric, they are waiting, as they waited four years ago, for a division in the North which will never come, and hailing in Andrew Johnson a scourge of God who is to avenge them in the desolation of our cities! Is it not time that these men were transplanted at least into the nineteenth century, and, if they cannot be suddenly Americanized, made to understand something of the country which was too good for them, even though at the cost of a rude shock to their childish self-conceit? Is that a properly reconstructed Union in the Southern half of which no Northern man's life is safe except at the sacrifice of his conscience, his freedom of speech, of everything but his love of money? To our minds the providential purpose of this intervention of Mr. Johnson in our affairs is to warn us of the solemn duty that lies upon us in this single crisis of our history, when the chance is offered us of stamping our future with greatness or contempt, and which requires something like statesmanship in the people themselves, as well as in those who act for them. The South insisted upon war, and has had enough of it; it is now our turn to insist that the peace we have conquered shall be so settled as to make war impossible for the future.

But how is this to be done? The road to it is a very plain one. We shall gain all we want if we make the South really prosperous; for with prosperity will come roads, schools, churches, printing-

presses, industry, thrift, intelligence, and security
of life and property.   Hitherto the prosperity of
the South has been factitious; it has been a prosperity of the Middle Ages, keeping the many poor
that a few might show their wealth in the barbarism of showy equipages and numerous servants, and
spend in foreign cities the wealth that should have
built up civilization and made way for refinement
at home.   There were no public libraries, no col-
leges worthy of the name; there was no art, no
science, — still worse, no literature but Simms's:
there was no desire for them.   We do not say it in
reproach; we are simply stating a fact, and are
quite aware that the North is far behind Europe in
these things.   But we are not behind her in the
value we set upon them; are even before her in the
price we are willing to pay for them, and are in the
way to get them.   The South was not in that way;
could not get into it, indeed, so long as the labor
that made wealth was cut off from any interest in
its expenditure, nor had any goal for such hopes as
soared away from the dreary level of its lifelong
drudgery but in the grave and the world beyond
it.   We are not blind to what may be said on
the other side, nor to that fatal picturesqueness,
so attractive to sentimental minds and so melancholy to thoughtful ones, which threw a charm over
certain exceptional modes of Southern life among
the older families in Virginia and South Carolina.
But there are higher and manlier kinds of beauty,
— barer and sterner, some would call them, — with
less softly rounded edges, certainly, than the Wolf's

Crag picturesqueness, which carries the mind with pensive indolence toward the past, instead of stirring it with a sense of present life, or bracing it with the hope of future opportunity, and which at once veils and betrays the decay of ancient civilizations. Unless life is arranged for the mere benefit of the novelist, what right had these bits of last-century Europe here? Even the virtues of the South were some of them anachronisms; and even those that were not existed side by side with an obtuseness of moral sense that could make a hero of Semmes, and a barbarism that could starve prisoners by the thousand.

Some philosophers, to be sure, plead with us that the Southerners are remarkable for their smaller hands and feet, though so good an observer as Thackeray pronounced this to be true of the whole American people; but really we cannot think such arguments as this will give any pause to the inevitable advance of that democracy, somewhat rude and raw as yet, a clumsy boy-giant, and not too well mannered, whose office it nevertheless is to make the world ready for the true second coming of Christ in the practical supremacy of his doctrine, and its incarnation, after so many centuries of burial, in the daily lives of men. We have been but dimly, if at all, conscious of the greatness of our errand, while we have already accomplished a part of it in bringing together the people of all nations to see each other no longer as aliens or enemies, but as equal partakers of the highest earthly dignity, — a common manhood. We have been forced, whether we would or no, first to endure, then to tolerate, and at last to like men from all the four corners of the world, and to see that each added a certain virtue of his own to that precious amalgam of which we are in due time to fashion a great nation. We are now brought face to face with our duty toward one of those dusky races that have long sat in the shadow of the world; we are to be taught to see the Christ disguised also in these, and to find at last that a part of our salvation is inextricably knit up with the necessity of doing them justice and leading them to the light. This is no sentimental fancy; it is written in plain characters upon the very surface of things. We have done everything to get rid of the negro; and the more we did, the more he was thrust upon us in every possible relation of life and aspect of thought. One thing we have not tried, — a spell before which he would vanish away from us at once, by taking quietly the place, whatever it be, to which Nature has assigned him. We have not acknowledged him as our brother. Till we have done so he will be always at our elbow, a perpetual discomfort to himself and us. Now this one thing that will give us rest is precisely what the South, if we leave the work of reconstruction in their hands, will make it impossible for us to do; and yet it must be done ere America can penetrate the Southern States. It is for this reason, and not with any desire of establishing a standing garrison of four hundred thousand loyal voters in the South, that we insist on the absolute necessity of justice to the black man. Not that we have not a perfect right to demand the reception of such a garrison, but we wish the South to govern itself; and this it will never be able to do, it will be governed as heretofore by its circumstances, if we allow it to replace slavery by the disenfranchisement of color, and to make an Ireland out of what should be the most productive, populous, and happy part of the Union. We may evade this manifest duty of ours from indolence, or indifference, or selfish haste; but if there is one truth truer than another, it is that no man or nation ever neglected a duty that was not sooner or later laid upon them in a heavier form, to be done at a dearer rate. Neither man nor nation can find rest short of their highest convictions.

This is something that altogether transcends any partisan politics. It is of comparatively little consequence to us whether Congress or the President carry the day, provided only that America triumph. That is, after all, the real question. On which side is the future of the country, — the future that we cannot escape if we would, but which our action may embarrass and retard? If we had looked upon the war as a mere trial of physical strength between two rival sections of the country, we should have been the first to oppose it, as a wicked waste of treasure and blood. But it was something much deeper than this, and so the people of the North instinctively recognized it to be from the first, — instinctively, we say, and not deliberately at first; but before it was over, their understandings had grasped its true meaning, as an

effort of the ideal America, which was to them half
a dream and half a reality, to cast off an alien
element.   It was this ideal something, not the less
strongly felt because vaguely defined, that made
them eager, as only what is above sordid motives
can, to sacrifice all that they had and all that they
were rather than fail in its attainment.   And it is to
men not yet cooled from the white-heat of this passionate mood that Mr. Johnson comes with his paltry offer of "my policy," in exchange for the logical
consequences of all this devotion and this sacrifice.
What is any one man's policy, and especially any
one weak man's policy, against the settled drift of a
nation's conviction, conscience, and instinct?   The
American people had made up not only their minds,
but their hearts, and no man who knows anything
of human nature could doubt what their decision
would be.   They wanted only a sufficient obstacle
to awaken them to a full consciousness of what was
at stake, and that obstacle the obstinate vanity of
the President and the blindness or resentment of
his prime minister have supplied.   They are fully
resolved to have the great stake they played for and
won, and that stake was the Americanization of
all America, nothing more and nothing less.   Mr.
Johnson told us in New York, with so profound a
misconception of the feeling of the Northern States
as was only possible to a vulgar mind, and that
mind a Southern one, that the South had set up
slavery as its stake, and lost, and that now the
North was in danger of losing the stake it had
risked on reconstruction in the national debt.   Mr.

Johnson is still, it would seem, under that delusion which led the South into the war; namely, that it was that section of the country which was the chief element in its wealth and greatness. But no Northern man, who, so long as he lives, will be obliged to pay his fine of taxes for the abolition of slavery which was forced upon us by the South, is likely to think it very hard that the South should be compelled to furnish its share toward the common burden, or will be afraid that the loyal States, whose urgent demands compelled a timid Congress at last to impose direct taxes, will be unable to meet their obligations in the future, as in the past.

We say again that the questions before the country are not to be decided on any grounds of personal prejudice or partiality. We are far from thinking that Congress has in all respects acted as became the dignity of its position, or seized all the advantage of the opportunity. They have seemed to us sometimes afraid of coming before the people with a direct, frank, and simple statement of what was not only the best thing that could be done, but the one thing that must be done. They were afraid of the people, and did not count securely, as they should have done, on that precious seeing which four years of gradually wakening moral sense had lent to the people's eyes. They should not have shrunk from taking upon themselves and their party all the odium of being in the right; of being on the side of justice, humanity, and of the America which is yet to be, whoever may fear to help and whoever may try to hinder. The vulgar cry would be against them, at any rate, and they might reckon on being accused of principles which they thought it prudent to conceal, whether they committed their party to them or not. With those who have the strong side, as they always do who have conscience for an ally, a bold policy is the only prosperous one. It is always wisest to accept in advance all the logical consequences that can be drawn from the principles we profess, and to make a stand on the extremest limits of our position. It will be time enough to fall back when we are driven out. In taking a half-way position at first, we expose ourselves to all the disadvantage and discouragement of seeming to fight on a retreat, and cut ourselves off from our supplies. For the supplies of a party which is contending for a clear principle, and not for its own immediate success, are always drawn from the highest moral ground included in its lines. We are not speaking here of abstractions or wire-drawn corollaries, but of those plain ethical axioms which every man may apprehend, and which are so closely involved in the question now before the country for decision. We at least could lose nothing by letting the people know exactly what we meant; for we meant nothing that could not claim the suffrage of sincere democracy, of prudent statesmanship, or of jealousy for the nation's honor and safety. That the Republican party should be broken up is of comparatively little consequence; for it would be merged in the stronger party of those who are resolved that no by-questions, no fallacies of gen-

erosity to the vanquished, shall turn it aside from
the one fixed purpose it has at heart; that the war
shall not have been in vain; and that the Rebel
States, when they return to the Union, shall return
to it as an addition of power, and under such terms
as that they *must*, and not merely *may*, be fixed
there. Let us call things by their right names,
and keep clearly in view both the nature of the
thing vanquished and of the war in which we were
victors. When men talk of generosity toward a
suppliant foe, they entirely forget what that foe
really was. To the people of the South no one
thinks of being unmerciful. But they were only
the blind force wielded by our real enemy, — an
enemy, prophesy what smooth things you will, with
whom we can never be reconciled and whom it
would be madness to spare. And this enemy was
not any body of kindred people, but that principle
of evil fatally repugnant to our institutions, which,
flinging away the hilt of its broken weapon, is now
cheating itself with the hope that it can forge a
new one of the soft and treacherous metal of
Northern disloyalty. The war can in no respect
be called a civil war, though that was what the
South, in its rash ignorance, threatened the North
with. It was as much a war between two different
nations, and the geographical line was as distinctly
drawn between them, as in the late war between
North and South Germany. They had been living,
it is true, under the same government, but the
South regarded this as implying no tie more intimate than that which brought the representatives

of Prussia and Austria together in the Frankfort
Diet. We have the same right to impose terms
and to demand guaranties that Prussia has, that
the victor always has.

Many people are led to favor Mr. Johnson's policy because they dislike those whom they please to
call the " Republican leaders." If ever a party existed that had no recognized leaders, it is the Republican party. Composed for the last five years,
at least, of men who, themselves professing all
shades of opinion, were agreed only in a determination to sustain the honor and preserve the existence of the nation, it has been rather a majority
than a party, employing the legislative machine to
carry out the purposes of public opinion. The
people were the true inspirers of all its measures, and accordingly it was left without a definite
policy the moment the mere politicians in its ranks
became doubtful as to what direction the popular mind would take. It had no recognized leader
either in the House or Senate just at the time when
it first stood in need of such. The majority of
its representatives there tried in vain to cast any
political horoscope by which it would be safe for
them individually to be guided. They showed the
same distrust of the sound judgment of the people
and their power to grasp principles that they
showed at the beginning of the war, and at every
discouraging moment while it was going on. Now
that the signs of the times show unmistakably to
what the popular mind is making itself up, they
have once more a policy, if we may call that so

which is only a calculation of what it would be " safe to go before the people with," as they call it. It is always safe to go before them with plain principles of right, and with the conclusions that must be drawn from them by common sense, though this is what too many of our public men can never understand. Now joining a Know-Nothing "lodge," now hanging on the outskirts of a Fenian "circle," they mistake the momentary eddies of popular whimsy for the great current that sets always strongly in one direction through the life and history of the nation. Is it, as foreigners assert, the fatal defect of our system to fill our highest offices with men whose views in politics are bounded by the next district election ? When we consider how noble the science is, — nobler even than astronomy, for it deals with the mutual repulsions and attractions, not of inert masses, but of bodies endowed with thought and will, calculates moral forces, and reckons the orbits of God's purposes toward mankind, — we feel sure that it is to find nobler teachers and students, and to find them even here.

There is another class of men who are honestly drawn toward the policy of what we are fain, for want of a more definite name, to call the Presidential Opposition party, by their approval of the lenient measures which they suppose to be peculiar to it. But our objection to the measures advocated by the Philadelphia Convention, so far as we can trace any definite shape amid the dust-cloud of words, is, not they would treat the Rebel States with moderation, but that they propose to take them back on trust. We freely admit that we should have been inclined to see more reasonableness in this course if we had not the examples of Jamaica and New Orleans before our eyes ; if we had not seen both there and in other instances with which history supplies us, that it is not safe to leave the settlement of such matters in the hands of men who would be more than human if they had not the prejudices and the resentments of caste. Here is just one of those cases of public concern which call for the arbitrament of a cool and impartial third party, — the very office expected of a popular government, — which should as carefully abstain from meddling in matters that may be safely left to be decided by natural laws as it should be prompt to interfere where those laws would to the general detriment be inoperative. It should be remembered that self - interest, though its requirements may seem plain and imperative to an unprejudiced bystander, is something which men, and even communities, are often ready to sacrifice at the bidding of their passions, and of none so readily as their pride. As for the attachment between master and slave, whose existence is sometimes asseverated in the face of so many glaring facts to the contrary, and on which we are asked to depend as something stronger than written law, we have very little faith in it. The system of clanship in the Scottish Highlands is the strongest case to which we can appeal in modern times of a truly patriarchal social order. In that, the pride of the chief was answered by the willing devotion of the sept, and the two were bound together as closely as kindred blood, immemorial tradition, and mutual dependence could link them; and yet, the moment it became for the interest of the chieftain, in whom alone was the landed title, to convert the mountain slopes into sheep-walks, farewell to all considerations of ancestral legend and ideal picturesqueness! The clansmen were dispossessed of their little holdings, and shipped off to the colonies like cattle, by the very men for whom they would have given their lives without question. The relation, just like that of master and slave, or the proposed one of superior and dependent, in the South, had become an anachronism, to preserve which would have been a vain struggle against that power of Necessity which the Greeks revered as something god-like. In our own case, so far from making it for the interest of the ruling classes at the South to elevate the condition of the black man, the policy of Mr. Johnson offers them a bribe to keep him in a state of hopeless dependency and subjection. It gives them more members of Congress in proportion as they have more unrepresented inhabitants. Mr. Beecher asks us (and we see no possible reason for doubting the honesty of his opinions, whatever may be their soundness) whether we are afraid of the South, and tells us that, if we allow them to govern us, we shall richly deserve it. It is not that we are afraid of, nor are we in the habit of forming our opinions on any such imaginary grounds; but we confess that we are afraid of committing an act of national injustice, of national dishonor, of national breach of faith, and therefore of national unwisdom and weakness. Moderation is an excellent thing; but taking things for granted is not moderation, and there may be such a thing as being immoderate in concession and confidence. Aristotle taught us long ago that true moderation was as far from the too-much of blind passion on the one hand as from that of equally blind luke-warmness on the other. We have an example of wise reconstructive policy in that measure of the Bourbon-restoration ministry, which compensated the returned emigrants for their confiscated estates by a grant from the public treasury. And the measure was wise, for the reason that it enabled the new proprietors and the ousted ones to live as citizens of the same country together without mutual hatred and distrust. We do not propose to compensate the slaveholder for the loss of his chattels, because the cases are not parallel, and because Mr. Johnson no less than we acknowledges the justice and validity of their emancipation. But the situation of the negro is strikingly parallel with that of the new holders of land in France. As they were entitled to security, so he has a right not only to be secured in his freedom, but in the consequences which legitimately flow from it. For it is only so that he can be insured against that feeling of distrust and uncertainty of the future which will prevent him from being profitable to himself, his former master, and the country. If we sought a parallel for Mr. Johnson's " policy," we should find it in James II., thinking his prerogative strong enough to overcome the instincts, convictions, and fears of England.

However much fair-minded men may have been wearied with the backing and filling of Congress, and their uncertainty of action on some of the most important questions that have come before them, — however the dignity, and even propriety, of their attitude toward Mr. Johnson may be in some respects honestly called in question, — no one who has looked fairly at the matter can pronounce the terms they have imposed on the South as conditions of restoration harsh ones. The character of Congress is not before the country, but simply the character of the plan they propose. For ourselves, we should frankly express our disgust at the demagogism which courted the Fenians; for, however much we may sympathize with the real wrongs of Ireland, it was not for an American Congress to declare itself in favor of a movement which based itself on the claim of every Irish voter in the country to a double citizenship, in which the adopted country was made secondary, and which, directed as it was against a province where Irishmen are put on equal terms with every other inhabitant, and where their own Church is the privileged one, was nothing better than burglary and murder. Whatever may be Mr. Seward's faults, he was certainly right in his dealing with that matter, unless he is to be blamed for slowness. But as regards the terms offered by Congress to the South, they are very far from harsh or unreasonable; they are lamb-like compared to what we had reason to fear from Mr. Johnson, if we might judge by his speeches and declarations of a year or two ago. But for the unhappy hallucination which led Mr. Johnson first to fancy himself the people of the United States, and then to quarrel with the party which elected him for not granting that he was so, they would not have found a man in the North to question their justice and propriety, unless among those who from the outset would have been willing to accept Mr. Jefferson Davis as the legitimate President of the whole country. The terms imposed by Congress really demand nothing more than that the South should put in practice at home that Monroe Doctrine of which it has always been so clamorous a supporter when it could be used for party purposes. The system of privileged classes which the South proposes to establish is a relic of old Europe which we think it bad policy to introduce again on this continent, after our so fresh experience in the war of the evil consequences that may spring from it. Aristocracy can form no more intimate and hearty union with democracy under one form than under another; and unless such a union be accomplished, or we can see some reasonable hope of its future accomplishment, we are as far from our object as ever.

The plan proposed disfranchises no one, does not even interfere with the right of the States to settle the conditions of the franchise. It merely asks that the privilege shall be alike within reach of all, attainable on the same terms by those who have shown themselves our friends as by those whose hands were so lately red with the blood of our nearest and dearest. We have nothing to do with the number of actual loyalists at the South, but with the number of possible ones. The question is not how many now exist there, and what are their rights, but how many may be made to exist there, and by what means. The duty of the country to itself transcends all private claims or class interests. And when people speak of "the South," do they very clearly define to themselves what they mean by the words? Do they not really mean, without knowing it, the small body of dangerous men who have misguided that part of the country to its own ruin, and almost to that of the Republic? In the mind of our government the South should have no such narrow meaning. It should see behind the conspirators of yesterday an innumerable throng of dusky faces, with their dumb appeal, not to its mercy, its generosity, or even its gratitude, but to its plighted faith, to the solemn engagement of its chief magistrate and their martyr. Any theory of the South which leaves out the negro is a scandal and reproach to our honesty; any attempt at another of those fatal compromises which ignore his claims upon us, but cannot ignore his claims upon nature and God and that inevitable future which we may hope to put far from us, but which is even now at our door, would be an imputation on our judgment, and an acknowledgment that we were unworthy to measure our strength with a great occasion when it met us face to face.

We are very far from joining in the unfeeling outcry which is sometimes raised by thoughtless persons against the Southern people, because they decorate with flowers the graves of their dead soldiers, and cherish the memory of those who fell in the defence of a cause which they could not see to be already fallen before they entered its service. They have won our respect, the people of Virginia especially, by their devotion and endurance in sustaining what they believed to be their righteous quarrel. They would rather deserve our reprobation, if they were wanting in these tributes to natural and human feeling. They are as harmless as the monument to the memory of those who fell for the Pretender, which McDonald of Glenaladale raised after the last of the Stuarts was in his grave. Let us sympathize with and respect all such exhibitions of natural feeling. But at the same time let us take care that it shall not be at the risk of his life that the poor black shall fling his tribute on the turf of those who died, with equal sacrifice of self, in a better cause. Let us see to it that the Union men of the South shall be safe in declaring and advocating the reasons of their faith in a cause which we believe to be sacred. Let us secure such opportunities of education to the masses of the Southern people, whether white or black, as shall make any future rebellion impracticable, and render it possible for the dead of both sides to sleep peaceably together under the safeguard of a common humanity, while the living dwell under the protection of a nationality which both shall value alike. Let us put it out of the power of a few ambitious madmen to shake, though they could not endanger, the foundations of a structure which enshrines the better hope of mankind. When Congress shall again come together, strong in the sympathy of a united people, let them show a dignity equal to the importance of the crisis. Let them give the President a proof of their patriotism, not only by allowing him the opportunity, but by making it easy for him, to return to the national position he once occupied. Let them not lower their own dignity and that of the nation by any bandying of reproaches with the Executive. The cause which we all have at heart is vulgarized by any littleness or show of personal resentment in its representatives, and is of too serious import to admit of any childishness or trifling. Let there be no more foolish talk of impeachment for what is at best a poor infirmity of nature, and could only be raised into a harmful importance by being invested with the dignity of a crime against the state. Nothing could be more unwise than to entangle in legal quibbles a cause so strong in its moral grounds, so transparent in its equity, and so plain to the humblest apprehension in its political justice and necessity. We have already one criminal half turned martyr at Fortress Monroe; we should be in no hurry to make another out of even more vulgar material, — for unhappily martyrs are not Mercuries. We have only to be unswervingly faithful to what is the true America of our hope and belief, and whatever is American will rise from one end of the country to the other instinctively to our side, with more than ample means of present succor and of final triumph. It is only by being loyal and helpful to Truth that men learn at last how loyal and helpful she can be to them.

www.ingramcontent.com/pod-product-compliance
Lightning Source LLC
Chambersburg PA
CBHW020937030726
47496CB00005B/1231